1st Joint Workshop on Statistical Parsing of Morphologically Rich Languages and Syntactic Analysis of Non-Canonical Languages

(SPMRL-SANCL 2014)

Held at COLING 2014

Dublin, Ireland
24 August 2014

ISBN: 978-1-63439-237-2

Printed from e-media with permission by:

Curran Associates, Inc.
57 Morehouse Lane
Red Hook, NY 12571

Some format issues inherent in the e-media version may also appear in this print version.

Printed by Curran Associates, Inc. (2014)

For permission requests, please contact the Association for Computational Linguistics at the address below.

Association for Computational Linguistics
209 N. Eighth Street
Stroudsburg, Pennsylvania 18360

Phone: 1-570-476-8006
Fax: 1-570-476-0860

acl@aclweb.org

Additional copies of this publication are available from:

Curran Associates, Inc.
57 Morehouse Lane
Red Hook, NY 12571 USA
Phone: 845-758-0400
Fax: 845-758-2634
Email: curran@proceedings.com
Web: www.proceedings.com

Introduction

The papers in these proceedings were presented at the First Joint Workshop on Statistical Parsing of Morphologically Rich Languages and Syntactic Analysis of Non-Canonical Languages (SPMRL-SANCL 2014), held in Seattle, USA, on October 18th, 2013, in conjunction with the 25th international Conference on Computational Linguistics (Coling 2014).

SPMRL-SANCL is endorsed by the ACL SIGPARSE interest group and provides a forum for research in parsing morphologically-rich languages and non-canonical language, with the goal of identifying cross-cutting issues in the annotation and parsing methodology, in the face of more flexible word order and/or higher word-form variation, or lexical sparseness and ad-hoc structures than English newspaper text.

SPMRL has also been host to discussions on realistic and appropriate evaluation methods that can be applied in the face of morphological and/or segmentation ambiguities; these discussions have culminated in the first shared task for parsing morphologically-rich languages, co-located with SPMRL 2013, and the second shared task for semi-supervised parsing of morphologically-rich languages, co-located with SPMRL 2014. The proceedings include nine contributions to the workshop as well as one system description from the shared task. The workshop included a keynote talk by Joakim Nivre (Uppsala).

We would like to thank all submitting authors for their contributions, the program committee for their fine work on reviewing the submissions, the participants of the shared task for their contributions and of course our invited speaker. For their precious help preparing the SPMRL 2014 Shared Task and for allowing their data to be part of it, we warmly thank and the Linguistic Data Consortium, the Knowledge Center for Processing Hebrew (MILA), the Ben Gurion University, Columbia University, Institute of Computer Science (Polish Academy of Sciences), Korea Advanced Institute of Science and Technology, University of the Basque Country, Uppsala University, University of Stuttgart, University of Szeged, University Paris Diderot (Paris 7), University of Marne La Vallée, and University of Tübingen. We gratefully acknowledge the contribution of Språkbanken and the University of Gothenburg for providing the PAROLE corpus and the help of Dr. Jungyeul Park and Prof. Key-Sun Cho for the KAIST annotated news corpus. Finally, we would also like to thank the ACL SIGPARSE interest group for their endorsement, for the support of INRIA's Alpage project, and everybody who participated in the workshop and contributed to the discussions.

Yoav Goldberg, Yuval Marton, Ines Rehbein, Yannick Versley, Özlem Çetinoğlu, Joel Tetrault
(Workshop organisers)

Sandra Kübler, Djamé Seddah and Reut Tsarfaty
(Shared Task organisers)

Workshop Organizers

Yoav Goldberg (Bar Ilan University, Israel)

Yuval Marton (Microsoft Corp., US)

Ines Rehbein (Potsdam University, Germany)

Yannick Versley (Heidelberg University, Germany)

Özlem Çetinoğlu (University of Stuttgart, Germany)

Joel Tetreault (Yahoo! Labs, US)

SANCL Special Track

Ines Rehbein (Potsdam University, Germany)

Djamé Seddah (Université Paris Sorbonne & INRIA's Alpage Project, France)

Özlem Çetinoğlu (University of Stuttgart, Germany)

Joel Tetreault (Yahoo! Labs, US)

SPMRL Shared Task

Sandra Kübler (Indiana University, US)

Djamé Seddah (Université Paris Sorbonne & INRIA's Alpage Project, France)

Reut Tsarfaty (Weizmann Institute of Science, Israel)

Invited Speaker:

Joakim Nivre (Uppsala University)

Program Committee:

Bernd Bohnet (University of Birmingham, UK)
Marie Candito (University of Paris 7, France)
Aoife Cahill (Educational Testing Service, US)
Jinho D. Choi (University of Massachusetts Amherst, US)
Grzegorz Chrupała (Tilburg University, Netherlands)
Markus Dickinson (Indiana University, US)
Stefanie Dipper (Ruhr-Universität Bochum, Germany)
Jacob Eisenstein (Georgia Institute of Technology, US)
Richárd Farkas (University of Szeged, Hungary)
Jennifer Foster (Dublin City University, Ireland)
Josef van Genabith (DFKI, Germany)
Koldo Gojenola (University of the Basque Country, Spain)
Spence Green (Stanford University, US)
Samar Husain (Potsdam University, Germany)
Sandra Kübler (Indiana University, US)
Joseph Le Roux (Université Paris-Nord, France)
John Lee (City University of Hong Kong, China)
Wolfgang Maier (University of Düsseldorf, Germany)
Takuya Matsuzaki (University of Tokyo, Japan)
David McClosky (IBM Research, US)
Detmar Meurers (University of Tübingen, Germany)
Joakim Nivre (Uppsala University, Sweden)
Kemal Oflazer (Carnegie Mellon University, Qatar)
Adam Przepiórkowski (ICS PAS, Poland)
Owen Rambow (Columbia University, US)
Kenji Sagae (University of Southern California, US)
Benoît Sagot (Inria, France)
Djamé Seddah (Univ. Paris Sorbonne, France)
Wolfgang Seeker (University of Stuttgart, Germany)
Anders Søgaard (University of Copenhagen, Denmark)
Reut Tsarfaty (Weizmann Institute of Science, Israel)
Lamia Tounsi (Dublin City University, Ireland)
Daniel Zeman (Charles University, Czech Republic)

Table of Contents

Conference Program

Sunday August 24, 2014

9:00 Opening

9:05 Invited Talk: Universal Dependency Parsing (Joakim Nivre)

SPMRL

10:00 *Parsing German: How Much Morphology Do We Need?*
Wolfgang Maier, Sandra Kübler, Daniel Dakota and Daniel Whyatt

10:30 (coffee break)

11:00 *Joint Ensemble Model for POS Tagging and Dependency Parsing*
Iliana Simova, Dimitar Vasilev, Alexander Popov, Kiril Simov and Petya Osenova

11:30 *Improving the parsing of French coordination through annotation standards and targeted features*
Assaf Urieli

12:00 *Experiments with Easy-first nonprojective constituent parsing*
Yannick Versley

12:25 (lunch)

SANCL

14:00 *Exploring Options for Fast Domain Adaptation of Dependency Parsers*
Viktor Pekar, Juntao Yu, Mohab El-karef and Bernd Bohnet

14:30 *Self-Training for Parsing Learner Text*
Aoife Cahill, Binod Gyawali and James Bruno

14:50 *The effect of disfluencies and learner errors on the parsing of spoken learner language*
Andrew Caines and Paula Buttery

15:30 Poster session (SPMRL short papers and shared task)

Sunday August 24, 2014 (continued)

SPMRL short papers

Initial Explorations in Two-phase Turkish Dependency Parsing by Incorporating Constituents
İlknur Durgar El-Kahlout, Ahmet Afşın Akın and Ertugrul Yılmaz

Experiments for Dependency Parsing of Greek
Prokopis Prokopidis and Haris Papageorgiou

SANCL special session

I lack words and I don't know why: Solving elliptical structures in the syntactic annotation of private letters (Clara Pinto and Catarina Carvalheiro)

SPMRL shared task

Introducing the IMS-Wrocław-Szeged-CIS entry at the SPMRL 2014 Shared Task: Reranking and Morpho-syntax meet Unlabeled Data
Anders Björkelund, Özlem Çetinoğlu, Agnieszka Faleńska, Richárd Farkas, Thomas Mueller, Wolfgang Seeker and Zsolt Szántó

Introducing the SPMRL 2014 Shared Task on Parsing Morphologically-rich Languages
Djamé Seddah, Sandra Kübler and Reut Tsarfaty

Parsing German: How Much Morphology Do We Need?

Wolfgang Maier
Heinrich-Heine-Universität Düsseldorf
Düsseldorf, Germany
maierw@hhu.de

Sandra Kübler
Indiana University
Bloomington, IN, USA
skuebler@indiana.edu

Daniel Dakota
Indiana University
Bloomington, IN, USA
ddakota@indiana.edu

Daniel Whyatt
Indiana University
Bloomington, IN, USA
dwhyatt@indiana.edu

Abstract

We investigate how the granularity of POS tags influences POS tagging, and furthermore, how POS tagging performance relates to parsing results. For this, we use the standard "pipeline" approach, in which a parser builds its output on previously tagged input. The experiments are performed on two German treebanks, using three POS tagsets of different granularity, and six different POS taggers, together with the Berkeley parser. Our findings show that less granularity of the POS tagset leads to better tagging results. However, both too coarse-grained and too fine-grained distinctions on POS level decrease parsing performance.

1 Introduction

German is a non-configurational language with a moderately free word order in combination with a case system. The case of a noun phrase complement generally is a direct indicator of the phrase's grammatical function. For this reason, a morphological analysis seems to be a prerequisite for a syntactic analysis. However, in computational linguistics, parsing was developed for English without the use of morphological information, and this same architecture is used for other languages, including German (Kübler et al., 2006; Petrov and Klein, 2008). An easy way of introducing morphological information into parsing, without modifying the architecture, is to attach morphology to the part-of-speech (POS) tagset. However, this makes POS tagging more complex and thus more difficult.

In this paper, we investigate the following questions: 1) How well do the different POS taggers work with tagsets of a varying level of morphological granularity? 2) Do the differences in POS tagger performance translate into similar differences in parsing quality? Complementary POS tagging results and preliminary parsing results have been published in German in Kübler and Maier (2013).

Our experiments are based on two different treebanks for German, TiGer (Brants et al., 2002) and TüBa-D/Z (Telljohann et al., 2012). Both treebanks are based on the same POS tagset, the Stuttgart-Tübingen Tagset (STTS) (Schiller et al., 1995). We perform experiments with three variants of the tagset: The standard STTS, the Universal Tagset (UTS) (Petrov et al., 2012) (a language-independent tagset), and an extended version of the STTS that also includes morphological information from the treebanks (STTSmorph). STTS consists of 54 tags, UTS uses 12 basic tags, and the morphological variants of the STTS comprise 783 and 524 POS tags respectively. We use a wide range of POS taggers, which are based on different strategies: Morfette (Chrupala et al., 2008) and RF-Tagger (Schmid and Laws, 2008) are designed for large morphological tagsets, the Stanford tagger (Toutanova et al., 2003) is based on a maximum entropy model, SVMTool (Giménez and Màrquez, 2004) is based on support vector machines, TnT (Brants, 2000) is a Markov model trigram tagger, and Wapiti (Lavergne et al., 2010) a conditional random field tagger. For our parsing experiments, we use the Berkeley parser (Petrov and Klein, 2007b; Petrov and Klein, 2007a).

First Joint Workshop on Statistical Parsing of Morphologically Rich Languages and Syntactic Analysis of Non-Canonical Languages, pages 1–14 Dublin, Ireland, August 23-29 2014.

Our findings for POS tagging show that Morfette reaches the highest accuracy on UTS and overall on unknown words while TnT reaches the best performance for STTS and the RF-Tagger for STTSmorph. These trends are stable across both treebanks. As for the parsing results, using STTS results in the best accuracies. For TiGer, POS tags assigned by the parser perform better in combination with UTS and STTSmorph. For TiGer in combination with STTS and all variants in TüBa-D/Z, there are only minor differences between the parser assigned POS tags and those by TnT.

The remainder of the article is structured as follows. In section 2, we review previous work. Section 3 presents the different POS tagsets. Section 4 describes our experimental setup. The POS tagging and parsing results are discussed in the sections 5 and 6, respectively. Section 7 concludes the article.

2 Previous Work

In this section, we present a review of the literature that has previously examined the correlation of POS tagging and parsing under different aspects. While this overview is not exhaustive, it presents the major findings related to our work. The issues examined can be regarded under two orthogonal aspects, namely, the parsing model used (data-driven or grammar-based), and the question of how to disambiguate between various tags for a single word.

Some work has been done on investigating different tagsets for individual languages. Collins et al. (1999) adapt the parser of Collins (1999) for the Czech Prague Dependency Treebank. Using an external lexicon to reduce data sparseness for word forms did not result in any improvement, but adding case to the POS tagset had a positive effect. Seddah et al. (2009) investigate the use of different parsers on French. They also investigate two tagsets with different granularity and come to the conclusion that the finer grained tagset leads to higher parser performance. The work that is closest to ours is work by Marton et al. (2013), who investigate the optimal POS tagset for parsing Arabic. They come to the conclusion that adding definiteness, person, number, gender, and lemma information to the POS tagset improve parsing accuracy. Both Dehdari et al. (2011) and Szántó and Farkas (2014) investigate automatic methods for selecting the best subset of morphological features, the former for Arabic, the latter for Basque, French, German, Hebrew, and Hungarian. However, note that Szántó and Farkas (2014) used the data from the SPMRL shared task 2013, which does not contain grammatical functions in the syntactic annotations. Both approaches found improvements for subsets of morphological features.

Other works examine, also within a "pipeline" method, possibilities for ambiguity reduction through modification of tagsets, or of the lexicon by tagset reduction, or through word-clustering. Lakeland (2005) uses lexicalized parsing à la Collins (1999). Similarly to the more recent work by Koo et al. (2008) or Candito and Seddah (2010), he addresses the question of how to optimally disambiguate for parsing on the lexical level by clustering. A word cluster is thereby seen as an equivalence class of words and assumes to a certain extent the function of a POS tag, but can be adapted to the training data. Le Roux et al. (2012) address the issue of data sparseness on the lexical level with PCFG parsing with the morphologically rich language Spanish. The authors use a reimplementation of the Berkeley parser. They show that parsing results can be improved by simplifying the POS tagset, as well as by lemmatization, since both approaches reduce data sparseness.

As already mentioned, a POS tag can be seen as an equivalence class of words. Since in the "pipeline" approach, the parse tree is built on POS tags, it is possible that a POS tagset is optimal from a linguistic point of view, but that its behavior is not optimal with respect to parsing results, because relevant lexical information is hidden from the parse tree by the POS tagset. While Koo et al. (2008) overcome this deficit by automatically searching for "better" clusters, other works copy certain lexical information into the actual tree, e.g., by using grammatical function annotation (Versley, 2005; Versley and Rehbein, 2009). Seeker and Kuhn (2013) complement the "pipeline" model (using a dependency parser (Bohnet, 2010)) by an additional component that uses case information as a filter for the parser. They achieve improvements for Hungarian, German and Czech.

A number of works develop models for simultaneous POS tagging or morphological segmentation and parsing. Based on work by Ratnaparkhi (1996) and Toutanova and Manning (2000), Chen and Kit (2011) investigate disambiguation on the lexical level. They assume that local, i.e., sequential but not

tag	description	tag	description	tag	description
NOUN	noun	PRON	pronoun	CONJ	conjunction
VERB	verb	DET	determiner, article	PRT	particle
ADJ	adjective	ADP	preposition, postposition	.	punctuation
ADV	adverb	NUM	numeral	X	everything else

Table 1: The 12 tags of the Universal Tagset.

hierarchical, features are decisive for the quality of POS tagging and note that a "pipeline" model does not take this into account since the parser effectively performs the POS disambiguation. On these grounds, they present a factorized model for PCFG parsing which separates parsing into a discriminative lexical model (with local features) and the actual parsing model, to be combined with a *product-of-experts* (Hinton, 1999).

Particularly in the dependency parsing literature, combined models for simultaneous POS tagging and parsing can be found. Research has concentrated on languages that require additional segmentation on the word level, such as Chinese (Hatori et al., 2011) or Hebrew (Goldberg and Tsarfaty, 2008). A new approach by Bohnet and Nivre (2012) was also evaluated on German. Results for POS tagging and parsing of German by means of a constraint grammar can be found in Daum et al. (2003) as well as in Foth et al. (2005). However, since these approaches are only marginally related to our approach, we forego a further overview.

3 The Three Tagset Variants

In our experiments, we use three POS tagset variants: The standard Stuttgart-Tübingen Tagset (STTS), the Universal Tagset (UTS) (Petrov et al., 2012), and an extended version of the STTS that also includes morphological information from the treebanks (STTSmorph). Since the two treebanks differ in their morphological annotation, in this variant, the tags differ between the two treebanks: For TiGer, we have 783 possible complex POS tags, and for TüBa-D/Z, there are 524. By complex tags, we mean a combination of an STTS tag with the morphological tag. Also, note that not all of the possible combinations are attested in the treebanks.

The UTS consists of 12 basic POS tags, shown in table 1[1]. It was developed for multilingual applications, in which a common tagset is of importance, such as for a multilingual POS tagger. The UTS only represents the major word classes. Thus, this tagset should result in a high POS tagging accuracy since only major distinctions are made. However, it is unclear whether these coarse distinctions provide enough information for a syntactic analysis.

The STTS is based on distributional regularities of German. It contains 54 tags and thus models more fine grained distinctions than the UTS. For a list of tags, see Schiller et al. (1995). The finer distinctions in STTS mostly concern word classes, but there is also a distinction between finite and infinite verbs. This distinction is important for the syntactic analysis, especially in TüBa-D/Z, but it can be difficult to make by a POS tagger with a limited context.

The STTS can be extended by a morphological component. Both treebanks provide a morphological analysis, but the analyses model different decisions. In TiGer, a set of 585 different feature combinations is used, which can be combined from the features listed in table 2. The sentence in (1) gives an example of the combination of the STTS and morphology, which are separated by the % sign. The feature – means that there are no morphological features for the given POS tag.

(1) Konzernchefs lehnen den Milliardär als
NN%Nom.Pl.Masc VVFIN%3.Pl.Pres.Ind ART%Acc.Sg.Masc NN%Acc.Sg.Masc APPR%–
US-Präsidenten ab /
NN%Acc.Sg.Masc PTKVZ%– $(%–
'Corporate CEOs disapprove of the billionaire as US president /'

[1]For a mapping from STTS to UTS, cf. `https://code.google.com/p/universal-pos-tags/`.

feature	description
ambiguous:	*
gender	masculine (Masc), feminine (Fem), neuter (Neut)
gradation	positive (Pos), comparative (Comp), superlative (Sup)
case	nominative (Nom), genitive (Gen), dative (Dat), accusative (Akk)
mode	indicative (Ind), conjunctive (Subj), imperative (Imp)
number	singular (Sg), plural (Pl)
person	1., 2., 3.
tense	present (Pres), past (Past)

Table 2: The morphological categories in TiGer.

feature	description
ambiguous	*
gender	masculine (m), feminine (f), neuter (n)
case	nominative (n), genitive (g), dative (d), accusative (a)
number	singular (s), plural (p)
person	1., 2., 3.
tense	present (s), past (t)
mode	indicative (i), conjunctive (k)

Table 3: The morphological categories in TüBa-D/Z.

Out of the 585 possible combinations of morphological features, 271 are attested in TiGer. In combination with the STTS, this results in 783 combinations of STTS and morphological tags. Out of those, 761 occur in the training set. However, we expect data sparseness during testing because of the high number of possible tags. For this reason, we calculated which percentage of the tags in the development and test set are known combinations. We found that 25% and 30%, respectively, do not occur in the training set. However, note that the number of tags in the development and test sets is considerably smaller than the number of tags in the training set.

In TüBa-D/Z, there are 132 possible morphological feature combinations which can be combined from the features listed in table 3. The sentence in (2) gives an example of the combination of the STTS and morphology.

(2) Aber Bremerhavens AfB fordert jetzt Untersuchungsausschuß
KON%– NE%gsn NE%nsf VVFIN%3sis ADV%– NN%asm
'But the Bremerhaven AfB now demands a board of inquiry'

Out of the 132 possible feature combinations, 105 are attested in TüBa-D/Z. In combination with the STTS, this results in 524 combinations of STTS and morphological tags. Out of those, 513 occur in the training set. For the development and test set, we found that 16% and 18% respectively do not occur in the training set. These percentages are considerably lower than the ones for TiGer.

Since the tagsets that include morphology comprise several hundred different POS tags, we expect tagging to be more difficult, resulting in lower accuracies. We also expect that the TüBa-D/Z tagset is better suited for POS tagging than the TiGer set because of its smaller tagset size and its higher coverage on the development and test set. It is, however, unknown whether this information can be used successfully in parsing.

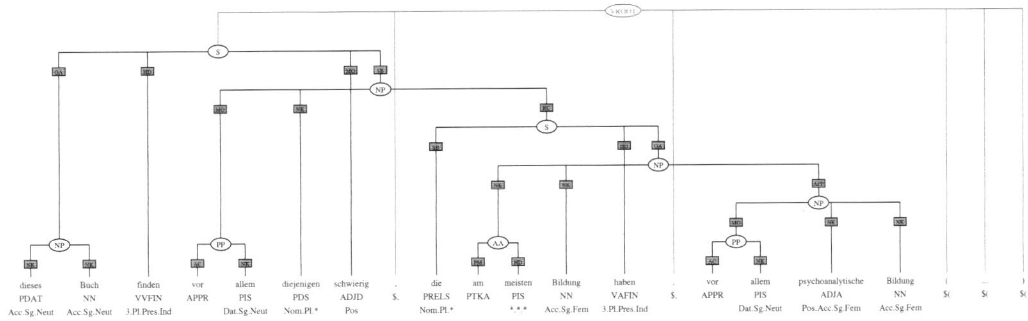

Figure 1: A sentence from TiGer.

4 Experimental Setup

4.1 Treebanks

We use the treebanks TiGer (Brants et al., 2002), version 2.2, and TüBa-D/Z (Telljohann et al., 2012), release 8. Both are built on newspaper text, *Frankfurter Rundschau* for TiGer and *taz* for TüBa-D/Z. Both treebanks use the same POS tagset with only one minor difference in the naming of one POS label. However, the treebanks differ considerably in the syntactic annotation scheme. While TiGer uses a very flat annotation involving crossing branches, the annotations in TüBa-D/Z are more hierarchical, and long distance relations are modeled via grammatical function labels rather than via attachment. Figures 1 and 2 show examples.

For preprocessing, we follow the standard practices from the parsing community. In both treebanks, punctuation and other material, such as parentheses, are not included in the annotation, but attached to a virtual root node. We attach the respective nodes to the tree using the algorithm described by Maier et al. (2012) so that every sentence corresponds to exactly one tree. In a nutshell, this algorithm uses the left and right terminal neighbors as attachment targets. In TiGer, we then remove the crossing branches using a two-stage process. In a first step, we apply the transformation described by Boyd (2007). This transformation introduces a new non-terminal for every continuous block of a discontinuous constituent. We keep a flag on each of the newly introduced nodes that indicates if it dominates the head daughter of the original discontinuous node. Subsequently, we delete all those nodes for which this flag is false.[2]

For both POS tagging and parsing, we use the same split for training, development, and test. We use the first half of the last 10 000 sentences in TiGer for development and the second half for testing. The remaining 40 472 sentences are used for training. Accordingly, in order to ensure equal conditions, we use the first 40 472 sentences in TüBa-D/Z for training, and the first and second half of the following 10 000 sentences for development and testing. The remaining sentences in TüBa-D/Z are not used.

4.2 POS Taggers

We employ six different POS tagger, each of them using a different tagging technique. Morfette (Chrupala et al., 2008), in its current implementation based on averaged Perceptron, is a tool designed for the annotation of large morphological tagsets. Since none of the other POS taggers have access to lemmas, we only provide full word forms to Morfette as well, which may inhibit its generalization capability. The RF-Tagger (Schmid and Laws, 2008) assumes a tagset in a factorized version. I.e., the POS tag VVFIN%3sis in sentence (2) would be represented as VVFIN.3.s.i.s, where the dots indicate different subcategories, which are then treated separately by the POS tagger. It is based on a Markov model, but the context size is determined by a decision tree. The Stanford tagger (Toutanova et al., 2003) is based on a maximum entropy model, and SVMTool (Giménez and Màrquez, 2004) is based on support vector machines. TnT (Brants, 2000; Brants, 1998), short for trigrams and tags, is a Markov model POS tagger.

[2] An implementation of all transformations is available at `http://github.com/wmaier/treetools`.

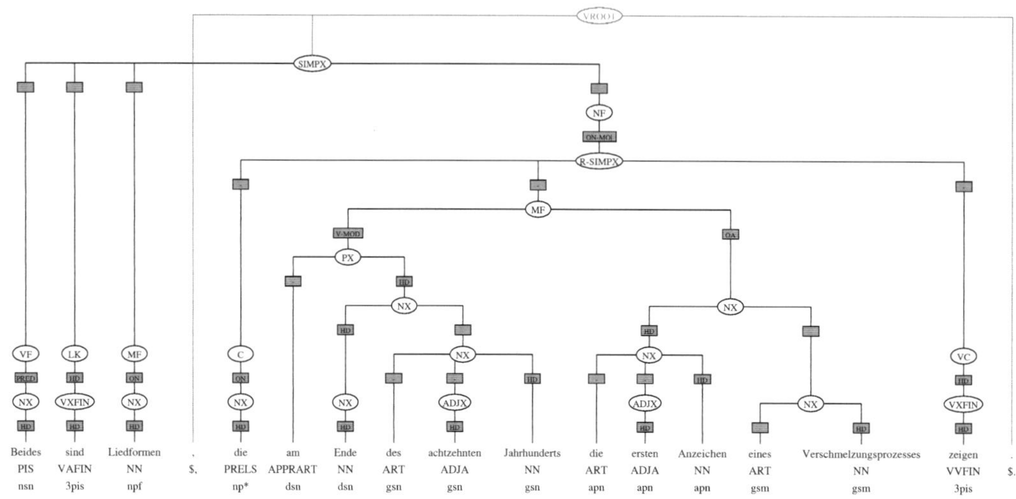

Figure 2: A sentence from TüBa-D/Z.

It uses an interpolation between uni-, bi- and trigrams as probability model. TnT has a sophisticated mechanism for tagging unknown words. We also use Wapiti (Lavergne et al., 2010) a conditional random field tagger. Since conditional random fields were developed for sequence tagging, this POS tagger is expected to perform well.

All POS taggers are used with default settings. For the Stanford tagger, we use the bi-directional model based on a context of 5 words. For SVMTool, we use the processing from left to right in combination with features based on word and POS trigrams and word length, prefix and suffix information. Wapiti is trained on uni-, bi-, and trigrams. Features used in training consist of tests concerning the alphanumeric, upper or lower case characteristics, prefixes and suffixes of length three, and all possible POS tags for a word.

For POS tagging evaluation, we use the script provided by TnT since it also allows us to calculate accuracy on known and unknown words.

4.3 Parser

We use the Berkeley parser (Petrov and Klein, 2007b; Petrov and Klein, 2007a). We chose the Berkeley parser because we are aware of the fact that there are considerable differences in the tagset sizes, which a plain PCFG parser cannot process successfully. The Berkeley parser split/merge capabilities provide a way of smoothing over these differences. For parser evaluation, we use our own implementation of the PARSEVAL metrics.[3] We report labeled precision (LP), labeled recall (LR), and the labeled F-score(LF1). Note that the labeled evaluation does not only look at constituent labels but also at grammatical functions attached to the constituents, e.g. NP-SBJ for a subject NP. This is a considerably more difficult task for German because of the relatively free word order. We also provide POS tagging accuracy in the parse trees since the Berkeley parser adapts POS tags from the input if they do not fit its syntax model.

5 POS Tagging Results

5.1 The Three Tagset Variants

The results for the POS tagging evaluation are shown in table 4. We are aware of the fact that the results are not directly comparable across the different POS tagsets and across different treebanks since the

[3] The implementation is available at `http://github.com/wmaier/evalb-lcfrs`. Note that we evaluate the trees as they are, i.e., we do not collapse or ignore tags.

Tagset	Tagger	TiGer		TüBa-D/Z	
		dev	test	dev	test
UTS	Morfette	98.51	**98.09**	**98.25**	**98.49**
	RF-Tagger	97.89	97.41	97.69	97.96
	Stanford	97.88	96.83	97.11	97.26
	SVMTool	**98.54**	98.01	98.09	98.28
	TnT	97.94	97.48	97.72	97.92
	Wapiti	97.54	96.67	97.47	97.80
STTS	Morfette	94.12	93.23	92.95	93.41
	RF-Tagger	97.04	96.24	96.68	96.84
	RF-Tagger (fact.)	97.05	96.26	96.69	96.85
	Stanford	96.26	95.15	95.63	95.79
	SVMTool	97.06	96.22	96.46	96.69
	TnT	**97.15**	**96.29**	**96.92**	**97.00**
	Wapiti	92.93	91.62	90.99	91.81
STTSmorph	Morfette	82.71	80.10	81.19	82.26
	RF-Tagger	**86.56**	**83.90**	**85.68**	**86.31**
	Stanford	–	–	–	–
	SVMTool	82.47	79.53	80.33	81.31
	TnT	85.77	82.77	84.67	85.45
	Wapiti	79.83	75.92	77.27	78.29
STTSmorph → STTS	TnT	97.08	96.15	96.78	96.82

Table 4: POS tagging results using three versions of the German POS tagset and two treebanks.

corresponding tagging tasks differ in the level of difficulty. Any interpretation must therefore be taken with a grain of salt, but we think that it is important to evaluate POS tagging on its own, especially since it is not always the case that a larger label set automatically results in a more difficult task. The results show that UTS, i.e., the variant with the least information, results in the highest POS tagging results, between 96.67% and 98.54%. In tagging with the STTS, we reach a lower accuracy between 90.99% and 97.15%. When we include the morphological information, we reach considerably lower results, between 75.92% and 86.56%. In other words, this shows that the more information there is in the POS tagset, the harder the POS tagging task is. POS tagging with morphological information is the most difficult task. We also see that there are no results for the Stanford POS tagger in the morphological setting. We were unable to run these experiments, even when we used a high-memory cluster with access to 120g of memory. It seems that the Stanford tagger is incapable of handling the large tagset sizes in the setting using morphological information. Additionally, our assumption that the morphological tagset of TüBa-D/Z is less difficult to annotate because of its smaller tagset size is not borne out. The variation of results on TüBa-D/Z is often less than between the treebanks, across POS taggers.

If we compare the result of the different POS taggers, we see that for the different tagset variants, different POS taggers perform best: For UTS, surprisingly, Morfette reaches the highest results, with the exception of the TiGer development set, for which SVMTool performs slightly better. In general, SVMTool is very close in accuracy to Morfette for this tagset variant. For STTS, TnT outperforms all other POS taggers, and SVMTool is a close second. For STTSmorph, the RF-Tagger reaches the highest results. For the RF-Tagger in combination with the STTS, we performed 2 experiments, one using the standard STTS and one in which the STTS tags are factored, such that VVFIN is factored into V.V.FIN. The latter variant reaches minimally higher results. In all settings, Wapiti is the weakest approach; the difference between Wapiti and the best performing POS tagger reaches 6-7 percent points for STTSmorph. This is rather surprising given that POS tagging is a typical sequence tagging task, for which CRFs were developed.

Another fact worth mentioning is that there are considerable differences in POS tagging accuracy

		TiGer				TüBa-D/Z			
		dev		test		dev		test	
Tagset	Tagger	Known	Unkn.	Known	Unkn.	Known	Unkn.	Known	Unkn.
UTS	Morfette	98.66	**96.74**	98.32	**96.04**	98.54	**95.46**	98.69	**96.39**
	RF-Tagger	98.15	94.64	97.82	93.65	98.28	92.02	98.35	93.85
	Stanford	**99.05**	91.85	**98.78**	87.70	**98.94**	79.30	**98.92**	79.69
	SVMTool	98.81	95.26	98.41	94.45	98.63	92.89	98.66	94.27
	TnT	98.06	96.50	97.67	95.74	98.07	94.28	98.25	95.25
	Wapiti	98.94	80.71	98.51	80.04	98.68	85.79	98.83	86.91
STTS	Morfette	94.42	**90.60**	93.56	**90.24**	93.17	**90.83**	93.59	**91.57**
	RF-Tagger	97.80	87.92	97.30	86.71	97.62	87.59	97.73	87.52
	RF-T. (fact.)	97.78	88.21	97.28	87.09	97.63	87.65	97.73	87.51
	Stanford	**98.16**	73.56	**97.75**	71.60	**97.96**	73.04	**97.97**	72.64
	SVMTool	97.86	87.41	97.26	86.82	97.50	86.47	97.60	87.05
	TnT	97.80	89.25	97.21	87.95	97.65	89.78	97.72	89.33
	Wapiti	94.51	73.78	93.48	74.83	93.21	69.45	93.71	71.74
STTSmorph	Morfette	84.30	63.50	82.43	58.98	82.91	64.53	83.95	64.42
	RF-Tagger	**88.34**	**65.09**	**86.38**	**61.47**	**87.70**	**66.20**	**88.25**	**65.80**
	SVMTool	84.67	55.89	82.40	53.58	82.87	55.81	83.61	57.01
	TnT	87.62	63.41	85.55	57.65	86.91	62.95	87.61	62.55
	Wapiti	83.91	30.51	81.43	26.08	82.05	31.05	82.83	30.29

Table 5: Results for the different POS taggers for known and unknown words.

between the development and test set in both treebanks. For both STTS variants, these differences are often larger than the differences between individual POS taggers on the same data set. Thus, in the STTSmorph setting, the difference for TnT between the development and test set in TiGer is 3 percent points while the differences between TnT and SVMTool and Morfette respectively are less.

One last question that we investigated concerns the effect of the morphological information on POS tagging accuracy. We know that when we use morphological information, the POS tagging task is more difficult. However, it is possible that the mistakes that occur concern only the morphological information while the POS tags minus morphology may be predicted with equal or even higher accuracy. In order to investigate this problem, we used the STTSmorph output of TnT and deleted all the morphological information, thus leaving only the STTS POS tags. We then evaluated these POS tags against the gold STTS tags. The results are shown in the last row in table 4, marked as STTSmorph → STTS. A comparison of these results with the TnT results for STTS shows that the POS tagger reaches a higher accuracy when trained directly on STTS rather than on STTSmorph, with a subsequent deletion of the morphological information. This means that the morphological information is not useful but rather harmful in POS tagging.

5.2 Evaluating on Known and Unknown Words

In a next set of experiments, we investigate how the different POS taggers perform on known and unknown words. We define all words from the development and test set as known if the appear in the training set. If they do not, they are considered unknown words. Note, however, that even if a word is known, we still may not have the full set of POS tags in its ambiguity set. This is especially relevant for the larger tagsets where the ambiguity rate per word is higher.

In TiGer, 7.64% of the words in the development set are unknown, 9.96% in the test set. In TüBa-D/Z, 9.36% of the words in the development set are unknown, 8.64% in the test set. Note that this corresponds to the levels of accuracy in table 4.

The results of the evaluation on known and unknown words are shown in table 5. These results show that the Stanford POS tagger produces the highest accuracies for known words for UTS and STTS (note

Morphology	TiGer dev	TiGer test	TüBa-D/Z dev	TüBa-D/Z test
STTS	**97.15**	**96.29**	**96.92**	**97.00**
STTSmorph	85.77	82.77	84.67	85.45
agreement	86.04	83.08	84.96	85.77
case	88.10	86.47	87.48	87.91
number	95.60	94.19	95.24	95.41
number + person	95.55	94.11	95.18	95.24
verbal features	97.03	96.02	96.55	96.44

Table 6: The results for TnT with different morphological variants.

that it could not be used for STTSmorph). For unknown words, Morfette reaches the highest results for UTS and STTS, with TnT reaching the second highest results. For STTSmorph, the RF-Tagger reaches the highest accuracy on both known and unknown words. The results for the RF-Tagger for STTS show that the factored version performs better on unknown words than the standard one. It is also noticeable that Wapiti, the CRF POS tagger, has the lowest performance on unknown words: For UTS, the results are 10-16 percent points lower that the ones by Morfette; for STTS, the difference reaches 16-23 percent points, and for STTSmorph, about 35 percent points. This shows that in order to reach a reasonable accuracy rate, Wapiti's unknown word handling model via regular expressions must be extended further. However, note that Wapiti's results on known words are also lower than the best performing system's, thus showing that CRFs are less well suited for POS tagging than originally expected.

5.3 Evaluating Morphological Variants

In this set of experiments, we investigate whether there are subsets of STTSmorph that are relevant for parsing and that would allow us to reach higher POS tagging and parsing accuracies than on the full set of morphological features. The subsets were chosen manually to model our intuition on which features may be relevant for parsing. We investigate the following subsets: all agreement features, case only, number only, number + person, and only verbal features. In this set of experiments, we concentrate on TnT because it has been shown to be the most robust across the different settings. The results of these experiments are shown in table 6. For comparison, we also list the results for the original STTS and STTSmorph settings from table 4.

The results show that there are morphological subsets that allow reliable POS accuracies: If we use verbal features, we reach results that are only slightly below the STTS results. For the subset using number + person features, the difference is around 2 percent points. However, all subsets perform worse than the STTS. The subsets that include case or all agreement features, which are the subsets most relevant for parsing, reach accuracies that are slightly above STTSmorph, but still more than 10 percent points below the original STTS.

6 Parsing Results

In this section, we report parsing results for TiGer in table 7 and for TüBa-D/Z in table 8. We again use the three POS tag variants as input, and we report results for 1) gold POS tags, 2) for tags assigned by TnT, which proved to be the most reliable POS tagger across different settings, and 3) for POS tags assigned by the Berkeley parser. Since the parser is known to alter POS tags given as input if they do not fit the syntax model, we also report POS tagging accuracy. Note that this behavior of the parser explains why we do not necessarily have a 100% POS tagging accuracy in the gold POS tag setting.

A first glance at the POS tagging results in the gold POS setting in tables 7 and 8 shows that for UTS and STTS, the decrease in accuracy is minimal. In other words, the parser only changes a few POS tags. When we compared the differences in POS tags between the output of the parser and the gold standard, we found that most changes constitute a retagging of common nouns (NN) as proper nouns (NE). In the STTSmorph setting, POS tagging accuracy is considerably lower, showing that the parser changed

Tag source	Tagset	dev				test			
		POS	LP	LR	LF1	POS	LP	LR	LF1
gold	UTS	100.00	77.97	77.23	77.60	99.97	71.80	70.26	71.02
	STTS	99.98	78.09	77.55	**77.82**	99.97	71.90	71.11	**71.50**
	STTSmorph	91.67	74.72	75.21	74.97	88.70	67.68	67.99	67.83
parser	UTS	**98.55**	77.75	76.84	77.29	**97.83**	71.13	69.50	70.30
	STTS	97.25	78.03	77.19	**77.60**	96.18	71.16	69.84	**70.49**
	STTSmorph	83.06	75.53	75.24	75.39	79.05	67.67	67.02	67.34
TnT	UTS	96.56	74.16	73.28	73.72	96.01	68.37	66.78	67.57
	STTS	97.26	78.03	77.19	**77.60**	96.19	71.16	69.84	**70.49**
	STTSmorph	77.94	73.06	72.69	72.88	75.05	65.43	64.78	65.10

Table 7: Parsing results for TiGer.

Tag source	Tagset	dev				test			
		POS	LP	LR	LF1	POS	LP	LR	LF1
gold	UTS	99.98	81.39	81.12	81.26	99.98	82.24	81.94	82.09
	STTS	100.00	83.60	83.58	**83.59**	99.99	84.54	84.46	**84.50**
	STTSmorph	89.75	82.27	78.85	80.53	90.55	83.57	79.91	81.70
parser	UTS	**98.35**	79.97	79.61	79.79	**98.58**	81.07	80.66	80.87
	STTS	97.20	81.84	81.65	**81.74**	97.39	82.93	82.78	**82.85**
	STTSmorph	81.03	80.85	77.22	78.99	81.68	81.89	78.20	80.00
TnT	UTS	**98.35**	79.97	79.61	79.79	**98.58**	81.07	80.66	80.87
	STTS	97.21	81.84	81.65	**81.74**	97.39	82.93	82.78	**82.85**
	STTSmorph	81.03	80.85	77.22	78.99	81.68	81.89	78.20	80.00

Table 8: Parsing results for TüBa-D/Z.

between 8% (UTS) and 25% (STTSmorph) of the POS tags. This is a clear indication that the parser suffers from data sparseness and has to adapt the POS tags in order to be able to parse the sentences.

We need to compare the POS tagging results based on automatically assigned POS tags; they show the following trends: For TiGer in the STTS setting, the results based on TnT and on the parser are very similar. For UTS and STTSmorph, the POS tags assigned by the parser reach a higher accuracy. For TüBa-D/Z, all the results are extremely similar.[4] If we compare the POS tagging accuracies of the parsed sentences and the accuracies of the original POS tags assigned by the tagger, we see that for TiGer, the accuracy decreases by approximately 1.5 percent points for UTS, 0.1 percent points for STTS and 9 percent points for STTSmorph. For TüBa-D/Z, the loss in the STTSmorph setting is smaller, at around 4 percent points. For UTS and STTS, there is a small improvement in POS tagging accuracy.

When we look at the parsing results, we see that gold POS tags always lead to the highest parsing results, across treebanks and POS tagsets. We also see that across all conditions, the parsing results for STTS are the highest. For TiGer, the results for UTS are only marginally lower, which seems to indicate that some of the distinctions made in STTS are important, but not all of them. For TüBa-D/Z, the loss for UTS is more pronounced, at around 2 percent points. This suggests that for the TüBa-D/Z annotation scheme, the more fined grained distinctions in STTS are more important than for UTS. One example would be the distinction between finite and infinite verbs, which is directly projected to the verb group in TüBa-D/Z (see the verb groups VXFIN and VXINF in figure 2). Note also that for Tüba-D/Z, the parsing based on automatic POS tagging outperforms parsing based on gold UTS tags, thus again confirming how important the granularity of STTS is for this treebank.

When we look at the parsing results for STTSmorph, it is obvious that this POS tagset variant leads to the lowest parsing results, even in the gold POS setting. This means that even though agreement

[4]Because of the (almost) identical results, we checked our results with extreme care but could not find any errors.

information should be helpful for assigning grammatical functions, the information seems to be presented to the parser in a form that it cannot exploit properly. We also performed preliminary experiments using the morphological variants discussed in section 5.3 in parsing, but the results did not improve over the STTS baseline.

When we compare the two sets of automatically assigned POS tags for TiGer, we see that the difference in POS accuracy for UTS is 1.8 percent points while the difference in F-scores is 2.5 percent points. This means that TnT tagging errors have a more negative impact on parsing quality than those in the POS tags assigned by the parser itself. For STTSmorph, the difference is more pronounced in POS accuracy (4 points as opposed to 2.2 in F-scores), which means that for STTSmorph, TnT errors are less harmful than for UTS. We assume that this is the case because in many instances, the POS tags themselves will be correct, and the error occurs in the morphological features. For TüBa-D/Z, the difference between UTS and STTSmorph is marginal; this is due to the fact that UTS results are much lower than for TiGer. Thus, the difference between STTS and STTSmorph is stable across both treebanks.

A more in-depth investigation of the results shows that the aggregate EVALB score tends to hide individual large differences between single sentences in the results. For example, in the results for the TiGer dev set with gold POS tags, there are 119 sentences in STTSmorph which have an STTS counterpart with an F-score that is at least 50 points higher. However, there are also 28 sentences for which the opposite holds, i.e., for which STTSmorph wins over STTS. In TüBa-D/Z, there are fewer sentences with such extreme differences. There are 28 / 11 sentences with a score difference of 50 points or more between STTS and STTSmorph in the TüBa-D/Z development set, and vice versa. A manual inspection of the results indicates that in some cases, the morphology is passed up into the tree and thereby contributes to a correct grammatical function of a phrase label (such as for case information) while in other cases, it causes an over-differentiation of grammatical functions and thereby has a detrimental effect (such as for PPs, which are attached incorrectly). In the case of TüBa-D/Z, this leads to trees with substructures that are too flat, while in the case of TiGer, it leads to more hierarchical substructures. This finding is corroborated by a further comparison of the number of edges produced by the parser, which reveals that for the case of TiGer, the number of edges grows with the size of the POS tagset, while for the case of TüBa-D/Z, the number of edges produced with STTS is higher than with UTS, but drops considerably for STTSmorph. The large differences in results for single sentences look more pronounced in TiGer due to the average number of edges per sentence (7.60/8.72 for dev/test gold), which is much lower than for TüBa-D/Z (20.93/21.16 for dev/test gold); in other words, because of its flat annotation. We suspect that there is data sparsity involved, but this needs to be investigated further.

7 Conclusion and Future Work

We have investigated how the granularity of POS tags influences POS tagging, and furthermore, how POS tagging performance relates to parsing results, on the basis of experiments on two German treebanks, using three POS tagsets of different granularity (UTS, STTS, and STTSmorph), and six different POS taggers, together with the Berkeley parser.

We have shown that the tagging task is easier the less granular the tagset is. Furthermore, we have shown that both too coarse-grained and too fine-grained distinctions on POS level hurt parsing performance. The results for the morphological tagset are thus in direct contrast to previous studies, such as (Dehdari et al., 2011; Marton et al., 2013; Seddah et al., 2009; Szántó and Farkas, 2014), which show for different languages that adding morphological information increases parsing accuracy. Surprisingly, given the STTS tagset, the Berkeley parser itself was able to deliver a POS tagging performance which was almost identical to the performance of the best tagger, TnT. Additionally, we can conclude that the choice of the tagset and of the best POS tagger for a given treebank does not only depend on the language but also on the annotation scheme.

In future work, we will undertake a systematic investigation of tag clustering methods in order to find a truly optimally granular POS tagset. We will also investigate the exact relation between annotation depth and the granularity of the POS tagset with regard to parsing accuracy and data sparsity. The latter may elucidate reasons behind the differences between our results and those of the studies mentioned above.

References

Bernd Bohnet and Joakim Nivre. 2012. A transition-based system for joint part-of-speech tagging and labeled non-projective dependency parsing. In *Proceedings of the Joint Conference on Empirical Methods in Natural Language Processing and Computational Natural Language Learning (EMNLP-CoNLL)*, pages 1455–1465, Jeju Island, Korea.

Bernd Bohnet. 2010. Very high accuracy and fast dependency parsing is not a contradiction. In *Proceedings of the 23rd International Conference on Computational Linguistics (IJCNLP)*, pages 89–97, Beijing, China.

Adriane Boyd. 2007. Discontinuity revisited: An improved conversion to context-free representations. In *Proceedings of The Linguistic Annotation Workshop (LAW) at ACL 2007*, pages 41–44, Prague, Czech Republic.

Sabine Brants, Stefanie Dipper, Silvia Hansen, Wolfgang Lezius, and George Smith. 2002. The TIGER treebank. In *Proceedings of the First Workshop on Treebanks and Linguistic Theories (TLT)*, pages 24–41, Sozopol, Bulgaria.

Thorsten Brants, 1998. *TnT–A Statistical Part-of-Speech Tagger*. Universität des Saarlandes, Computational Linguistics, Saarbrücken, Germany.

Thorsten Brants. 2000. TnT–a statistical part-of-speech tagger. In *Proceedings of the 1st Conference of the North American Chapter of the Association for Computational Linguistics and the 6th Conference on Applied Natural Language Processing (ANLP/NAACL)*, pages 224–231, Seattle, WA.

Marie Candito and Djamé Seddah. 2010. Parsing word clusters. In *Proceedings of the NAACL HLT 2010 First Workshop on Statistical Parsing of Morphologically-Rich Languages*, pages 76–84, Los Angeles, CA.

Xiao Chen and Chunyu Kit. 2011. Improving part-of-speech tagging for context-free parsing. In *Proceedings of 5th International Joint Conference on Natural Language Processing (IJCNLP)*, pages 1260–1268, Chiang Mai, Thailand.

Grzegorz Chrupala, Georgiana Dinu, and Josef van Genabith. 2008. Learning morphology with Morfette. In *Proceedings the Fifth International Conference on Language Resources and Evaluation (LREC)*, Marrakech, Morocco.

Michael Collins, Jan Hajič, Lance Ramshaw, and Christoph Tillmann. 1999. A statistical parser for Czech. In *Proceedings of the 37th Annual Meeting of the Association for Computational Linguistics*, pages 505–512, College Park, MD.

Michael Collins. 1999. *Head-Driven Statistical Models for Natural Language Parsing*. Ph.D. thesis, University of Pennsylvania, Philadelphia, PA.

Michael Daum, Kilian Foth, and Wolfgang Menzel. 2003. Constraint based integration of deep and shallow parsing techniques. In *Proceedings of the 10th Conference of the European Chapter of the Association for Computational Linguistics (EACL)*, Budapest, Hungary.

Jon Dehdari, Lamia Tounsi, and Josef van Genabith. 2011. Morphological features for parsing morphologically-rich languages: A case of Arabic. In *Proceedings of the Second Workshop on Statistical Parsing of Morphologically Rich Languages*, pages 12–21, Dublin, Ireland.

Kilian Foth, Michael Daum, and Wolfgang Menzel. 2005. Parsing unrestricted German text with defeasible constraints. In H. Christiansen, P. R. Skadhauge, and J. Villadsen, editors, *Constraint Solving and Language Processing*, pages 140–157. Springer.

Jesús Giménez and Lluís Màrquez. 2004. SVMTool: A general POS tagger generator based on Support Vector Machines. In *Proceedings of the 4th International Conference on Language Resources and Evaluation (LREC)*, pages 43–46, Lisbon, Portugal.

Yoav Goldberg and Reut Tsarfaty. 2008. A single generative model for joint morphological segmentation and syntactic parsing. In *Proceedings of The 46th Annual Meeting of the Association for Computational Linguistics: Human Language Technologies (ACL:HLT)*, pages 371–379, Columbus, OH.

Jun Hatori, Takuya Matsuzaki, Yusuke Miyao, and Jun'ichi Tsujii. 2011. Incremental joint POS tagging and dependency parsing in Chinese. In *Proceedings of 5th International Joint Conference on Natural Language Processing (IJCNLP)*, pages 1216–1224, Chiang Mai, Thailand.

Geoffrey Hinton. 1999. Products of experts. In *Proceedings of the Ninth International Conference on Artificial Neural Networks*, pages 1–6, Stockholm, Sweden.

Terry Koo, Xavier Carreras, and Michael Collins. 2008. Simple semi-supervised dependency parsing. In *Proceedings of The 46th Annual Meeting of the Association for Computational Linguistics: Human Language Technologies (ACL:HLT)*, pages 595–603, Columbus, OH.

Sandra Kübler and Wolfgang Maier. 2013. Über den Einfluss von Part-of-Speech-Tags auf Parsing-Ergebnisse. *Journal for Language Technology and Computational Linguistics. Special Issue on "Das Stuttgart-Tübingen Wortarten-Tagset – Stand und Perspektiven"*, 28(1):17–44.

Sandra Kübler, Erhard W. Hinrichs, and Wolfgang Maier. 2006. Is it really that difficult to parse German? In *Proceedings of the 2006 Conference on Empirical Methods in Natural Language Processing (EMNLP)*, pages 111–119, Sydney, Australia.

Corrin Lakeland. 2005. *Lexical Approaches to Backoff in Statistical Parsing*. Ph.D. thesis, University of Otago, New Zealand.

Thomas Lavergne, Olivier Cappé, and François Yvon. 2010. Practical very large scale CRFs. In *Proceedings the 48th Annual Meeting of the Association for Computational Linguistics (ACL)*, pages 504–513, Uppsala, Sweden.

Joseph Le Roux, Benoit Sagot, and Djamé Seddah. 2012. Statistical parsing of Spanish and data driven lemmatization. In *Proceedings of the ACL 2012 Joint Workshop on Statistical Parsing and Semantic Processing of Morphologically Rich Languages*, pages 55–61, Jeju, Republic of Korea.

Wolfgang Maier, Miriam Kaeshammer, and Laura Kallmeyer. 2012. Data-driven PLCFRS parsing revisited: Restricting the fan-out to two. In *Proceedings of the Eleventh International Conference on Tree Adjoining Grammars and Related Formalisms (TAG+11)*, Paris, France.

Yuval Marton, Nizar Habash, and Owen Rambow. 2013. Dependency parsing of Modern Standard Arabic with lexical and inflectional features. *Computational Linguistics*, 39(1):161–194.

Slav Petrov and Dan Klein. 2007a. Improved inference for unlexicalized parsing. In *Proceedings of Human Language Technologies 2007: The Conference of the North American Chapter of the Association for Computational Linguistics*, pages 404–411, Rochester, NY.

Slav Petrov and Dan Klein. 2007b. Learning and inference for hierarchically split PCFGs. In *Proceedings of AAAI (Nectar Track)*, Vancouver, Canada.

Slav Petrov and Dan Klein. 2008. Parsing German with language agnostic latent variable grammars. In *Proceedings of the ACL Workshop on Parsing German*, pages 33–39, Columbus, OH.

Slav Petrov, Dipanjan Das, and Ryan McDonald. 2012. A universal part-of-speech tagset. In *Proceedings of the Eight International Conference on Language Resources and Evaluation (LREC)*, Istanbul, Turkey.

Adwait Ratnaparkhi. 1996. A maximum entropy model for part-of-speech tagging. In *Proceedings of the Empirical Methods in Natural Language Processing Conference (EMNLP)*, pages 133–142, Philadelphia, PA.

Anne Schiller, Simone Teufel, and Christine Thielen. 1995. Guidelines für das Tagging deutscher Textkorpora mit STTS. Technical report, Universität Stuttgart and Universität Tübingen.

Helmut Schmid and Florian Laws. 2008. Estimation of conditional probabilities with decision trees and an application to fine-grained POS tagging. In *Proceedings of the 22nd International Conference on Computational Linguistics (COLING)*, pages 777–784, Manchester, UK.

Djamé Seddah, Marie Candito, and Benoît Crabbé. 2009. Cross parser evaluation: A French Treebanks study. In *Proceedings of the 11th International Conference on Parsing Technologies (IWPT)*, pages 150–161, Paris, France.

Wolfgang Seeker and Jonas Kuhn. 2013. Morphological and syntactic case in statistical dependency parsing. *Computational Linguistics*, 39(1):23–55.

Zsolt Szántó and Richárd Farkas. 2014. Special techniques for constituent parsing of morphologically rich languages. In *Proceedings of the 14th Conference of the European Chapter of the Association for Computational Linguistics (EACL)*, pages 135–144, Gothenburg, Sweden.

Heike Telljohann, Erhard W. Hinrichs, Sandra Kübler, Heike Zinsmeister, and Kathrin Beck, 2012. *Stylebook for the Tübingen Treebank of Written German (TüBa-D/Z)*. Seminar für Sprachwissenschaft, Universität Tübingen, Germany.

Kristina Toutanova and Christopher D. Manning. 2000. Enriching the knowledge sources used in a maximum entropy part-of-speech tagger. In *Proceedings of the Joint SIGDAT Conference on Empirical Methods in Natural Language Processing and Very Large Corpora (EMNLP/VLC)*, Hong Kong.

Kristina Toutanova, Dan Klein, Christopher Manning, and Yoram Singer. 2003. Feature-rich part-of-speech tagging with a cyclic dependency network. In *Proceedings of the Human Language Technology Conference of the North American Chapter of the Association for Computational Linguistics (HLT-NAACL)*, pages 252–259, Edmonton, Canada.

Yannick Versley and Ines Rehbein. 2009. Scalable discriminative parsing for German. In *Proceedings of the 11th International Conference on Parsing Technologies (IWPT)*, pages 134–137, Paris, France.

Yannick Versley. 2005. Parser evaluation across text types. In *Fourth Workshop on Treebanks and Linguistic Theories (TLT 2005)*, Barcelona, Spain.

Joint Ensemble Model for POS Tagging and Dependency Parsing

Iliana Simova **Dimitar Vasilev** **Alexander Popov** **Kiril Simov** **Petya Osenova**
Linguistic Modelling Laboratory, IICT-BAS
Sofia, Bulgaria
{iliana|dvasilev|alex.popov|kivs|petya}@bultreebank.org

Abstract

In this paper we present several approaches towards constructing joint ensemble models for morphosyntactic tagging and dependency parsing for a morphologically rich language – Bulgarian. In our experiments we use state-of-the-art taggers and dependency parsers to obtain an extended version of the treebank for Bulgarian, BulTreeBank, which, in addition to the standard CoNLL fields, contains predicted morphosyntactic tags and dependency arcs for each word. In order to select the most suitable tag and arc from the proposed ones, we use several ensemble techniques, the result of which is a valid dependency tree. Most of these approaches show improvement over the results achieved individually by the tools for tagging and parsing.

1 Introduction

Language processing pipelines are the standard means for preprocessing natural language text for various natural language processing (NLP) tasks. A typical pipeline applies the following modules sequentially: a tokenizer, a part-of-speech (POS) tagger, a lemmatizer, and a parser. The main drawback of such an architecture is that the erroneous output of one module in the pipeline propagates through to its final step. This usually has a more significant impact on the processing of languages with segmentation issues, like Chinese, or languages with rich morphological systems, like the Slavic and Romance ones, which exhibit greater morphological and syntactic ambiguity due to the high number of word forms and freer word order.

In this paper we present several experiments in which we simultaneously solve two of the aforementioned tasks – tagging and parsing. The motivation behind this idea is that the two tasks are highly dependent on each other when working with a morphologically rich language, and thus a better solution could be found for each if they are solved jointly. We assemble the outputs of three morphosyntactic taggers (POS taggers) and five dependency parsers in a single step. The ensemble approach uses weights in order to select the best solution from a number of alternatives. We follow (Surdeanu and Manning, 2010) and use two classes of approaches for selecting weights for the alternatives: *voting*, where the weights are assigned by simple calculations over the number of used models and their performance measures; *machine learning weighting*[1], where machine learning is exploited in order to rank the alternatives on the basis of a joint feature model. We refer to both types of approaches as *ranking*. The language of choice in our experiments is Bulgarian, but the techniques presented here are easily applicable to other languages, given the availability of training data.

The interaction between the two levels – morphology and syntax – is carried out via a joint model of features for machine learning. Its aim is to determine the best possible combination out of the predictions of the different taggers and dependency parsers. Working only with the outputs of the taggers and parsers, instead of considering all possibilities for tag, head and syntactic relation for each word in the sentence, reduces the search space and allows us to experiment with more complex features. One limitation of this approach is that the correct combination of an POS tag and a dependency arc might not have been

[1] Surdeanu and Manning (Surdeanu and Manning, 2010) call them *meta-classification*.

First Joint Workshop on Statistical Parsing of Morphologically Rich Languages and Syntactic Analysis of Non-Canonical Languages, pages 15–25 Dublin, Ireland, August 23-29 2014.

predicted by any of the tools in the first place. Therefore the ensemble approach can be beneficial only to a certain extent.

The data used throughout our experiments consists of the dependency conversion[2] of the HPSG-based Treebank of Bulgarian – the BulTreeBank. This data set contains non-projective dependency trees, which are more suitable for describing the relatively free word order of Bulgarian sentences.

The structure of the paper is as follows: in Section 2 we introduce related work on joint models and ensemble models; in Section 3 we introduce related work on Bulgarian parsing and POS tagging; in Section 4 we present our ensemble model; in Section 5 we report on our current experimental setup, including the construction of a parsebank of parses and tagging results; Section 6 presents the results from our ensemble experiments; the last section concludes the paper.

2 Related Work

Our work on ensemble systems for dependency parsing is inspired by the in-depth performance analysis of two of the most influential dependency parsing models: transition-based and graph-based (McDonald and Nivre, 2007). This analysis shows that the two frameworks make different errors when trained and tested on the same datasets. The authors conclude the paper by proposing three approaches for using the advantages of both frameworks: (1) ensemble systems – weighted combinations of the output of both systems; (2) hybrid systems – a single system designed to integrate the strengths of the individual ones; and (3) novel approaches – based on a combination of new training and inference methods. In their further work (Nivre and McDonald, 2008) on the subject they present a hybrid system that combines the two models. The work presented in this paper is along the lines of their first suggestion – a system to facilitate the combination of the outputs of several parsing and tagging models, in order to find an optimal solution.

An experiment with ensemble systems is presented in (Surdeanu and Manning, 2010). This work describes several approaches to the combination of dependency parsers via different types of voting and meta-classification. Voting determines the correct dependency arcs by choosing the ones that are selected by the majority of parsers. Weighted voting uses the accuracy of each parser in order to choose between their predictions for each arc. We also employ these two ranking techniques in our current experiment. Surdeanu and Manning (Surdeanu and Manning, 2010) conclude that meta-classification does not improve the results in comparison to voting. They divide the dependencies in two categories: majority dependencies and minority dependencies. Their conclusion is that meta-classification cannot provide a better selection of minority dependencies, and in this way is comparable to voting. In our work we show that depending on the feature selection for meta-classification, it can actually outperform the voting approach. The experiments presented in (Surdeanu and Manning, 2010) do not use a specific algorithm for the selection of dependencies, and do not ensure that the result of voting is a well-formed dependency tree. In our work we use two algorithms to ensure the construction of trees. We show that the results also depend on the algorithm for tree construction.

Joint models have been successfully used for processing other morphologically rich languages. For instance, (Lee et al., 2011) propose a joint model for inference of morphological properties and syntactic structures, which outperforms a standard pipelined solution when tested on highly-inflected languages such as Latin, Czech, Ancient Greek and Hungarian. It uses a graphical model that employs "local" and "link" factors to impose local word context constraints and to handle long-distance dependencies.

(Cohen and Smith, 2007) and (Goldberg and Tsarfaty, 2008) focus on a joint model for morphological segmentation and syntactic parsing with application to Hebrew. The authors argue that syntactic context is crucial for the correct segmentation of tokens into lexemes and that a model wherein the segmentation and parsing modules share information during processing is better suited to carry out the task. To solve the two tasks jointly, the different morphological analyses of a given utterance are represented simultaneously in a lattice structure; a path through the lattice corresponds to a specific morphological segmentation of the utterance. In (Cohen and Smith, 2007), paths in the lattice and parse trees are combined through a joint probability model and the best combination is found through chart parsing.

[2]www.bultreebank.org/dpbtb/

(Hatori et al., 2012) employ an incremental joint approach to solve three tasks in Chinese: word segmentation, POS tagging, and dependency parsing. The motivation for solving them simultaneously is that some segmentation ambiguities in the language cannot be resolved without considering the surrounding grammatical constructions, while syntactic information can improve the segmentation of out-of-vocabulary words. Parsing is done through a dynamic programming framework – a version of the shift-reduce algorithm.

Joint morphological and syntactic analysis of several morphologically rich languages is presented in (Bohnet et al., 2013). They use an extended transition system for dependency parsing to incorporate POS tagging, tagging with morphological descriptions and lemmas. In addition they define new evaluation metrics. They include the standard POS accuracy, Labeled and Unlabled Arc Accuracy, but also accuracy of combination of features like POS tags, morphological description, lemmas and dependency arcs. Several experiments with different parameters controlling the selection of best tags and morphosyntactic descriptions are presented.

The approach presented in our work is joint in the sense that we solve two tasks simultaneously – the choice for POS tag is dependent on the choice for dependency arc, and vice versa. However, our approach is also ensemble, since it combines the outputs of several systems for solving the two tasks, instead of exploring the whole search space of all combinations of tags and arcs. In this way, the approach is better described as a *joint ensemble model*.

3 Related Work on Bulgarian

Bulgarian is still under-studied with respect to parsing. Although several systems were trained on the BulTreeBank treebank during the CoNLL-X 2006 Shared Task (Buchholz and Marsi, 2006) and after it, a pipeline including a dependency parser with state-of-the-art performance does not exist. A state-of-the-art POS tagger with nearly 98% accuracy is available for Bulgarian (Georgiev et al., 2012). The best result for dependency parsing of Bulgarian reported in literature is 93.5% UAS (Martins et al., 2011). The best result for a pipeline including POS tagging and dependency parsing for Bulgarian is not known because most available tools were trained on the whole BulTreeBank and there is no way to measure their actual performance.

Our work is motivated by previous efforts to solve several NLP tasks simultaneously with application to Bulgarian (Zhikov et al., 2013). The presented joint model for POS tagging, dependency parsing, and co-reference resolution achieved results comparable to a state-of-the-art pipeline with respect to dependency parsing. This pipeline, however, used gold standard POS tags as input to the parser. Note that in the current work we do not rely on gold standard POS tags in the dependency parsing step in order to achieve more realistic results.

The usefulness of the ensemble parsing approach for Bulgarian is investigated in our previous works – (Simov et al., 2013) and (Simov et al., 2014). We trained 21 dependency parsing models with different configurations (parsing algorithm settings and features), including 12 MaltParser (Nivre et al., 2006) models, 6 MSTParser (McDonald, 2006) models, two TurboParser (Martins et al., 2010) models, and one Mate-tools parser (Bohnet, 2010) model. The best achieved ensemble result was 93,63% UAS, but gold POS tags were used as input for parsing. In our current work the best result is slightly lower, but more realistic, since no gold POS tags were used.

In this work as well as in the previous mentioned works we use Chu-Liu-Edmonds algorithm for maximum spanning tree as implemented in the MSTParser to ensure the construction of complete dependency trees. In (Zhikov et al., 2013), POS tags and the co-referential chains are encoded as an extension of the dependency tree in order to apply the same algorithm. We make use of this representation in the current work, as described in the following lines.

4 Ensemble Model

Our ensemble model works over extended dependency trees and graphs. First we define a dependency tree. Then we extend the dependency tree to include alternative POS tags for each wordform node and alternative dependency arcs.

Let us have a set D of dependency tags ($ROOT \in D$) and a sentence $x = w_1, ..., w_n$. A *dependency tree* is a tree $T = (V, A, \delta)$ where:

1. $V = \{0, 1, ..., n\}$ is an ordered set of nodes, that corresponds to an enumeration of the words in the sentence (the root of the tree has index 0);
2. $A \subseteq V \times V$ is a set of arcs;
3. $\delta : A \rightarrow D$ is a labeling function for arcs;
4. 0 is the root of the tree.

In order to extend the tree, we assume a range of possible POS tags for each wordform in the sentence. Such a range of tags has to contain the correct tag for the wordform in the given context. In this work we assume they are coming from results of several POS taggers. These tags are included in the tree as service nodes. In the linear representation of the sentence, they are inserted after the node for the corresponding wordform, and before the node for the next wordform to the right. They are connected to the corresponding wordform with a special link \$TAG. In order to indicate the correct tag, we introduce another type of service node. In the linear representation of the sentence, it is inserted after the last POS tag candidate node, and before the one corresponding to the next wordform to the right. This node is connected to the correct tag via a special arc \$CTAG (correct tag). In this way, all information about the potential tags and the correct tag is represented in the form of a subtree, attached to the wordform. Figure 1 depicts the encoding of a word with POS tag ambiguity as a tree. The correct tag is indicated: verb, personal, perfective, transitive, finite, aorist, third person, singular, or "Vpptf-03s". The `TAG` arcs are represented as red links. The `CTAG` arc is represented as an oval.

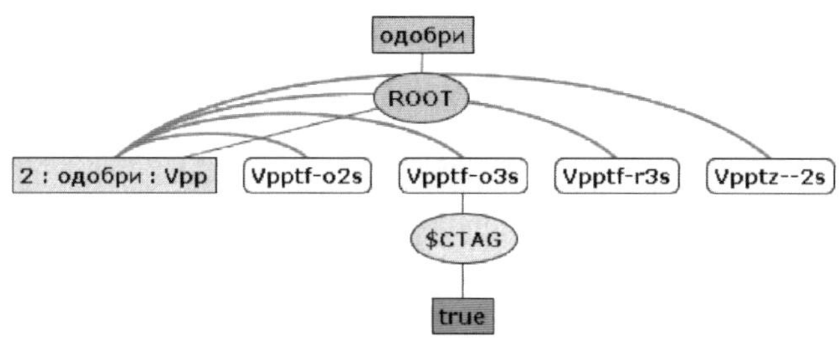

Figure 1: Subtree of a word with candidate POS tags and the correct tag.

Our ensemble model starts working on a set of extended dependency trees from which it to select the an extended tree. We represent this set as an extended dependency graph.

Let us have a set G of POS tags, and a set D of dependency tags ($ROOT \in D$). Let us have a sentence $x = w_1, ..., w_n$. An *extended dependency graph* is a directed graph $Gr = (V_e, A, \pi, \delta, \rho)$ where:

1. $V_e = \{0, 1, \$TAG1_1, TAG1_2, ..., TAG1_{j_1}, TT1, ..., n, TAGn_1, TAGn_2, ..., TAGn_{j_n}, TTn\}$ is an ordered set of nodes, that corresponds to an enumeration of the words in the sentence (the root of the tree has index 0), additional nodes for alternative POS tags - $TAGk_j$, such that for each wordform k there is at least one such node and for each wordform k there is one TTk selecting its correct POS tag;
2. $V = \{0, 1, ..., n\}$ is the ordered subset of V_e corresponding to words in the sentence including the root element;
3. $A \subseteq V \times V$ is a set of arcs;
4. $\pi : TAGk_j \rightarrow G$ is a labeling function from tag nodes to POS tags (node 0 does not have POS tag). These nodes are called POS nodes;
5. $TAGk_j$ is connected by an arc with label \$TAG to the wordform k;
6. TTk is connected each $TAGk_j$ by an arc with label \$CTAG, where k is the number of the wordform;

7. $\delta : A \rightarrow D$ is a labeling relation for arcs. Each arc has at least one label;
8. $\rho : \langle a, l \rangle \rightarrow R$, is a ranking function, where a is either an arc in A and $l \in \delta(a)$ or $a = \langle TAGk_j, k \rangle$ and $l = \$CTAG$. ρ assigns to each labeled dependency arc or tagging arc a rank. The arcs from POS tags nodes to wordform node always have rank 1;
9. 0 is the root of the graph.

We use an extended dependency graph *Gr* to represent the initial data from which we select an analysis. Each extended dependency graph could incorporate the results from several POS taggers and several dependency parsers. At the beginning each node for true tag is connected to all corresponding tagger predictions, and after ensemble is assigned to a single parent node, the correct tag. In this way, all information about the potential tags and the correct tag is represented in the form of a subtree, attached to the word form.

Our ensemble model starts from an extended dependency graph *Gr* and constructed an extended tagged dependency tree T which is a subgraph of *Gr*. In the rest of the paper we will use just dependency tree and dependency graph terms to denote the extended ones. We use two algorithms for the construction of a single dependency tree from the predictions of all tagger and parser models (dependency graph).

The first algorithm, denoted `LocTr`, is presented in (Attardi and Dell'Orletta, 2009). It constructs the dependency tree incrementally, starting from an empty tree and then selecting the arc with the highest rank that could extend the current partial tree. The arcs are selected from the extended dependency graph. The algorithm chooses the best arc *locally*.

The second algorithm, denoted `GloTr`, is the Chu-Liu-Edmonds algorithm for maximal spanning tree implemented in the MSTParser (McDonald, 2006). This algorithm starts with a complete dependency graph including all possible dependency arcs. Then it selects the maximal spanning tree on the basis of the ranks assigned to the potential arcs. The arcs that are not proposed by any of the parsers are deleted (or we could think about them as having infinite small rank). The arcs for the service nodes include only the once from the definition of extended dependency graph. The algorithm is *global* with respect to the selection of arcs. In our scenario, however, we do not construct a full graph, but one containing only the suggestions of the parsers and taggers.

These two ensemble algorithms are included in our system for experiments with dependency parsers. The user can specify which one should be used in their experiments, or alternatively compare the performance of both. Making choice for each of the TT nodes both algorithms select the best POS tag for the corresponding wordform.

In the next section we define the experimental setup: the creation of parsebank where for each tree in the original treebank a dependency graph is created; the definition of voting approaches and the machine learning weighting.

5 Experimental Setup

In this section we present in detail the way in which our ensemble experiment was set up, including the data format and choice of ranking and features for machine learning.

5.1 Tagger and Parser Models and Parsebank

In the current experiments we use the five parsing models which achieved the highest LAS and UAS scores for the BulTreeBank data in previous experiments[3] (Simov et al., 2014). They include two MaltParser models, `MLT07` and `MLT09`, one MSTParser model, `MST05`, one TurboParser model, `Turbo02`, and one Mate-tools Parser model, `MATE01`. The following configurations were used for each model:

1. `MLT07` - Convington non-projective algorithm with extended feature set for lemmas.
2. `MLT09` - Stack eager algorithm with extended feature set for morphosyntactic descriptions.
3. `MST05` - default parser settings, with the exception of the order of features. The parser was set to use features over pairs of adjacent edges (*second-order*: true).

[3]The names of the models were left unchanged for easier reference to previous work.

4. MATE01 - default parser settings.
5. Turbo02 - the parser was set to use a complex set of features (*model_type*=full), which include arbitrary sibling parts, non-projectivity parts, grand-sibling third-order parts, and tri-sibling third-order parts.

The models were initially trained on the gold standard values for lemma, part-of-speech tags and features, from the dependency version of the BulTreeBank. The best performing model in a 10-fold cross validation is MATE01, with 92.9% UAS, followed by TURBO02 with 92.7% UAS.

In addition to the parsing models, three part-of-speech taggers were trained to predict the morphosyntactic tags from the BTB-tagset (Simov et al., 2004) for the data. They include a baseline tagger which makes use of a lexicon (BLL tagger), the morphology tagger of Mate-tools, and the TreeTagger (Schmid, 1994).

The standard approach for setting up a POS tagging baseline – selection of the most frequent tag – cannot be applied for our experiment with Bulgarian, because of the rich morphosyntactic tagset of 680 tags. We construct a baseline tagger on the basis of the corpus and a morphological lexicon. This baseline ignores context altogether and assigns each word type the POS tag it was most frequently seen with in the training dataset; ties are broken randomly. For words not seen in the training dataset we use a simple guesser which assigns POS tags on the basis of the word suffix. We first built two frequency lists, containing respectively (1) the most frequent tag in the training dataset for each word type, as before, and (2) the most frequent tag in the training dataset for each class of tags that can be assigned to some word type, according to the lexicon. Given a target word type, this new baseline first tries to assign to it the most frequent tag from the first list. If this is not possible, which happens (i) in case of ties or (ii) when the word type was not seen during training, it extracts the tag class from the lexicon and consults the second list. If there is a single most frequent tag in the corpus for this tag class, it is assigned; otherwise a random tag from this tag class is selected. This strategy gives us a very high accuracy for this tagger. Although we refer to it as a baseline, it achieves the best score among the taggers we used in these experiments. Our explanation for this is the fact that we are using a morphological lexicon to predict the possible tags for the unseen words in the test sets.

The Mate morphology tagger constitutes one step of the processing pipeline in Mate-tools, and makes use of previously predicted values for lemma and tag. Therefore, we trained a Mate-tools lemmatizer and tagger in addition, so that no gold standard data is used directly to obtain the morphological information for each word in our experiment.

The third tagger trained on the BulTreeBank data and used in the experiments is TreeTagger, a tool that estimates transition probabilities via decision trees. In training mode it was run with its default options. The tagger takes as parameters a lexicon of all the words that are found in the training corpus, one per line, followed by the respective POS tags encountered in the corpus and, optionally, by the lemmas for those forms. We extracted this information from our training data, but skipped the optional training for lemma, since lemmas can be automatically generated for each word form using the predicted BTB tag.

Using the taggers in a 10-fold experiment, we obtained three new versions of the dependency treebank, with predicted values for the fields lemma, tag, and features, which brings us closer to a real-world parsing scenario with unseen data. The output of the Mate morphology tagger is a prediction of the values in the features field of the CoNLL dependency format. The BLL and TheeTagger predictions for morphosyntactic tags were used to generate the fields lemma, tag, and features, for each word in the original treebank. The taggers achieved accuracy of 95.91% (BLL Tagger), 94.92% (Mate morphology tagger), and 93.12% (TreeTagger). Each of the five parsing models was evaluated on the new data sets (Table 1). This evaluation exemplifies the extent to which a decrease in tagger accuracy can influence parsing accuracy. There is a decrease in performance in terms of UAS score ranging from 1.6% to 4.6%, compared to the performance of the models when using the gold data fields.

We define an upper bound for the potential improvement through ensemble for each task as the percentage of words in the parsebank for which there is at least one correct prediction by a tagger or parser. The upper bound for the combination of taggers is 98.38%. For the parses the upper bound is 96.95 %

MLT07	MLT09	MATE01	MST05	Turbo02	training data
0.900	0.908	0.929	0.911	0.927	gold
0.881	0.890	0.910	0.890	0.911	BLL tagger
0.881	0.889	0.908	0.890	0.910	Mate tagger
0.857	0.865	0.883	0.865	0.883	TreeTagger

Table 1: Average UAS scores from the 10-fold cross validation of the parsing models trained on gold data and on data containing automatically generated fields obtained using the outputs of three taggers.

for UAS and 95.38 % for LAS. These upper bounds can be reached if the algorithm is able to select the correct solution in all cases.

A rich search space of possible combinations of POS tags and parses is available for the voting and machine learning weighting modules to choose from. An increase in tagging accuracy through ensemble can lead to obtaining better parsing results. In order to allow for ensemble to be performed on the output of several POS taggers and parsers, the tree that stores the POS tags and the head and relation predicted by each parsing model was represented in a dependency graph.

Thus, the parsebank consists of dependency graphs constructed by the three POS tagging models and the five dependency parsing models. All the models are trained on gold data from the original treebank. Because the parsing depends on the POS tags assigned to the wordform we applied the parsing models for the results from each POS taggers. In this way we potentially up to fifteen arcs per wordform.

5.2 Combining Parses by Voting

We investigate three voting modes for the calculation of the weight assigned to each candidate dependency arc: (1) the arcs are ranked by the number of parsers/taggers that predicted them (Rank01); (2) the arcs are ranked by the sum of the accuracy of all parsers/taggers that predicted them (these metrics include the LAS and UAS measures from the 10-fold cross validation and the tagger accuracies individually achieved by each tool) (Rank02); and (3) the arcs are ranked by the average of the accuracy of the parsers/taggers that predicted them (Rank03).

5.3 Combining Taggers and Parsers by Machine Learning Weighting

In order to evaluate the interaction between morphosyntactic information and the dependency parsing, we conducted an experiment in which a machine learning technique was used for ranking the tags and arcs suggested by the different models. This was done with the help of the package `RandomForest`[4] of the system R[5]. The parsebank was once again divided into training and test parts, using the same proportion, but orthogonally: 90% and 10%.

For each word node there are up to three different tags and for each tag there are up to five arcs. We constructed pairs of tags and arcs on the basis of these suggestions. Each pair was compared with the gold data and classified as correct or incorrect for a given context. To each pair (`Tag` , `Arc`) a vector of features was assigned. `Arc` was modelled by three features: relation (`Rel`), distance in words to the parent node (`Dist`) and direction of the parent node (`Dir`) – `Left`, meaning that the parent node is on the left, and `Right`, meaning that the parent node is on the right. `Tag` was represented as a vector of its grammatical features including POS, gender, number, etc. In this way the agreement features were represented explicitly. We also included the word form string as a feature, as well as the corresponding information for the word form context – words before and after it, and the same for the parent node in the dependency tree.

A representation of this data as a value vector for `RandomForest` is given in Table 2.

[4]http://cran.r-project.org/web/packages/randomForest/randomForest.pdf
[5]http://www.r-project.org/

Feature	Value
Word	the current node
WordBefore	the word before the current node
WordAfter	the word after the current node
ParentWord	the parent word
PWordBefore	the word before the parent word
PWordAfter	the word after the parent word
SelectedArc	one of the arcs suggested by one of the models for the node
SelectedTag	one of the arcs suggested by one of the models for the node
CorrectIncorrect	true or false depending on whether the selected pair is the correct one for the node

Table 2: Feature vector used with RandomForest for the experiment.

The tuples generated from the training part of the treebank were used to train the RandomForest in regression mode, then the model was applied to the test set to rank each pair. After this the ranks were distributed to tags and arcs. These weights were used by the algorithms LocTr and GloTr.

Each tag and arc for a given word could participate in several different feature vectors. Thus each of them could receive different weights from the evaluation of the vectors. In our view, the best selection among these weights could be determined only through experimentation. We have tested three rankings: WMax – the maximum tag weight for all word vectors, WMin – the minimum tag weight for all word vectors, and MSum – the sum of all tag weights for all word vectors.

6 Experiments

We ran both algorithms (LocTr and GloTr) for construction of dependency trees using various combinations of the outputs of our dependency parsing and tagging models. Table 3 shows the parsing accuracy results when combining all models (1), only the models of the two best performing parsers, Turbo02 and Malt01 (2), and the best combination we have found by trying all possible combinations (around 32K) (3). We included the results for (1) and (2) to demonstrate that the best combination cannot be predicted in advance by simply selecting the candidate with the largest number of models, or the one with the best performing individual parsers.

The best combination in this experiment in terms of UAS score is: MLT09+BLL, Mate01+BLL, MST05+BLL, Turbo02+BLL, MLT07+MateTagger, Mate01+MateTagger, Turbo02+MateTagger. This combination achieves better UAS score (92.47%) than any of the individual parsers (see Table 1).

There was an improvement of 1.37% over the best performing individual parser Turbo01+BLL, which achieves 91.10% UAS. The unlabelled accuracy after voting is, however, still 0.43% lower than the best result on the gold data achieved by an individual model Mate01. We suspect that this is due to having only three tagger models in the current experiment, and that adding a few more tagger models for voting can help improve the result.

Table 4 presents the accuracy achieved for all possible combinations of the three taggers by voting per rank. We have to stress the fact that the selection of the morphosyntactic tag in the extended dependency tree is independent from the selection of dependency arcs, because each new tag node is connected to the word node by equal weight. The interaction between dependency arcs and morphosyntactic arcs is ensured by the features used in machine learning weighting. The results for the combination improve the individual accuracy for all taggers.

The results in Table 4 show that it is hard to predict the best combinations in advance without enumerating all possibilities. Note that for voting (Rank01, Rank02, and Rank03) it is meaningless to investigate

Models		Algorithm	Rank01		Rank02		Rank03	
			Number		Sum		Average	
			LAS	UAS	LAS	UAS	LAS	UAS
(1)	all models	LocTr	88.55	92.05	88.61	92.10	85.57	88.82
		GloTr	88.55	91.96	88.65	92.04	84.54	88.75
(2)	all Mate01 and Turbo02 models	LocTr	87.68	91.38	87.80	91.48	86.94	90.55
		GloTr	87.58	91.21	87.82	91.45	86.84	90.62
(3)	best combination	LocTr	88.90	92.34	89.05	**92.47**	86.19	89.40
		GloTr	88.94	92.31	89.14	**92.45**	85.23	89.27

Table 3: UAS and LAS obtained after voting using the algorithms LocTr and GloTr for tree construction. (1) All 18 models; (2) A combination of the best individual models: Mate01 and Turbo02 + each tagger; (3) best combination: MLT09+BLL, Mate01+BLL, MST05+BLL, Turbo02+BLL, MLT07+MateTagger, Mate01+MateTagger, Turbo02+MateTagger;

Voting	Rank01	Rank02	Rank03
	Number	Sum	Average
BLL, Mate, TreeTagger	96.24	96.24	95.22
MLearning	**WMax**	**WMin**	**WSum**
BLL, Mate, TreeTagger	96.10	96.20	96.25
BLL, Mate	96.62	96.59	**96.63**
BLL, TreeTagger	95.89	96.08	96.09
Mate, TreeTagger	95.29	95.40	96.25

Table 4: Tagger accuracy after voting and machine learning weighting.

the combinations involving only two taggers, because in this case the output of voting will always be the same as the output of the better tagger.

Table 5 presents the UAS and LAS measures achieved using machine learning weighting. In this case the best combination is Mate01+BLL, Turbo02+BLL, Mate01+MateTagger, Turbo02+MateTagger. Again, the results are better than the ones obtained by the individual parsing models. They also demonstrate some small improvement over the voting ranking.

Model	Algorithm	LAS	UAS
all	LocTr	89.17	92.46
	GloTr	89.23	92.27
all Mate01 and Turbo02 models	LocTr	88.26	91.81
	GloTr	88.32	91.87
best combination	LocTr	89.76	93.18
	GloTr	89.81	93.22

Table 5: Results from the experiments with RandomForest. The best combination is Mate01+BLL, Turbo02+BLL, Mate01+MateTagger, Turbo02+MateTagger.

These experiments show the following: (1) the combination of taggers and parsers is a feasible task; (2) the combination improves the accuracy of both the taggers and the parsers; (3) the combination of both tasks is better than the pipeline approach; (4) there is room for improvement in order to reach the upper bounds presented in Section 5.1.

7 Conclusion and Future Work

In this paper we have presented several approaches for combining parses produced by five parsing models and tagging results from three taggers. The motivation behind a joint ensemble model is the interaction between the morphosyntactic features of the word forms and the dependency relations between them. The interaction could be considered as local and global interaction. The local interaction is usually captured by n-gram models for tagging. The global interaction is represented by such phenomena like subject – verb agreement, verb clitic – object – indirect object agreement, agreement between head noun and relative pronouns, agreement between secondary predication, agreement within co-reference chains, agreement within NPs. With relation to these cases, our current model deals with local interaction on the basis of an n-gram model. Global agreement phenomena are currently modeled via dependency arcs between word forms that agree in their grammatical features.

We deal with some of the interaction between local and some global patterns via a machine learning approach in which the appropriateness of the MorphoSyntactic tag and the dependency arc for a given word form are evaluated in conjunction. The appropriateness is expressed as a number between 0 and 1, where 0 means inappropriate and 1 means appropriate. This number is used as a rank for the ensemble algorithms.

Some of the global agreement phenomena such as verb clitic – object – indirect object agreement, secondary predication and relative pronoun agreement are not covered by the current model. In the future we plan to extend the model with global features defined not by arcs in the dependency tree, but by patterns of dependency paths. These feature patterns will depend on the grammatical characteristics of the given word form. In some cases they might not be directly related to the word form in the tree.

Our experiments show that a joint architecture is a good alternative to a pipeline architecture. There is an improvement in accuracy for both tasks in our joint model. However, this approach has its limitations with respect to possible improvement.

Future extensions of the experiments in several directions are envisaged. First, more linguistic knowledge will be included from the morphological lexicon, valency lexicon and semantic categories of the words as features for machine learning. Second, we plan to extend the experiments by including more tagger and parser models, which could lead to an increase in the upper bound for potential improvement in accuracy. In future work we envisage to compare our work with the work of (Bohnet et al., 2013) applied on Bulgarian data. Also we will would like to include as features word clusters as they suggested in the paper and as we did in parsing context (Ghayoomi et al., 2014).

Acknowledgements

This research has received partial funding from the EC's FP7 (FP7/2007-2013) under grant agreement number 610516: "QTLeap: Quality Translation by Deep Language Engineering Approaches" and grant agreement number 611760: "EUCases: EUropean and National CASE Law and Legislation Linked in Open Data Stack".

References

Giuseppe Attardi and Felice Dell'Orletta. 2009. Reverse revision and linear tree combination for dependency parsing. In *Proceedings of Human Language Technologies: The 2009 Annual Conference of the North American Chapter of the Association for Computational Linguistics, Companion Volume: Short Papers*, pages 261–264, Boulder, Colorado.

Bernd Bohnet, Joakim Nivre, Igor Boguslavsky, RichÃ¡rd Farkas, Filip Ginter, and Jan Hajic. 2013. Joint morphological and syntactic analysis for richly inflected languages. *TACL*, 1:415–428.

Bernd Bohnet. 2010. Very high accuracy and fast dependency parsing is not a contradiction. In *Proceedings of the 23rd International Conference on Computational Linguistics*, COLING '10, pages 89–97, Stroudsburg, PA, USA.

Sabine Buchholz and Erwin Marsi. 2006. Conll-x shared task on multilingual dependency parsing. In *Proceedings of the Tenth Conference on Computational Natural Language Learning (CoNLL-X)*, pages 149–164, New York City.

Shay B Cohen and Noah A Smith. 2007. Joint morphological and syntactic disambiguation. Proceedings of the 2007 Joint Conference on Empirical Methods in Natural Language Processing and Computational Natural Language Learning (EMNLP-CoNLL). Prague, Czech Republic.

Georgi Georgiev, Valentin Zhikov, Kiril Ivanov Simov, Petya Osenova, and Preslav Nakov. 2012. Feature-rich part-of-speech tagging for morphologically complex languages: Application to Bulgarian. In *EACL'12*, pages 492–502.

Masood Ghayoomi, Kiril Simov, and Petya Osenova. 2014. Constituency parsing of bulgarian: Word- vs class-based parsing. Proceedings of LREC 2014.

Yoav Goldberg and Reut Tsarfaty. 2008. A single generative model for joint morphological segmentation and syntactic parsing. In *ACL 2008*, pages 371–379.

Jun Hatori, Takuya Matsuzaki, Yusuke Miyao, and Jun'ichi Tsujii. 2012. Incremental joint approach to word segmentation, pos tagging, and dependency parsing in chinese. In *Proceedings of the 50th Annual Meeting of the Association for Computational Linguistics: Long Papers-Volume 1*, pages 1045–1053.

John Lee, Jason Naradowsky, and David A Smith. 2011. A discriminative model for joint morphological disambiguation and dependency parsing. In *Proceedings of the 49th Annual Meeting of the Association for Computational Linguistics: Human Language Technologies-Volume 1*, pages 885–894.

André F. T. Martins, Noah A. Smith, Eric P. Xing, Pedro M. Q. Aguiar, and Mário A. T. Figueiredo. 2010. Turbo parsers: Dependency parsing by approximate variational inference. In *Proceedings of the 2010 Conference on Empirical Methods in Natural Language Processing*, EMNLP '10, pages 34–44, Stroudsburg, PA, USA.

Andre Martins, Noah Smith, Mario Figueiredo, and Pedro Aguiar. 2011. Dual decomposition with many overlapping components. In *Proceedings of the 2011 Conference on Empirical Methods in Natural Language Processing*, pages 238–249, Edinburgh, Scotland, UK.

Ryan McDonald and Joakim Nivre. 2007. Characterizing the errors of data-driven dependency parsing models. In *Proceedings of the 2007 Joint Conference on Empirical Methods in Natural Language Processing and Computational Natural Language Learning (EMNLP-CoNLL)*, pages 122–131.

Ryan McDonald. 2006. *Discriminative Training and Spanning Tree Algorithms for Dependency Parsing*. Ph.D. thesis.

Joakim Nivre and Ryan McDonald. 2008. Integrating graph-based and transition-based dependency parsers. In *Proceedings of ACL-08: HLT*, pages 950–958, Columbus, Ohio.

Joakim Nivre, Johan Hall, and Jens Nilsson. 2006. Maltparser: a data-driven parser-generator for dependency parsing. In *Proceedings of LREC-2006*.

Helmut Schmid. 1994. Probabilistic part-of-speech tagging using decision trees. In *Proceedings of international conference on new methods in language processing*, volume 12, pages 44–49. Manchester, UK.

Kiril Simov, Petya Osenova, and Milena Slavcheva. 2004. BTB:TR03: BulTreeBank morphosyntactic tagset BTB-TS version 2.0.

Kiril Simov, Ginka Ivanova, Maria Mateva, and Petya Osenova. 2013. Integration of dependency parsers for Bulgarian. In *The Twelfth Workshop on Treebanks and Linguistic Theories*, pages 145–156, Sofia, Bulgaria.

Kiril Simov, Iliana Simova, Ginka Ivanova, Maria Mateva, and Petya Osenova. 2014. A system for experiments with dependency parsers. In *Proceedings of LREC 2014)*, Reykjavik, Iceland.

Mihai Surdeanu and Christopher D. Manning. 2010. Ensemble models for dependency parsing: Cheap and good? In *Proceedings of the North American Chapter of the Association for Computational Linguistics Conference (NAACL-2010)*, Los Angeles, CA.

Valentin Zhikov, Georgi Georgiev, Kiril Simov, and Petya Osenova. 2013. Combining pos tagging, dependency parsing and coreferential resolution for Bulgarian. In *Proceedings of the International Conference Recent Advances in Natural Language Processing RANLP 2013*, pages 755–762, Hissar, Bulgaria.

Improving the parsing of French coordination through annotation standards and targeted features

Assaf Urieli
CLLE-ERSS
Université de Toulouse
assaf.urieli@univ-tlse2.fr
Joliciel Informatique
Foix, France
assaf@joli-ciel.com

Abstract

In the present study we explore various methods for improving the transition-based parsing of coordinated structures in French. Features targeting syntactic parallelism in coordinated structures are used as additional features when training the statistical model, but also as an efficient means to find and correct annotation errors in training corpora. In terms of annotation, we compare four different annotations for coordinated structures, demonstrate the importance of globally unambiguous annotation for punctuation, and discuss the decision process of a transition-based parser for coordination, explaining why certain annotations consistently out-perform others. We compare the gains provided by different annotation standards, by targeted features, and by using a wider beam. Our best configuration gives a 37.28% reduction in the coordination error rate, when compared to the baseline SPMRL test corpus for French after manual corrections.

1 Introduction

Coordinated structures (CS) are recognised as one of the main difficulties for automatic syntax parsers. They are particularly challenging for transition-based parsers, which operate sequentially from sentence start to end: indeed, even for a simple coordinated structure, it is virtually impossible to determine the first conjunct of the structure without examining the rest of the sentence. Consider the following three sentences, identical in French up to the coordinating conjunction:

Example 1.1 - J'ai mangé une pomme rouge et mûre. *(I ate a red and ripe apple)*
- J'ai mangé une pomme rouge et une orange. *(I ate a red apple and an orange)*
- J'ai mangé une pomme rouge et Georges a bu du thé. *(I ate a red apple and George drank some tea)*

In the above cases, selecting the correct conjuncts is simply a matter of examining the parts-of-speech immediately following the coordinating conjunction, except in the last case, where we have to decide whether or not George gets eaten. Nevertheless, nothing preceding the conjunction can help us make the decision. Often the situation is more complex, with adjuncts intervening between the conjunction and second conjunct, not to mention cases such as various forms of ellipsis, CSs with 3 or more conjuncts, and modifiers shared by two or more conjuncts.

In this article, after reviewing related work (section 2) and introducing CS annotation and transition-based parsing (section 3) and our data set and software (section 4), we follow a chronological outline in terms of our own research. In a previous study (Urieli, 2014) we successfully applied knowledge-rich targeted features to the pos-tagging of ambiguous functional words. In the present study we turn to parsing (section 5.1), and attempt to apply knowledge-rich targeted features for coordination to the SPMRL 2013 dependency corpus for French (Seddah et al., 2013). Although the results are not fully satisfactory, we discover while tuning the features that they can be very useful for pinpointing and correcting many of the coordination errors in the training and evaluation corpora (section 5.2). Also, while exploring the reason behind failure to coordinate correctly, we note that the way in which coordination is annotated in the corpus is responsible for a sizable proportion of errors. We then attempt automatic transformations

First Joint Workshop on Statistical Parsing of Morphologically Rich Languages and Syntactic Analysis of Non-Canonical Languages, pages 26–38 Dublin, Ireland, August 23-29 2014.

of this annotation and compare results for six different annotations (section 5.3). Finally, we combine annotation schemes with targeted features and a wider beam to find the maximal gain that can be attained (section 5.4).

2 Related work

Several studies have explored the annotation standards for coordination in English. However, the original Penn Treebank annotates only a subset of simple coordinated structures implicitly by grouping the items together in a single phrase. Maier et al. (2012) present an annotation scheme for Penn Treebank coordination which includes punctuation, critical in the case of constituency treebanks. They then (Maier and Kübler, 2013) train a classifier to attempt to recognise coordinating vs. non-coordinating commas, and achieve an f-score of 89.22 for the coordinating (difficult) class. Many of the phenomena they are trying to disambiguate in the constituency treebank by annotating punctuation are disambiguated in dependency treebanks more simply by using an appropriate set of dependency labels, e.g. in the case of apposition vs. coordination. In the present study, we thus take a somewhat opposite approach by removing annotation from punctuation in the dependency treebank context, in order to concentrate the decision-process on the conjuncts themselves.

Ivanova et al. (2013) measure performance for English using three different annotations for coordination, all of which are covered by the present study. With respect to annotation, they come to similar conclusions for English to ours for French, but concentrate on the lowest-accuracy conjunction-headed approach, as it is proned by the grammar-based parser in which they specialize.

Popel et al. (2013) perform a survey of many different dependency annotations for coordination, and develop a tool for lossless transformation between these annotations. They also describe in detail the various difficulties involved in annotating coordination, including the role of punctuation.

Schwartz et al. (2012) compare the "learnability" of various possible annotations for 6 structures in English, including coordination, where learnability is defined both by the annotation giving the highest attachment accuracy, and by the annotation which attains a target accuracy with the fewest training examples. They compare 2 possible annotations for coordination, and find, as we do, that using one of the conjuncts as head is far more learnable than using the conjunction as the head, across a variety of parsers. However, since the Penn Treebank does not annotate coordinated structures with more than 2 conjuncts, they explore fewer annotation possibilites than in the present study.

Tsarfaty et al. (2011) raise a similar question of evaluating parsers trained on different annotation standards, including for coordination, but take a radically different approach. They convert all annotations to directly comparable generalised functional trees, and find that apparent major differences in performance are considerably attenuated or disappear when considered in such a light. It would be interesting to apply their method to our different annotations for French data, and see to what extent it affects results.

In terms of annotation standards, the present study extends previous work by (a) applying similar experiments to French and consolidating certain conclusions, while concentrating on the case of 3 or more conjuncts, (b) highlighting the importance of a systematic annotation for punctuation, which is only possible when punctuation is not explicitly used to indicate coordination, and (c) comparing gains from annotation changes to those made by the addition of targeted coordination features or using a wider beam.

In terms of specific targeted features for coordination, Hogan (2007) achieves statistically significant improvements in noun phrase (NP) coordination in English, in the context of a history-based constituency parser, by introducing features for NP head semantic similarity. Shimbo and Hara (2007) leave out semantics, and instead use features incorporating the syntactic "edit-distance" between competing structures. Both studies apply to consitituency parsers with a higher complexity than our linear transition-based parser.

Other studies have attempted introducing generic "rich" features without specifically aiming at parallelism in coordination. Kübler et al. (2009) propose a method whereby the n-best PCFG parses are reranked, in order to improve the parsing of coordination in German. Their features are generic, but can cover the full parse trees since they are applied in reranking rather than during parsing. Our study differs

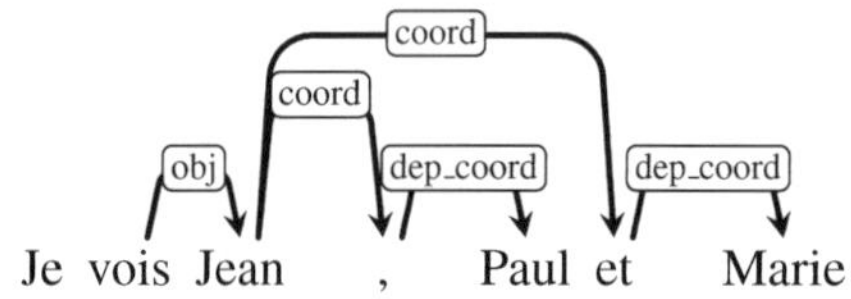

Figure 1: French SPMRL annotation for coordination

from theirs by applying the features during the first parsing pass of a linear-complexity transition-based parser, rather than requiring a large beam of n-best solutions at the outset.

Zhang and Nivre (2011; 2012) have shown the usefulness of generic "rich" features such as the valency (number of dependents) of a given token, the distance between two tokens, a list of current unique modifier labels for a token, and features looking at various characteristics a token's second order governor (its governor's governor). They find that these features are particularly useful for global-learning based parsers with a very high beam width (64)—this however comes with certain practical disadvantages, since parsing speed is linearly correlated to beam width, and analysing with a beam of 64 takes 64 times as long. In our study, we do not explore beam widths beyond 5 and do not apply global learning, and show nevertheless that highly specific targeted features give considerable gain even in such a context.

In terms of French, De la Clergerie (2014) introduces rich symbolic features into statistical transition-based parsing indirectly, by parsing each sentence first using FRMG, a TAG parser, and injecting features based on the FRMG parse into the transition-based parser. He attains excellent results for French (LAS=90.25 for the SPMRL `test` corpus with guessed pos-tags). However, given the need to parse with a TAG parser, this system is not directly comparable to linear-time transition-based parsing.

3 Annotations and analysis mechanisms

Let us consider the following sentence containing a 3-conjunct coordinated structure:

Example 3.1 Je vois Jean, Paul et Marie. *(I see John, Paul and Mary)*

Figure 1 shows the French SPMRL dependency annotation for this sentence: all conjuncts are governed by the first conjunct via the preceding comma or conjunction.

The next question is: how is such an annotation parsed? In this study we concentrate purely on transition-based parsing (Kübler et al., 2009). Parsing is thus defined as a series of transitions leading from one parse configuration to the next, where a parse configuration is defined as follows:

- σ: a stack, or ordered sequence of tokens which have been partially processed
- β: a buffer, or ordered sequence of tokens which have not yet been processed
- Δ: a set of dependency arcs of the form *label(governor, dependent)* that have already been added
- τ: a sequence of transitions allowing us to reach the current configuration from an initial one

We will use σ_0 to indicate the token currently on top of the stack, and $\sigma_{1..n}$ for tokens deeper in the stack. Similarly, β_0 indicates the next token to be processed on the buffer, and $\beta_{1..n}$ for tokens farther down the buffer. Parsing begins with *root* artefact on the stack and all other tokens on the buffer. Parsing ends when the buffer is empty. Our study uses the arc-eager transition system (Nivre, 2008), which defines the four transitions shown in table 1 for moving from one configuration to the next.

It is well known that transition-based parsers tend to favour short-distance dependencies over longer distance ones (McDonald and Nivre, 2007; Candito et al., 2010), since they will always compare two closer tokens before comparing two tokens which are farther away, and the decision regarding the two closer tokens is taken independently given the information available at this point. Thus, a closer token is never directly compared to a token farther away when making an attachment decision. This tendency can be somewhat curtailed by applying a beam search (Urieli and Tanguy, 2013).

transition	effect	precondition
left-arc$_{label}$	Create the dependency arc *label*(β_0,σ_0) and pop the stack	The reverse dependency *any*(σ_0,β_0) does not exist, and σ_0 is not the *root* node
right-arc$_{label}$	Create the dependency arc *label*(σ_0,β_0), and push the head of the buffer to the top of the stack	
reduce	Pop the top of the stack	The top-of-stack has a governor
shift	Push the head of the buffer to the top of the stack	

Table 1: The arc-eager transition system for shift-reduce dependency parsing

Now, as already seen in example 1.1, forward-looking features are required to correctly identify the first conjunct by guessing the second conjunct. Table 2 shows the exact sequence of transitions required for parsing the 3rd example sentence from example 1.1, from the moment when we first encounter the coordinating conjunction on the buffer to the moment when the CS itself has been fully parsed. Difficult decisions are shown in bold. Among these, the `reduce` transitions on lines n+1 and n+2 both require us to look farther down the buffer to guess the most likely second conjunct, since we can only reduce when there are no more dependents to be attached. The `shift` transitions on lines n+4 and n+5 are simpler, since we already know that the first conjunct is a verb. Still, we have to recognise that the second verb is composite, which is governed by convention by the past participle rather than the helper verb.

	transition	stack	buffer	dependencies added
n		*root*, mangé, pomme, rouge	et, Georges, a, bu, du, thé	
n+1	**reduce**	*root*, mangé, pomme	et, Georges, a, bu, du, thé	
n+2	**reduce**	*root*, mangé	et, Georges, a, bu, du, thé	
n+3	right-arc$_{coord}$	*root*, mangé, et	Georges, a, bu, du, thé	coord(mangé,et)
n+4	**shift**	*root*, mangé, et, Georges	a, bu, du, thé	
n+5	**shift**	*root*, mangé, et, Georges, a	bu, du, thé	
n+6	left-arc$_{aux_tps}$	*root*, mangé, et, Georges	bu, du, thé	aux_tps(bu, a)
n+7	left-arc$_{suj}$	*root*, mangé, et	bu, du, thé	suj(bu, Georges)
n+8	right-arc$_{dep_coord}$	*root*, mangé, et, bu	du, thé	dep_coord(et, bu)

Table 2: Arc-eager transition sequence for coordination, with difficult decisions in bold

The case of a CS with 3 or more conjuncts is even more complicated, since it requires lookahead features for the first two conjuncts, looking farther ahead than in the case of the 2-conjuct CS. In all cases, correctly guessing the final conjunct ahead of time is critical information to correctly annotating the coordination.

4 Data and software

4.1 Talismane

All of the experiments in this study use the Talismane parser[1]. Talismane (Urieli, 2013) is an NLP toolkit including a sentence detector, tokeniser, pos-tagger and transition-based parser. All four modules use a statistical supervised machine learning approach, and it is possible to apply a beam search to the last three modules, as well as defining sophisticated features and rules using an expressive feature definition syntax. For all experiments in the present study, we used a linear SVM model with $C = 0.25$ and $\epsilon = 0.01$. We applied a cutoff of 5, so that a feature has to appear at least 5 times in the training corpus to be considered.

4.2 French Treebank

The original input for this study is the dependency annotation for the French section of SPMRL (Seddah et al., 2013), itself derived from the French Treebank (Abeillé et al., 2003), via an automatic conversion of constituency structures to dependencies. We use the `train` (14,759 sentences, 412,879 tokens), `dev` (1,235 sentences, 36,272 tokens) and `test` (2,541 sentences, 69,922 tokens) divisions of this corpus as defined for SPMRL. All of our studies use the gold pos-tags from the treebank, in order to make an abstraction of pos-tagger errors and concentrate on parsing. The baseline LAS excluding punctuation is 89.57% (`dev`) and 89.45% (`test`). The baseline f-score for coordinated structures, calculated as the f-score for all individual coordination arcs, is 84.35% (`dev`) and 85.16% (`test`).

4.3 Initial error classification

We began this study by analysing coordination errors performed by Talismane in the `dev` corpus. Out of 240 errors analysed, 24% were annotation errors (of which over 60% were correctly annotated by Talismane), 14% were artefacts of the annotation scheme (the 2nd and 3rd conjunct were directly coordinated by Talismane unlike the original annotation), and 30% were errors where Talismane coordinated two different pos-tags, whereas the correct coordination involved the same pos-tag. If we group this together with other cases of simple parallelism (e.g. cases where Talismane coordinated different prepositions instead of the same prepostion), this climbs up to 38%. The remaining 24% covered various difficult cases, including elliptical coordinations. Only 12% involved cases where semantics were required to make the correct choice.

The cases where the mildly rich French morphology might help us are very rare: only three cases among the `dev` corpus errors. In the examples below and elsewhere in this article, the guessed conjuncts are shown in *italics* (non-italics for the English translation), the correct conjuncts are <u>underlined</u>, and the conjunction is shown in **bold**. In the first example, the feminine demonstrative pronoun *celle* indicates that we are coordinating with the feminine noun *présidence* rather than with *M. Michel Albert*:

Example 4.1 [...] on avait parlé <u>de la présidence</u> des AGF à la place *de M. Michel Albert* **ou** <u>*de celle*</u> du GAN occupée par M. François Heilbronner. *(... they spoke <u>of the presidency</u> of the AGFs instead* of Mr Michel Albert ***or*** <u>of that</u> *of the GAN occupied by Mr François Heilbronner.)*

In the second case, the masculine past participle *rejeté* should coordinate with the masculine past participle *opté* rather than the feminine *faite*:

Example 4.2 Le conseil d'administration [...] a <u>opté</u> pour la proposition de reprise *faite* par Bongrain **et** <u>*rejeté*</u> celle de Besnier. *(The board of directors <u>chose</u> the takeover proposal* made *by Bongrain* ***and*** <u>rejected</u> *the one made by Besnier.)*

In the final example, a plural adjective *répétitifs* is coordinated with a plural adjectival past participle *construits*, rather than a previous morphologically unadorned past participle *découvert* in a conjugated construction:

Example 4.3 [...] les Européens ont *découvert/VPP* l'immensité du stock japonais : [...] scénarios <u>répétitifs/ADJ</u> **mais** habilement <u>*construits/VPP*</u> [...] *(the Europeans* discovered *the immensity of the Japanese stock: <u>repetitive</u>* ***and*** *skillfully* <u>constructed</u> *scenarios...)*

[1] `http://redac.univ-tlse2.fr/applications/talismane.html`

Because of the rarity of such cases, we decided not to include morpholigical features in our experiments.

5 Experiments

5.1 Initial experiment with targeted features

We first decided to target the 38% of errors relating to simple parallelism (e.g. parallelism errors related to mismatched pos-tags or prepositions, rather than semantics).

Because of the importance of identifying a second conjunct before identifying the first one, we first constructed the following targeted feature:

- **Second conjunct identification:** attempts to correctly identify the second conjunct. Since all subsequent features depend on this second conjunct feature, it was critical to attain high accuracy. Also, since the feature is a component of features used to select the first conjunct, it can only make use of information available when a first conjunct candidate is at σ_0 and the conjunction at β_0 (steps 1, 2 and 3 in table 2): critically, it tries to guess the second conjunct with no knowledge of the correct first conjunct.

The most difficult cases for this feature are verbs, since both coordinated verbs need to be outside of subordinate, relative or comment phrases. Comment phrases, particularly numerous in journalistic text, and marked only by punctuation, word order, and lexical choices, are the most difficult to recognise. The following list shows examples of sentences with two conjugated verbs (in italics), and with the conjuncts underlined.

1. **Verb coordination**: Il s'*agit* ici d'un jour normal de la semaine **et** un inventaire scrupuleux *exigerait* que l'on prenne également en compte l'offre accrue du mercredi. *(We are* dealing *here with a normal weekday,* ***and*** *a scupulous inventory would* require *us to take into account the increased offer on Wednesdays.)*

2. **Verb coordination**: Les chiffres parlent d'eux-mêmes : les Japonais *occupent* 30 % du marché américain **et** leurs exportations *représentent* près de 75 % du déficit commercial global annuel. *(The numbers speak for themselves: the Japanese* occupy *30% of the American market* ***and*** *their exports* represent *almost 75% of the annual global commercial deficit.)*

3. **Comment phrase**: A Lourdes, nous *signale* notre correspondant Jean-Jacques Rollat, la venue **et** la circulation des pèlerins ont été très *perturbées*. *(At Lourdes,* signals *our correspondent Jean-Jacques Rollat, the* *arrival* ***and*** *circulation* *of pilgrims was considerably* disrupted.*)*

4. **Relative clause**: Les émissions d'éveil qui ont *fait* la richesse des chaînes de service public entre 1975 **et** 1985 ont toutes *disparu*. *(The discovery programmes which* constituted *the richness of public channels between 1975 and 1985 have all* disappeared.*)*

We tested this feature on the training corpus, by applying it whenever a conjunction was found in σ_0, and seeing how often it correctly guessed "true" when the token in β_0 was the second conjunct, and "false" when the token in β_0 was not the second conjunct, while ignoring knowledge of the first conjunct. The accuracy for the "true" result is 99.07%, and for the "false" result is 94.54%.

We then used this feature to construct various features attempting to recognise parallelism in CS within the framework of transition-based parsing. Most of these features compare the item currently at the top-of-stack to the second conjunct guess, and check to see if there is a better candidate deeper in the stack. The following features were used:

- **Pos-tag mismatch:** if the first conjunct candidate at the top-of-stack has a different pos-tag from the second conjunct guess, does a candidate with the same pos-tag exist deeper on the stack?

- **Mismatched prepositions:** if the first candidate at the top-of-stack and the second conjunct guess are two different prepositions, does the same preposition exist deeper on the stack?

- **Pos-tag match:** if the first conjunct candidate at the top-of-stack is the same pos-tag as the second conjunct guess, are there any other candidates with this pos-tag deeper on the stack?

- **3 conjunct parallelism:** when two tokens of the same pos-tag, separated by a comma, are being compared, is the second token followed by a coordinating conjunction and then a third token with the same pos-tag as the first two? We allow for various intervening modifiers depending on the pos-tag being considered.

- **Parentheses:** is the first conjunct candidate at the top-of-stack inside parentheses and the second conjunct guess outside of them?

When we first attempted to apply these features to our `dev` (and `test`) corpora, our f-score for coordination (`coord` and `dep_coord` combined) improved from 84.34% to 85.52% (85.16% to 86.97% for `test`), giving a fairly modest error reduction of 7.54% (12.20% for `test`). In terms of significance, McNemar's test gives a p-value < 0.001 for coordination label changes in both `dev` and `test`.

Now, there are of course cases in the training corpus with valid non-parallel structures, such as the following coordination between an adjective and prepositional phrase:

Example 5.1 Au mieux, la reprise sera lente/ADJ **et** de/P faible ampleur. *(At best, the recovery will be slow* ***and*** *of limited extent.)*

These, however, are few and far in between when compared to the very large number of errors concerning clear pos-tag parallelism. We will examine some errors introduced by applying targeted parallelism features to non-parallel CSs in our final error analysis found in section 5.4.

5.2 Improvements through manual correction

The targeted feature definition involved several iterations in which features were projected onto the training corpus, and any unexpected results were analysed. Among the unexpected results were a very large number of annotation errors. Given that 24% of the original errors in the `dev` corpus were annotation errors, and our efficient method for pinpointing and correcting such errors by projecting targeted features, we decided to apply these targeted manual corrections to the entire SPMRL French corpus (`train`, `dev` and `test`).

Specifically, these manual corrections involved:

- Fixing any coordination where the dependent preceded the governor (impossible in the original annotation standard)

- Reviewing and standardizing all cases of *ni…ni…* (neither…nor…) and *soit…soit…* (either…or…).

- Projecting the above targeted features onto the corpus via Talismane, and correcting any items where the feature yielded unexpected results.

The total corrections are 1,488 for `train` (out of 21,061 coordination relations = 7.07%), 106 for `dev` (out of 1,743 coordination relations = 6.08%) and 274 for `test` (out of 3,420 coordination relations = 8.01%). Multi-word expressions (MWEs) were left as is, except on rare cases where a modifier inside the MWE was coordinated to a modifier outside of it.

	dev base	dev fix	test base	test fix
train base	*84.34*	85.08	*85.16*	85.54
train fix	83.99	**85.75**	84.99	**86.75**

Table 3: Coordination f-score after targeted manual error correction

Table 3 shows the coordination f-score with and without targeted error correction in both training and evaluation. Fixing errors in the training corpus is only useful when equivalent errors are fixed in the

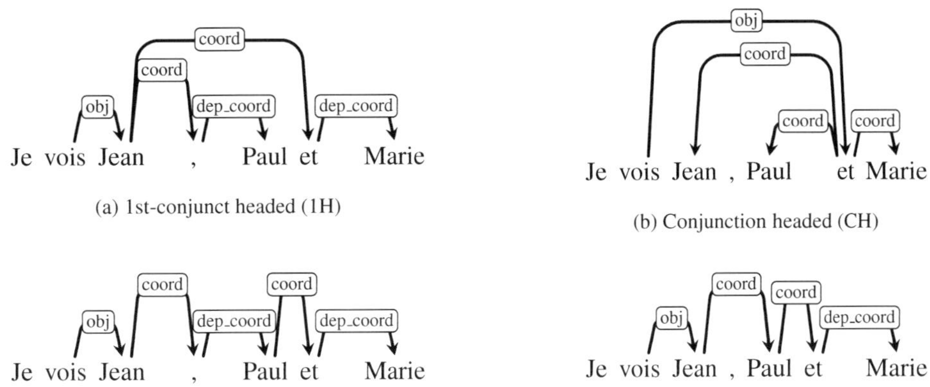

(a) 1st-conjunct headed (1H)

(b) Conjunction headed (CH)

(c) Previous conjunct headed (PH)

(d) Previous conjunct headed 2 (PH2)

Figure 2: Different annotations for coordination

evaluation corpora. If we consider the corrected evaluation corpora only, fixing errors in the training corpus gives an f-score error reduction of 4.49% for `dev` (8.37% for `test`).

The remainder of this study uses the manually corrected corpora as a baseline. Although this is not satisfying in terms of comparisons with other studies, we found ourselves constrained to do so because our automatic conversions from one annotation scheme to another required a clean and consistent annotation to begin with. In order to simplify comparisons, we have generated a difference file to apply to the original SPMRL corpus, available upon request.

5.3 Comparing annotation schemes

As seen in section 4.3, over 14% of the initial errors were artefacts of the annotation scheme for a CS with more than 2 conjuncts, where Talismane systematically attached the conjunct to the previous conjunct, whereas the original annotation scheme systematically attaches it to the first conjunct. Indeed, the previous conjunct attachment is more natural for transition-based parsers: since the comma is a highly ambiguous indicator for coordination, the coordination is often missed between the first and second conjuncts, and the first conjunct is reduced. By the time the parser reaches the coordinating conjunction, only the second conjunct is left on the stack. This suggested that changing the CS annotation scheme could lead to considerable improvements.

We therefore decided to experiment with four different equivalent CS annotation schemes, as shown in figure 2. Subfigure 2a gives the original **1H** (1st conjunct headed) annotation used in the SPMRL 2013 dependency corpus for French. The first conjunct always heads the CS, and governs the coordinating commas and conjunction with a `coord` label, which in turn govern the remaining conjuncts with a `dep_coord` label. Subfigure 2b shows the **CH** (conjunction headed) annotation, used by a wide variety of grammars: the conjunction governs all of the conjuncts with a `coord` label. Subfigure 2c shows the **PH** (previous conjunct headed) annotation, in which each conjunct governs the following coordinator (whether a comma or a conjunction) with the `coord` label, and the coordinator governs the following conjunct with the `dep_coord` label. Finally, subfigure 2d shows the **PH2** annotation, in which we skip the comma, so that conjuncts separated by a comma are directly governed by the previous conjunct using the `coord` label. In the case of a simple CS with 2 conjuncts, the PH and PH2 annotations are identical to the 1H annotation.

Notice that there is no loss of information between these four annotations, so that round-trip conversions can restore the original annotation. Post-positioned shared modifiers (e.g. *"Jean, Paul et Marie Dupont"*, where all three are members of the Dupont family) can be indicated by having the conjunction govern the shared modifier in the CH annotation, and having the 1st conjunct govern it in the other annotations. This annotation becomes non-projective (i.e. involves crossed dependency arcs) in 1H, PH and PH2 when the modifier applies to the objects of a prepositional phrase coordination, e.g. *"Je parle de Jean, de Paul, et de Marie Dupont"* ("I'm talking about John, Paul and Marie Dupont"). Since we use a projective parser in the present study, we change the governor to the final conjunct when required to avoid non-projectivity, thus losing some information. The 1H, PH and PH2 have no simple way of distinguishing ante-positioned shared modifiers from modifiers of the first conjunct, e.g. *"Chers Jean, Paul et Marie"* ("Dear John, Paul and Mary"). Moreover, none of these annotation schemes provide a clear solution for elliptical coordinations, e.g. *"J'ai vu Jean et Paul hier, et Marie aujourd'hui"* ("I saw John and Paul yesterday, and Mary today").

Another possibility for annotation was suggested by detailed analysis of the actual transition sequences for the first 20 coordination errors, revealing two cases in which, if a comma followed the first conjunct, the first conjunct was erroneously reduced. This suggested that having to take a decision when the comma was found at β_0 led to errors which could be eliminated if the comma were immediately attached and only used as a feature for further decisions. Now, if we look at the French Treebank annotation for punctuation outside of coordinated structures, the label is always `ponct`, but the choice of the punctuation's governor seems fairly arbitrary. Parser confidence is thus very low for punctuation attachment decisions, and as a result, when applying a beam search, the beam is often filled with alternative arbitrary punctuation attachment decisions instead of true syntactic ambiguities. We therefore decided to experiment as well with attaching punctuation systematically to the previous non-punctation token (or to the root artefact when punctuation opens the sentence), except in the case of coordinating commas for the 1H and PH annotations. Indeed, for the CH and PH2 schemes, we were forced to apply this punctuation "fix" in order to avoid generating a large number of non-projective punctuation arcs when transforming the corpus. In these latter two annotations, where coordinated commas are not used to annotate the CS, applying a punctuation fix results in systematic annotation for all punctuation in the corpus, thus resulting in a systematic application of the `right-arc`$_{\text{ponct}}$ and `reduce` transitions.

We thus make the hypothesis that transition-based parsers will favour those annotations which rely on shorter-distance dependencies, specifically PH and PH2. Our second hypothesis is that systematic annotation for commas (PH2) helps improve annotation by removing a needless source of ambiguity.

Scheme:	**1H**	**1H+P**	**CH+P**	**PH**	**PH+P**	**PH2+P**
Dev						
Coord f-score	85.75	85.60	73.20	86.68	86.96	89.21
Coord prec.	99.55	99.55	98.88	99.49	99.49	99.41
Coord recall	75.31	75.09	58.11	76.79	77.24	80.91
LAS no punct.	89.69	89.69	87.44	89.74	89.82	90.11
UAS no punct.	91.71	91.64	89.39	91.74	91.78	92.02
LAS	87.34	91.00	89.13	87.38	91.11	91.45
UAS	89.10	92.69	90.81	89.12	92.82	93.10
Test						
Coord f-score	86.75	86.94	73.09	88.20	88.44	90.29
Coord prec.	99.70	99.52	99.38	99.75	99.50	99.71
Coord recall	76.78	77.18	57.80	79.04	79.59	82.50
LAS no punct.	89.63	89.81	87.19	89.76	89.94	90.16
UAS no punct.	91.63	91.79	89.17	91.75	91.94	92.13
LAS	87.19	91.12	88.93	87.29	91.24	91.49
UAS	88.93	92.85	90.64	89.01	92.98	93.20

Table 4: Comparing CS annotation

Table 4 shows results for the six annotation schemes (where +P indicates the punctuation fix was applied): 1H, 1H+P, CH+P, PH, PH+P, PH2+P. All results are after targeted manual correction. For ease of comparison with previous studies, we show LAS and UAS both with and without punctuation. Unsurprisingly, in the schemes without the punctuation fix, hence with arbitrary attachment for punctuation, we systematically lose 2% when we include punctuation in the LAS/UAS, whereas in the schemes with the punctuation fix we systematically gain over 1%.

In the coordination results, we include both the `coord` and `dep_coord` labels, since different schemes have different proportions for these. Precision is very high because of the strong markers for coordination. Recall is much lower, because of the difficulty of finding the first conjunct. The conjunction-headed scheme CH+P is a clear loser in transition-based parsing—hardly a surprising result, since it requires far more lookahead features. All of the previous-conjunct headed schemes (PH, PH+P, PH2+P) outperform the first-conjunct headed schemes (1H, 1H+P) by over 1.5% when it comes to the coordination f-score, which validates our hypothesis based on the analysis of errors in section 4.3. Finally, the clear winner is the PH2+P scheme, where all attachment ambiguity is transposed from punctuation to the conjuncts, with 2.0% gain in coordination f-score with respect to the PH+P scheme. The coordination f-score error reduction between the original 1H scheme and PH2+P is 24.28% for `dev` (26.72% for `test`). In terms of statistical significance for both the `dev` and `test` corpora (McNemar's test applied to identifying individual conjuncts), the differences between 1H, 1H+P, PH and PH+P are not significant (p-value > 0.05). The differences between any other schema and CH+P or PH2+P are highly significant (p-value < 0.001).

5.4 Combining with targeted features

In our final experiment, we combine the PH2+P annotation scheme with the targeted features presented in section 5.1, to see to what extent the gains are cumulative. We also test at different beam widths to see how much additional gain can be had at higher beams.

Beam:	**Beam 1**				**Beam 2**				**Beam 5**			
Scheme:	**1H**		**PH2+P**		**1H**		**PH2+P**		**1H**		**PH2+P**	
Features:	∅	+	∅	+	∅	+	-∅	+	∅	+	∅	+
Dev												
Coord f-score	85.8	86.4	89.2	90.0	87.0	87.2	90.3	90.5	87.2	87.4	90.8	90.7
Coord prec.	99.6	99.4	99.4	99.4	99.6	99.5	99.5	99.5	99.4	99.4	99.6	99.5
Coord recall	75.3	76.3	80.9	82.2	77.2	77.5	82.7	83.0	77.6	78.0	83.3	83.4
LAS no pnct	89.7	89.7	90.1	90.3	90.2	90.3	90.5	90.6	90.4	90.4	90.7	90.7
UAS no pnct	91.7	91.8	92.0	92.2	92.2	92.3	92.5	92.6	92.4	92.5	92.6	92.7
LAS	87.3	87.4	91.5	91.6	88.0	88.1	91.8	91.9	88.2	88.3	91.9	92.0
UAS	89.1	89.2	93.1	93.2	89.8	89.9	93.5	93.6	90.0	90.1	93.6	93.7
Test												
Coord f-score	86.8	88.5	90.3	91.3	87.8	89.3	90.5	91.6	88.6	89.6	90.6	91.7
Coord prec.	99.7	99.6	99.7	99.7	99.8	99.7	99.6	99.6	99.8	99.6	99.6	99.6
Coord recall	76.8	79.5	82.5	84.3	78.4	80.9	83.0	84.8	79.6	81.5	83.1	85.0
LAS no pnct	89.6	89.9	90.2	90.3	90.3	90.4	90.6	90.7	90.5	90.6	90.6	90.8
UAS no pnct	91.6	91.9	92.1	92.2	92.2	92.4	92.5	92.6	92.5	92.6	92.6	92.7
LAS	87.2	87.4	91.5	91.6	88.0	88.2	91.8	92.0	88.4	88.4	91.9	92.0
UAS	88.9	89.2	93.2	93.3	89.7	89.9	93.5	93.6	90.0	90.1	93.6	93.7

Table 5: Combining annotation schemes and targeted features at different beam widths

Table 5 shows the results at beams 1, 2 and 5, for the original scheme 1H and the best scheme PH2+P, and with (+) or without (∅) targeted features. Gains are clearly centered on coordination recall. Table 6 shows the same information in terms of f-score error reduction with respect to the baseline configuration (1H annotation, baseline features, beam 1), with a maximal reduction of 35.09% for the `dev` corpus, and 37.28% for `test`. The three parameters tested are to a large extend cumulative. Individually, changing the annotation standard gives the most gain, followed by targeted features and then increasing the beam size to 2. In terms of statistical significance for the test corpus (McNemar's test applied to identifying individual conjuncts), all combinations are significant (p-value < 0.05) except for: PH2+P/∅/1-2 to PH2+P/∅/5; PH2+P/+/2 to PH2+P/+/5; and a few other combinations going from 1H/+ to PH2+P/∅.

	None	Features	Scheme	Both
Dev: base f-score = 85.75				
Beam 1	0.00	4.28	24.28	29.89
Beam 2	8.49	9.82	32.14	33.40
Beam 5	9.82	11.44	35.09	34.95
Test: base f-score = 86.75				
Beam 1	0.00	12.91	26.72	34.64
Beam 2	8.15	19.02	28.53	36.83
Beam 5	13.58	21.81	28.98	37.28

Table 6: Coordination f-score error reduction with respect to 1H, baseline features, beam 1

In terms of time performance, these changes have a vastly different cost. All tests were run on an Intel Xeon E3-1245 V2 machine, with a 3.4GHz clock speed, 4 cores, 8 threads, and 8 Mb cache, running the Ubuntu 12.04.2 LTS 64-bit operating system. The baseline setup takes 171 seconds to parse the `test` corpus (+133 seconds to load the model and lexicon), giving about 400 tokens/second. Changing the schema from 1H to PH2+P speeds up analysis slightly ($\times 0.93$). Changing the beam width results in a linear increase in time, $\times 2$ for a beam of 2, and $\times 5$ for a beam of 5. Finally, targeted features result in a $\times 22$ increase in time.

We also performed a detailed error analysis for `dev` corpus, on the remaining errors in the PH2+P corpus with targeted features at beam 1. Although the number of erroneous coordinations analysed has reduced from 241 to 151, the percentage of errors relating to simple parallelism (pos-tag mismatch, preposition mismatch, etc.) remains stable, down from 38% to 36%. Annotation errors are reduced from 24% to 11%. Artefacts of the annotation scheme in which conjuncts are attached to the first or second conjunct are reduced from 15% to 5%. Finally, the complicated cases have climbed significantly, with ellipses climbing from 5% to 13% and cases where only semantics can help us decide climbing from 12% to 23%. The latter results indicates that introducing semantic resources might be worthwhile for the remaining errors.

There are a few cases of CSs coordinating unlike categories, where the new features introduced errors. We have a two cases of true non-parallelism, as in the following case, where an adjectival past participle is coordinated with a prepositional phrase:

Example 5.2 [...] celle *d'/P* une part significative des programmes et des productions réalisées/VPP **ou** *en cours de/P* réalisation. *(... that* of *a significant part of programs and productions that are already finished **or** currently* being *prepared.)*

We have a similar valid case of a non-parallel copula coordinating an adjective with a pronoun :

Example 5.3 Ce n'*est/V* pas forcément la plus économiquement souhaitable/ADJ, **mais** celle/PRO qui fera le moins de vagues, compte tenu de l'agitation dans les campagnes, *entendait/V*-on [...] *(It's not necessarily the most economically desirable, **but** the one which will make the least waves, given the restlessness in the countryside, we were* told... *)*

The remaining cases are related to spelling errors in the original text, or to tokenisation and pos-tag errors in the gold pos-tags. For example, in the following case, the journalist misspelt the second *baisser* (to lower) as an infinitive verb whereas it should have been the homophone past participle *baissé*:

Example 5.4 Quant au dollar lui-même, il a monté/V quand on croyait qu'il allait *baisser/VINF* [...] **et** *baisser/VINF* derechef quand le marché commençait à se convaincre... *(As for the dollar itself, it rose when we thought it would* lower, ***and*** lower[ed] *once again when the market started to convince itself...)*

A second case involves the MWE *conformément aux* (in conformance with), which should probably be marked as a single preposition rather than ADV+P:

Example 5.5 *Dans le cas des/P* céréales, **et** conformément/ADV *aux/P* orientations souhaitées par les organisations professionnelles [...] *(*In the case of *cereals, **and** in conformance* with *the desires of professional organisations, ...)*

Similar cases involve the pos-tagging of *généraux* as a noun (generals in an army) rather than an adjective (general):

Example 5.6 [...] à l'ensemble des *présidents/NC* des conseils régionaux/ADJ et *généraux/NC*. *(... to all of the* presidents *of regional* ***and*** general *councils.)*

6 Conclusions and perspectives

In the present study, we attempted to improve the parsing of coordinated structures in French through changes to the annotation scheme and the application of targeted features. Both methods were successful, with annotation scheme changes reducing the `test` corpus coordination f-score error rate by 26.72%, targeted features reducing it by 12.91%, and the two combined reducing it by 34.64% (36.83% at beam 2, 37.28% at beam 5).

However, the application of targeted features comes at a considerable practical cost in terms of time performance ($\times 22$ increase in time). This is partly due to the fact that features are described in configuration files using a declarative syntax, so that certain operations (e.g. looking forward in the buffer) are repeated thousands of times. Indeed, forward-looking features do not rely on partial parsing information, and could even be cached for any given token for the entire sentence parse, across parse configurations. If features were programmed and compiled, this could be made far more efficient, but we would lose the advantage of external configuration files.

In addition, we introduced a method for efficiently correcting training corpus errors through the projection of targeted features, a method which could be extremely useful for corpus constructors. Finally, we highlighted the usefulness of removing all ambiguity from the annotation of punctuation.

In a future study, we would need to test these methods with guessed pos-tags rather than gold pos-tags in order to check their sensitivity to pos-tag errors. It would also be interesting to apply our methods to other languages, and to include targeted semantic features based on semantic resources automatically constructed using semi-supervised methods. For languages with a richer morphology than French, it might well be worthwhile to introduce features based on morphological parallelism as well. Finally, various methods would have to be explored for improving the time performance of targeted features, if possible without losing the configurability and flexibility of declarative feature files.

Acknowledgements

I would like to thank the anonymous reviewers for their in-depth reading and many helpful suggestions.

References

Anne Abeillé, Lionel Clément, and François Toussenel. 2003. Building a treebank for French. In Anne Abeillé, editor, *Treebanks*. Kluwer.

Marie Candito, Joakim Nivre, Pascal Denis, and Enrique Henestroza Anguiano. 2010. Benchmarking of statistical dependency parsers for french. In *Proceedings of the 23rd International Conference on Computational Linguistics: Posters*, pages 108–116. Association for Computational Linguistics.

Deirdre Hogan. 2007. Coordinate noun phrase disambiguation in a generative parsing model. In *Annual Meeting - Association for Computational Linguistics*, volume 45, page 680.

Angelina Ivanova, Stephan Oepen, and Lilja Øvrelid. 2013. Survey on parsing three dependency representations for english. *ACL 2013*, page 31.

Sandra Kübler, Ryan McDonald, and Joakim Nivre. 2009. *Dependency parsing*. Morgan & Claypool Publishers.

Sandra Kübler, Wolfgang Maier, Erhard Hinrichs, and Eva Klett. 2009. Parsing coordinations. In *Proceedings of the 12th Conference of the European Chapter of the Association for Computational Linguistics*, pages 406–414. Association for Computational Linguistics.

Wolfgang Maier and Sandra Kübler. 2013. Are all commas equal? detecting coordination in the penn treebank. In *The Twelfth Workshop on Treebanks and Linguistic Theories (TLT12)*, page 121.

Wolfgang Maier, Erhard Hinrichs, Sandra Kübler, and Julia Krivanek. 2012. Annotating coordination in the penn treebank. In *Proceedings of the Sixth Linguistic Annotation Workshop*, pages 166–174. Association for Computational Linguistics.

Ryan T McDonald and Joakim Nivre. 2007. Characterizing the errors of data-driven dependency parsing models. In *EMNLP-CoNLL*, pages 122–131.

Joakim Nivre. 2008. Algorithms for deterministic incremental dependency parsing. *Computational Linguistics*, 34(4):513–553.

Martin Popel, David Marecek, Jan Štepánek, Daniel Zeman, and Zdeněk Žabokrtský. 2013. Coordination structures in dependency treebanks. In *Proceedings of the 51st Annual Meeting of the Association for Computational Linguistics*.

Éric Villemonte de la Clergerie. 2014. Jouer avec des analyseurs syntaxiques. In *Actes de la 21e conférence sur le Traitement Automatique des Langues Naturelles (TALN'2014)*, pages 67–78, Marseille, France.

Roy Schwartz, Omri Abend, and Ari Rappoport. 2012. Learnability-based syntactic annotation design. In *COLING*, pages 2405–2422.

Djamé Seddah, Reut Tsarfaty, Sandra Kübler, Marie Candito, Jinho Choi, Richárd Farkas, Jennifer Foster, Iakes Goenaga, Koldo Gojenola, Yoav Goldberg, Spence Green, Nizar Habash, Marco Kuhlmann, Wolfgang Maier, Joakim Nivre, Adam Przepiorkowski, Ryan Roth, Wolfgang Seeker, Yannick Versley, Veronika Vincze, Marcin Woliński, Alina Wróblewska, and Eric Villemonte de la Clérgerie. 2013. Overview of the spmrl 2013 shared task: A cross-framework evaluation of parsing morphologically rich languages. In *Proceedings of the 4th Workshop on Statistical Parsing of Morphologically Rich Languages: Shared Task*, Seattle, WA.

Masashi Shimbo and Kazuo Hara. 2007. A discriminative learning model for coordinate conjunctions. In *EMNLP-CoNLL*, pages 610–619.

Reut Tsarfaty, Joakim Nivre, and Evelina Andersson. 2011. Evaluating dependency parsing: robust and heuristics-free cross-nnotation evaluation. In *Proceedings of the Conference on Empirical Methods in Natural Language Processing*, pages 385–396. Association for Computational Linguistics.

Assaf Urieli and Ludovic Tanguy. 2013. L'apport du faisceau dans l'analyse syntaxique en dépendances par transitions : études de cas avec l'analyseur Talismane. In *Actes de la 20e conférence sur le Traitement Automatique des Langues Naturelles (TALN'2013)*, pages 188–201, Les Sables d'Olonne, France.

Assaf Urieli. 2013. *Robust French syntax analysis: reconciling statistical methods and linguistic knowledge in the Talismane toolkit*. Ph.D. thesis, Université de Toulouse II le Mirail.

Assaf Urieli. 2014. Améliorer l'étiquetage de "que" par les descripteurs ciblés et les règles. In *Actes de la 21e conférence sur le Traitement Automatique des Langues Naturelles (TALN'2014)*, pages 56–66, Marseille, France.

Yue Zhang and Joakim Nivre. 2011. Transition-based dependency parsing with rich non-local features. In *ACL (Short Papers)*, pages 188–193.

Yue Zhang and Joakim Nivre. 2012. Analyzing the effect of global learning and beam-search on transition-based dependency parsing. In *COLING (Posters)*, pages 1391–1400.

Experiments with Easy-first nonprojective constituent parsing

Yannick Versley
Department of Computational Linguistics
University of Heidelberg
versley@cl.uni-heidelberg.de

Abstract

Less-configurational languages such as German often show not just morphological variation but also free word order and nonprojectivity. German is not exceptional in this regard, as other morphologically-rich languages such as Czech, Tamil or Greek, offer similar challenges that make context-free constituent parsing less attractive.

Advocates of dependency parsing have long pointed out that the free(r) word order and non-projective phenomena are handled in a more straightforward way by dependency parsing. However, certain other phenomena in language, such as gapping, ellipses or verbless sentences, are difficult to handle in a dependency formalism.

In this paper, we show that parsing of discontinuous constituents can be achieved using easy-first parsing with online reordering, an approach that previously has only been used for dependencies, and that the approach yields very fast parsing with reasonably accurate results that are close to the state of the art, surpassing existing results that use treebank grammars. We also investigate the question whether phenomena where dependency representations may be problematic – in particular, verbless clauses – can be handled by this model.

1 Introduction

Automatic syntactic parsing has been fruitfully incorporated into sytems for information extraction (Miyao et al., 2008), question answering, machine translation (Huang and Chiang, 2007), among others, but we also see syntactic structures being used to communicate facts about language use in the digital humanities or in investigations of the language of language learners. In all of these applications, we see fruitful use both of constituent trees, and of dependency trees.

Depending on the application, different criteria may become important: on one hand, the ability to produce structures that are (intuitively) compatible with semantic composition, or where arguments and adjuncts are related to their predicate in the tree, which commonly requires dealing with nonprojectivity. Such a formalism should also deal with a wide range of constructions including verbless clauses. Finally, parsing speed is somewhat important for many application cases, and a parser that changes the tokenization of the input or inserts additional "null" tokens runs afoul many of the fundamental assumptions in pipelines for semantic processing or information extraction.

If we look at the current three largest treebanks for German, namely the Hamburg Dependency Treebank (Foth et al., 2014) with 101 000 sentences, the TüBa-D/Z treebank (Telljohann et al., 2009) with 85 000 sentences or the Tiger treebank (Brants et al., 2002) with about 50 000 sentences, we see find a continuum of the nonprojective single-parent dependencies of the HDT on one side and projective phrase structures of TüBa-D/Z, with Tiger straddling in the middle with a scheme that is neither projective nor limited to dependencies, and which represents, we'll argue, both the best and the worst of both worlds.

First Joint Workshop on Statistical Parsing of Morphologically Rich Languages and Syntactic Analysis of Non-Canonical Languages, pages 39–53 Dublin, Ireland, August 23-29 2014.

Because of its expressivity, the Negra/Tiger scheme has also been used for other languages such as Swedish Volk and Samuelsson (2004) as well as Georgian/Russian/Ukrainian (Kapanadze, 2012), and as Early New High German (Pauly et al., 2012).

The Tiger scheme is arguably more expressive than either of the alternatives since it can capture both elliptic clauses (which are difficult to represent in normal dependency schemes) and nonprojective constructions (which have to be added as a second annotation layer in purely projective treebanks such as TüBa-D/Z). It also makes it the most difficult to provide good automatic tool support, in terms of effective parsing components or of annotation tools, since parsing of discontinuous constituents has only recently become practical.

The straightforward approach of Kallmeyer and Maier (2013) to use a treebank-derived linear context-free rewriting system suffers from near-exponential observed time consumption in practice. Approaches that use context-free grammar approximation such as the ones of Schmid (2006), Cai et al. (2011) or van Cranenburgh and Bod (2013), still have cubic time complexity; especially in the latter case, it is not clear whether techniques that allow fast PCFG parsing such as those of Bodenstab et al. (2011) would be suitable for the subsequent steps with increased grammar complexity.

In this paper, we present a novel application of the easy-first parsing principle of Goldberg and Elhalad (2010) to discontinuous constituent parsing, which performs fast enough for interactive use (about 40 sentences per second) while giving an acceptable accuracy that is within the range normally seen with unmodified treebank grammars.

In the remainder of the paper, we will include a short discussion of the interrelation between constituency and dependency relations of syntax, as well as relevant prior work in section 2, and discuss the construction of the parser in section 3. Section 4 and following contain a discussion of quantitative results on the Tiger corpus, whereas the penultimate section contains a more detailed analysis of the parser behaviour on constructions that are problematic for either dependency parsers or projective constituent parsing.

2 Constituency and Dependency: Good friends?

Constituency and dependency structures are two formalisms that are frequently used for theory-neutral description of syntactic structures. In constituent structures, usually influenced by some version of X-bar theory (see Kornai and Pullum, 1990 for a discussion; most notably, phrases are supposed to be projections of a head), whereas in dependency structures it is usually assumed that each word has exactly one governor (except one or more words that are attached to a virtual *root* node).

The common subset of both can be described (in the words of Hockenmaier, 2007) as "Heads, arguments, modifiers, conjuncts", which includes the grammatical function labels that are added in dependency structures, and to varying extent in phrase structure treebanks. Nivre (2011) goes further and asks whether we need constituents at all, since pure dependency parsing recovers arguments and adjuncts while being generally faster (and, at least for results published on Czech and French which Nivre cites, more accurate). Versley and Zinsmeister (2006) similarly argue that even "deep" dependency relations (including nonlocal ones) can be recovered from single-parent dependencies if subsequent disambiguation steps identify the scope of conjunctions, argument sharing in coordination, passive identification, and lexicalized control phenomena. However, verbless clauses as they may occur in coordination pose a problem to the idea that every phrase is headed by a preterminal, or the equivalent assumption in dependency grammar that every argument has a governing head word.

In constituent treebanks, the solution to this problem is rather simple: deviate from the descriptive-Xbar schema outlined earlier on and introduce headless projections for these clauses. Dependency treebanks lack this additional degree of freedom, and the choice is usually to either attach the respective nodes somewhere else (Böhmova et al., 2001; Foth, 2006) or introduce empty nodes that are the governors of the orphaned subtrees (Bosco and Lombardo, 2006; Vincze et al., 2010; Dipper et al., 2013).

In dependency parsing, good solutions for nonprojective edges have been found, including pseudoprojective parsing (Nivre and Nilsson, 2005), approximate weighted constraint solving (Koo et al., 2010), as well as deterministic online reordering (Nivre, 2009), which also has been applied to easy-first decoding strategies (Tratz and Hovy, 2011). Seeker et al. (2012) additionally employs an *attach-inner* operation which allows non-projective insertion into a structure that has already been built. Despite these very reasonable solutions, the treatment of elliptic phrases, whether it is done using the somewhere-else approach or by introducing empty nodes (see Seeker et al., 2012 and references therein) yields uninformative structures for subsequent processing components or even makes it necessary to re-engineer subsequent processing stages for dealing with the newly introduced empty nodes, or (equally impractical) require the refactoring of annotated corpus resources to accommodate a new tokenization whenever a null element is introduced or changed.

In constituency parsing, the problem of discontinuous constituents in parsing has, at least in German, first been met with a proposals of raising degrees of complexity (among others, van Noord, 1991; Plaehn, 2000) and then silently been ignored both in the building of parsers and in their evaluation: researchers from Dubey and Keller (2003) to the present day cite bracketing scores based on structures that would make the reconstruction of "Heads, arguments, modifiers, and conjuncts" – usually – rather difficult.

Only relatively recently has the problem of discontinuous constituent parsing been tackled head-on. Kallmeyer and Maier (2013) propose an approach that extracts a treebank LCFRS grammar, which is then used for probabilistic parsing, albeit with near-exponential time consumption. Maier et al. (2012) present an approach to make parsing in this approach more efficient by flattening coherent structures in a sentence to one single sentence node and thus eliminating scrambling as a source of discontinuities, together with other transformations, which allows a time complexity of $O(n^6)$ and parsing times of about 2 minutes for a 40-word sentence. van Cranenburgh and Bod (2013) use a more practical approach that first creates phrase candidates from the n-best list of a projective constituent parser, and uses these to construct LCFRS items that do not necessarily correspond to grammar rules seen in the training set, but which are then matched against a collection of tree fragments extracted from the training set.

There exists some work on transforming dependency structures into constituents that may help in the recovery of discontinuous constituents: Hall and Nivre (2008) propose to encode information about node labels in the dependency labels, whereas Carreras et al. (2008) show that an ILP-based combination of finding dependencies and adding phrase projections and adjunctions to a dependency backbone works well for constructing structures matching those of the Penn Treebank. Seddah (2010) found that similar spinal structures can be used for the French Treebank.

3 Incremental parsing

In general, statistical parsing follows one of several general approaches: one is the approach of item-based decoding, which is centered around the creation of a parse forest that implicitly stores a very large number of possible trees, followed by either dynamic programming in the case of projective parsing (e.g. (Collins, 2003)) or techniques that provide an approximate or exact solution to the intractable problem in the case of nonprojective parsing with second-order factors (Koo et al., 2010). The second large group of approaches is based on incremental structure building, including the approaches of Magerman (1995) or Sagae and Lavie (2006) in the case of constituent parsing, or of Nivre (2003) and following in the case of dependency parsing, with approaches such as Stolcke (1995) or Huang and Sagae (2010) occupying a middle ground.

While the idea of head lexicalization has played a large role in projective constituent parsing, there are rather few approaches that attempt to bridge the gap between dependency and constituency representations in a way that could be exploited for the efficient building of discontinuous constituent structures.

Among these, both the approaches of Hall and Nivre (2008) and of Carreras et al. (2008) could be described in terms of a **spinal transform**: each terminal in the input string is assigned a set of governing nodes that form its *spine*; parsing then consists of assigning a dependency structure among the terminal nodes and of assigning spines and the relation to each other.

In the remainder of this section, we describe two approaches that we used to perform nonprojective constituent parsing in expected linear time: one is relatively close to the approach of Hall and Nivre (2008), but instead of assigning nodes to the first terminal of their yield, uses a strategy more like the spinal tree adjoining grammr of Carreras et al. (2008). The other is an application of the principle

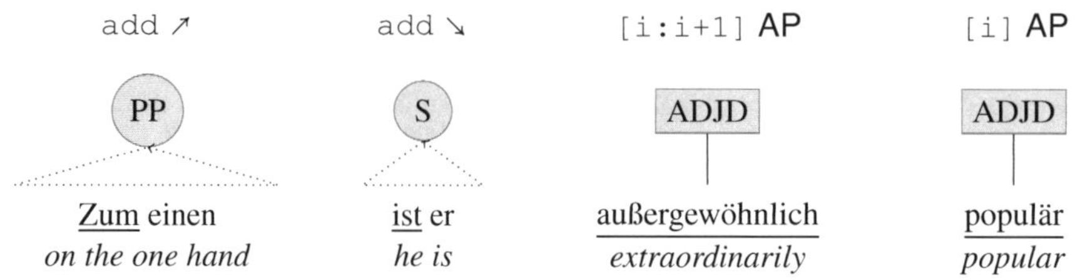

Figure 1: Example for an intermediate state in EaFi, with the preferred action candidates for each position

of easy-first parsing, which has been used for unlabeled dependency parsing by Goldberg and Elhalad (2010), and for non-projective labeled dependency parsing by Tratz and Hovy (2011), towards discontinuous constituency parsing. Because computed feature vectors can be memorized and only have to be recomputed in a small window around the last parser action, this latter approach, just as a left-to-right transition-based parser, has an expected time consumption that is linear in the number of words to be parsed.

3.1 ADG: Constituency-to-Dependency Reduction

Our baseline is an approach close in spirit to Hall and Nivre (2008): The tree with node labels is turned into a dependency graph that encodes, on the governor edge of each terminal, a combination of (i) the node labels on the spine of this node, and (ii) the level at which this node attaches to its parent's spine.

We change two parameters of Hall and Nivre's approach: on one hand, we do not use the first terminal in the yield of a node as its representative but the head according to the head table that we also use to assign the head in the easy-first parser. The reason for this is a practical one: using the head, we get a distribution of 531 different spine/level combinations when we use the head, whereas we would get about 1525 categories when we use the first terminal.

To ensure efficient parsing, this list is further pared down to 100 entries, with the remaining entries being replaced by an UNK placeholder. In decoding, terminals with these entries are assigned the most frequent combination of spine and parent category for the POS tags of the node and its governor, and the topmost spine node with a matching category (or simply the topmost one) would be chosen.

The decoding algorithm and parameter settings for MaltParser were then determined using the MaltOptimizer software (Ballesteros and Nivre, 2012). The settings selected use the stack-projective algorithm with head+path marking strategy for pseudoprojective parsing.[1]

Hall and Nivre's approach is more complex than the approach presented here, and involves interleaving of identifying dependency edges (using the nonprojective Covington parsing scheme) and the stepwise determination of the topmost edge label, then the path of edge labels, and finally the path of constituent labels and its attachment. However, we find that this approach of dependency reduction constitutes a very reasonable intelligent baseline, and is able to perform at a similar speed than our approach.

3.2 EaFi: Easy-first Constituency Parsing

The main approach that we will present here constitutes an adaptation of the *Easy-First* approach to nonprojective constituent parsing. The parser keeps track of a sequence of nodes, beginning with the terminals that are output by the preprocessing consisting of morphological analyzer and lemmatization, and at each point applies one of several actions:

- **Reduce-Unary**: one node is grouped under a unary node of a given category, with the restriction that the corresponding unary rule must have been observed in the treebank. (Additionally, we collapse any two nodes with the same category embedding each other, which sometimes occurs in the Tiger treebank when several empty-headed phrases are assumed to embed each other in coordination).

[1]MaltParser is able to do direct nonprojective parsing using the reordering approaches of Nivre (2009) and Nivre et al. (2009), however the pseudoprojective approach was selected in MaltOptimizer's parameter selection.

Basic featureset		
Unigram:	$n \in n_{i-2} \ldots n_{i+3}$	CnPn CnWn CnMn CnLn
Left/Right Children:	$n \in n_{i,L} n_{i,R} n_{i+1,L} n_{i+1,R}$	CnPn
Bigram:	$m, n \in n_{i-1} n_i \ldots n_{i+2} n_{i+3}$	WmWn WmCn CmWn WmWn
Trigram:	$r, m, n \in n_{i-1} n_i n_{i+1} \ldots n_{i+1} n_{i+2} n_{i+3}$	
Medium featureset		
Bigram+Child:	$m, n, r \in \{n_i n_{i+1} n_{i+1,L}; n_i n_{i+1} n_{i,R}; n_{i+1} n_{i+2} n_{i+1,R}; n_i n_{i-1} n_{i,L}\}$	CmCnCr CmCnPr
Distance:	$\Delta \in \{\mathrm{dist}(n_i, n_{i+1}), \mathrm{gap}(n_i, n_{i+1})\}$	ΔCm ΔCn ΔPm ΔPn
	$m, n = n_i, n_{i+1}$	ΔFm ΔFn
Large featureset		
Gap bigram:	$m, n \in n_{i-1} n_{i+2}, n_i n_{i+2}$	WmWn WmCn CmWn WmWn
Bigram+2child:	$m, n \in n_{i-1} n_i \ldots n_{i+2} n_{i+3}; C, D \in \mathrm{L}, \mathrm{R}$	CmCnCm_CCn_D CmCnCm_CPn_D CmCnPm_CCn_D
Bigram-Dist	$m, n \in n_{i-1} n_i \ldots n_{i+2} n_{i+3}$	Δ
	$\Delta = \mathrm{dist}(m, n)$	ΔPmPn

Table 1: Features used: W=word, C=phrase label, M=head morph, P=head pos

- **Reduce-Binary**: two nodes are grouped under one node, with the head of the new node being determined by a head table.
- **Add-Left/Add-Right**: one node is added as a child to a node on its left/to its right.
- **Swap**: if two nodes are in surface order (i.e., the head of the first node being left of the head of the second node in the normal word ordering), they can be swapped.

In addition, we experimented with a **retag** action which allows the parser to change the tag of a word that has been mistagged. While this has a positive effect on the parser's accuracy for verb phrases, it also results in a slight deterioration of other phrases, resulting in a very slight decline in performance.

To decide among different parsing actions, the parser uses a linear classifier with a pre-defined feature set (POS, word form, morphological tag and lemma in a two-token window around the two nodes that are being considered, the category and part-of-speech tag of the leftmost and rightmost dependent of the nodes that are being considered; bigrams of words, categories, and one of each, in a window of one around the two nodes being considered, and trigrams consisting of two category and one category, part-of-speech tag, or word form within said window).

Weights are learned by performing online learning with early stopping, similar to the strategy employed by Collins and Roark (2004). We use the Adaptive Gradients method (Duchi et al., 2011) for weight updates and averaging of the weight vector (in a fashion identical to the averaged perceptron). We found that 5-10 epochs of training on Tiger were sufficient to get a mostly usable model, and used 15 epochs of training for the results reported in the later section. Considering that Goldberg and Elhalad (2010) use a learning strategy that performs multiple perceptron updates until the constraint violation is fixed, we also tried this strategy but did not achieve convergence.

3.3 Reordering Oracles for Constituents

The basic idea for reordering oracles in deterministic dependency parsing has been presented by Nivre (2009). In the following, we present a straightforward adapation of the idea to constituent trees.

Given a set of terminals $T = \{w_1, \ldots, w_n\}$ that is totally ordered by a relation $<$, an unordered tree graph is a directed graph $(NT \cup T, \triangleleft)$ with nonterminal (NT) and terminal nodes (T), where the transitive hull $\triangleleft^*$ of the parent relation $\triangleleft$ is acyclic, no node has a parent from T, and exactly one node, v_{root}, has no parent.

An **node ordering** $\prec$ is *consistent* with $\triangleleft$ whenever, for any node u and an descendant $u' \triangleright^* u$, and a node v with an descendant $v' \triangleright^* v$, $u \prec v$ entails $u' \prec v'$.

A **tree cut** of a tree is a sequence $v_1, \ldots, v_n$ that contains exactly one node from each path $v_{\text{root}}, \ldots w_i$ from the root to a terminal. Nivre's insight, applied to constituent structures, is that sorting the terminals in a $\lhd$-compatible order $\prec$ will allow us to use normal projective parsing techniques to find a sequence of reductions that parses this tree, since any needed reduction would reduce one $\prec$-ordered cut to another $\prec$-ordered cut. In the following, two orderings $\prec$, $\prec'$ are considered equivalent iff they only differ on pairs of nodes u, v where one is the ancestor of the other.

Two subtrees under nodes u and v with yields $\text{yield}(u) = \{u' \in T | u' \lhd^* u\}$ and $\text{yield}(v) = \{v' \in T | v' \lhd^* v\}$ are *separated* by a surface ordering $<$ whenever any two terminals u' of u and v' of v fulfill $u' < v'$. Note that two nodes without gaps (i.e. block-degree one) either embed each other (in which case $u \lhd^* v$ or $v \lhd^* u$ is the case) or they are separated by $<$. In a slight abuse of notation, we extend $<$ from a total order of the terminals to a partial order of the nonterminals by writing $u < v$ whenever u and v are separated. For projective trees, this extension of $<$ specifies exactly one total relation (modulo equivalence), and which is also $\lhd$-compatible.

For trees that are non-projective, we can have the situation where two nodes u and v are *overlapping* in that u has descendants u', u'' and v has a descendant v' with $u' < v' < u''$. Then we cannot extend $<$ to an ordering of nodes that is $\lhd$-compatible. However, we can always find an ordering that respects $<$ locally such that, for two children u' and u'' of u, $u' < u''$ entails $u' \prec u''$. Nivre proposes the sequence assigned by an in-order traversal of the dependency tree. In our case, any function $h : NT \rightarrow (NT \cup T)$ that assigns a "head" child to each node will do the same, with an extension $h^*(w) = w$ for all terminals and $h^*(v) = h^*(h(v))$ otherwise, through $u \prec v :\Rightarrow h^*(u) \prec h^*(v)$.[2]

A transition sequence for parsing a tree is then a sequence consisting of **reductions** (leading from a cut $\ldots v_i, u', \ldots u'', v_j, \ldots$ with a contiguous subsequence of the children of u to the sequence $\ldots v_i, u, v_j, \ldots$ that contains u instead) and **swaps** (leading from a cut $\ldots v_i, v_j \ldots$ that has $h^*(v_i)$ and $h^*(v_j)$ ordered with respect to $<$ but not with respect to $\prec$ to a cut $\ldots v_j, v_i \ldots$ that is orders $h^*(v_i)$ and $h^*(v_j)$ with respect to $\prec$ but not $<$).

Nivre (2009) defines an oracle for shift-reduce parsing that is **swap-eager** in that it always allows swapping. In Nivre's case, the oracle is deterministic and always performs the swapping before any reduction.

Nivre et al. (2009) note that the swap-eager oracle performs too many swaps because it swaps groups of words that are later reduced. They propose a **swap-lazy** algorithm that does not swap two nodes if one of them is adjacent to another node that is within the same maximal projective subtree.

The perspective of parsing as a series of swap and reduce actions allows us to specify a strategy that performs less reductions in some cases: Consider that we need to reorder the $<$-contiguous sequence of terminals to the $\prec$-contiguous sequence that is needed for reducing the tree to its final form. The number of swaps performed, if we assume that we always swap adjacent constituents, is exactly equal to the number of terminal pairs v_i, v_j that are $<$-ordered but not $\prec$-ordered. Any reduction of the number of swaps relative to this baseline will come from a group of nodes with heads $v_{i1}, \ldots v_{ik}$ that are reduced to their parent v_i before being swapped with a node v_j.

We can take advantage of this fact by using any node with blockdegree one as a **barrier**: no node that is a descendant of this node can be swapped with a node that is not a descendant before the reduction that results in the barrier node has been carried out. Because any projective subtree has all nodes as barrier nodes, any pair of nodes whose swapping is delayed by the swap-lazy approach will be kept from swapping by a barrier. Conversely, nodes with a block-degree of one can also occur higher-up in the tree (e.g. as clause or sentence nodes), in which case they can act as a barrier even when their subtrees are not projective.

4 Quantitative Evaluation

In order to evaluate our approach, we used the Tiger treebank, with the split used in the SPMRL'2013 shared task (about 40 000 training sentences and 5 000 development and test sentences each; see also

[2] Note that the concrete choice of h is quite arbitrary: we could take the actual head child, but also the first or last child of a node.

	$\ell \leq 30$	$\ell \leq 40$					
	F_1	F_1	LA	EX	NP	PP	VP
EaFi: Preprocessing (large, barrier, noretag)							
gold	77.95	76.64	92.17	41.71	75.0	82.8	56.6
marmot	75.51	73.97	91.08	38.48	72.7	81.3	48.3
pred	74.71	73.18	90.81	37.67	72.1	80.6	48.9
ADG, marmot preprocessing							
marmot	73.42	72.24	90.95	33.77	68.0	77.4	52.1
EaFi: Train projective, evaluate on real data							
gold	76.86	75.50	92.13	38.38	74.4	81.7	48.2
marmot	74.43	72.98	91.20	36.52	72.1	79.8	42.6
pred	73.75	72.32	90.72	35.55	71.8	79.2	42.4
EaFi: Train projective, evaluate on projective							
gold	79.95	78.59	93.40	44.20	76.1	83.0	68.7
marmot	77.00	75.64	92.38	40.79	73.8	81.1	59.1
pred	76.25	74.94	91.87	39.60	73.5	80.5	58.4

Table 2: Results on SPMRL'13-dev (German, Tiger treebank) with varying preprocessing

	$\ell \leq 30$	$\ell \leq 40$					
	F_1	F_1	LA	EX	NP	PP	VP
EaFi: Feature set (barrier, noretag)							
basic	70.26	68.60	89.03	34.03	69.1	77.1	40.1
medium	73.31	71.75	90.13	36.22	70.5	79.9	45.8
large	74.71	73.18	90.81	37.67	72.1	80.6	48.9
EaFi: Reordering (large, noretag)							
eager	73.33	71.66	90.33	37.43	71.7	80.6	47.8
lazy	74.85	73.37	90.85	38.08	72.2	80.8	49.0
barrier	74.71	73.18	90.81	37.67	72.1	80.6	48.9
EaFi: Tag correction (large, barrier)							
noretag	74.71	73.18	90.81	37.67	72.1	80.6	48.9
retag	74.62	73.16	90.83	37.51	71.5	80.3	49.4

Table 3: Results on SPMRL'13-dev (German, Tiger treebank) with *pred* preprocessing

Seddah et al., 2013 for a more extensive description), with the state-of-the-art preprocessing results for part-of-speech and morphological tags[3] which were produced by Björkelund et al. (2013) using the MarMoT tagger (Müller et al., 2013), in addition to the gold-standard preprocessing (*gold*) and automatic predictions (*pred*) that are part of the official dataset of the SPMRL shared task.

We applied two transformations to the data, which are automatically reversed in the parser output: one is adding NPs into PPs, which is also done by Seeker et al. (2012), and the other is that we make parenthetical material subordinate to its embedding clause, as Maier et al. (2012) also advocate.

Evaluation was performed using the evaluator from the DiscoDop package of van Cranenburgh and Bod (2013), excluding punctuation and the ROOT label added by disco-dop from the evaluation. Training was run for 15 epochs. Parsing the 5000 development sentences took about 90-120 seconds for EaFi, which corresponds to 40-55 sentences per second (on a Core i7 2GHz) and is slightly faster than MaltParser using the ADG-derived model and a LibLinear classifier.

In the results in table 2, we see the results for the dependency-to-constiuents approach, as well as for the easy-first parsing with different reordering heuristics. As in Nivre et al. (2009), we notice that the *lazy* strategy that keeps projective constituents together yields better results than the *eager* strategy which allows moving right away. The overall results – around 76.6% f-score on gold tags and 73.1% f-score on predicted tags in sentences of 40 words and below – indicate the promise of this approach, even though they are significantly below the results of van Cranenburgh and Bod (2013) who achieve more than 78% f-measure using predicted tags on a different split of the Tiger treebank. Van Cranenburgh's approach is about 15-20 times slower than ours, using 10 seconds for a 40-word sentence.

For informative purposes, we also included results for projective parsing in table 2, using a conversion that first attaches punctuation and then projectivizes the tree by detaching non-head children.[4] Comparing the nonprojective parser and a variant that was trained on the projectivized version of the dataset, we see that the projective parser is about 1-2 percent worse than the nonprojective one, corresponding to our intuition that the reordering part improves the parsing on average. We also see that the projective evaluation yields an estimate of parser performance that is substantially more optimistic than evaluating on the original treebank.

4.1 Comparison with Related work

Tables 4 and 5 show previous results for discontinous constituent parsing on the Tiger and Negra treebanks. The current best results on the Tiger treebank have been achieved by van Cranenburgh and Bod (2013), whose approach yields 78.8% Parseval F_1 measure on the Tiger treebank in the split by Hall and Nivre (2008), and 76.8% on the Negra treebank, in both cases with above 40% of exact matches among the sentences of up to 40 words. Kallmeyer and Maier (2013) only report results on shorter sentences in Negra for their approach using a modified treebank LCFRS. They achieve 75.6% on sentences of up to 30 words.

A recent approach that attempts to speed up discontinuous constituent parsing is the one by Angelov and Ljunglöf (2014), whose parser takes about 100 seconds for a length-40 sentence, which can be reduced to 10 seconds for a length-40 sentence with an approximate search strategy. For sentences between 5 and 60 tokens, their approach reaches an F_1 score of 69.3%, which however deteriorates quickly when approximate search is used, to 61.9% F_1 in the latter case.

It is quite evident that pushing for more speed in these formalisms forcibly leads to a deterioration in the quality of the results. As such, we think that the speed/quality tradeoff achieved in our system is quite useful.

5 Qualitative Analysis

In the following, we will provide a categorization of the phenomena concerning verbless clauses on one hand, and discontinuous constituents on the other. Table 6 contains a breakdown on these types of

[3]Data from `http://www.cis.lmu.de/~muellets/marmot/marmot_spmrl.tar.bz2`, version with file dates of June 13th 2014. See `http://code.google.com/p/cistern/wiki/marmotSPMRL`

[4]The SPMRL shared task dataset is idiosyncratic in that it deprojectivizes before attaching punctuation, which leads to a result that is rather dissimilar to the original treebank.

	$\ell \leq 30$		$\ell \leq 40$	
	F_1	EX	F_1	EX
Hall and Nivre (2008), gold[a]	—	—	79.93	37.78
Hall and Nivre (2008), pred[a]	—	—	75.33	32.63
van Cranenburgh and Bod (2013), pred[a]	—	—	78.8	40.8
This work, gold[a]	76.47	40.61	74.23	37.32
Maier (2010), LCFRS gold[c]	73.43	29.87	—	—
Maier (2010), CFG gold[c]	75.57	31.80	—	—
This work, gold[b]	77.95	43.81	76.64	41.71
This work, gold, eval w/ ROOT[bc]	81.13	43.81	79.80	41.71

[a]) Hall&Nivre split [b]) SPMRL split [c]) includes the ROOT node in the evaluation

Table 4: Previous results on the Tiger treebank

	$\ell \leq 30$		$\ell \leq 40$	
	F_1	EX	F_1	EX
Maier (2010), LCFRS gold[c]	71.52	31.65	—	—
Maier (2010), CFG gold[c]	74.04	33.43	—	—
van Craenburgh (2012), LCFRS, gold	—	—	67.26	27.90
van Craenburgh (2012), Disco-DOP, gold	—	—	72.33	33.16
Maier et al. (2012)	74.5	—	—	—
Kallmaier and Maier (2013), LCFRS, gold	75.75	—	—	—
van Cranenburgh and Bod (2013), gold	—	—	76.8	40.5

[c]) includes the ROOT node in the evaluation

Table 5: Previous results on the NeGra treebank

phenomena according to whether they are:

- **correctly parsed** (+): when the incredients for the construction are present in the parse and they are combined in a suitable fashion.
- **missed** (o): when the ingredients for the construction are present, but combined in another way – for example, an extraposition where the extraposed item is misattached
- **broken** (-): when the ingredients for the construction are not present and the parse has a completely different structure.

Many of the same categories are discussed by Seeker and Kuhn (2012), who only discuss examples, and by Maier et al. (2014), who published a list of sentence numbers for each phenomenon that is, however, disjoint with the development portion considered here. Although the distinctions between "missed" and "broken" analyses are somewhat subjective, we think that it is still informative in the sense that it helps to compare the relative difficulty of the problems involved.

5.1 Types of Verbless Clauses

In their conversion Seeker and Kuhn (2012) found 3 035 sentences that contain at least one empty node in the Tiger treebank, or about one every 16 sentences. While this phenomenon may be more frequent in spontaneously-produced text such as it may occur in user-generated content, it is still quite frequent.

Seeker et al. only distinguish among edge labels, followed by a guess on the clause type that they need in order to place the inserted null element.

In this work, we will concentrate on verbless VP and S nodes, with rougly three categories:

The first consists of **verbless copula clauses** that mostly occur at top level,[5] and where the most obvious way to build a complete clause would be to add a *be* copula to the clause.

[5]sentences 40499, 41442, 41468, 41676, 41682, 41736, 41743, 42566, 42606, 42738

	ADG/marm			large/pred		
	+	o	-	+	o	-
copula clauses	3	4	3	2	5	3
gapping/ellipsis	0	4	6	0	4	6
parentheticals	1	6	4	0	4	6
extraposition	1	7	2	0	7	3
scrambling	3	2	4	3	1	5
topicalization	3	6	1	4	4	2

+) construction parsed ok, o) construction missed, −) broken parse

Table 6: Qualitative analysis: Counts for *ok/missed/broken* examples

A second group consists of clauses with **gapping/ellipsis** which occur in a coordinated structure, but do not have a verb of their own.[6] Such cases can occur with a final constituent in clause coordination as well as with a non-final constituent in verb-last clauses:

(1) a. Die Anstalt soll [Anfang 1998 noch 1200 Beschäftigte] und [ein Jahr später 600 zählen].
the institution shall start 1998 still 1200 employees and one year later 600 count.
"*The institution will count 1200 employees at the start of 1998 and one year later, 600*".

b. [Die Zahl der Urlaubsreisen im Inland fiel laut Schörcher um zwei Prozent] und [damit nicht mehr so stark wie im Vorjahreszeitraum] .
the number of holiday trips in interior fell according to Schörcher by two percent and hence not anymore as strong as in the previous year period
"*The national number of holiday trips fell by two percent according to Schorcher, and hence not as strongly anymore as in the corresponding period from last year*".

Finally, we have **parentheticals**, which are rather rather similar to the examples listed under *verbless copula clauses*, except that they occur as parenthetical material in a larger clause rather than by themselves.[7]

5.2 Types of Non-projectivity Phenomena

For the purpose of this paper, we will make a three-way distinction in the phenomena that create discontinuities, according to the following questions:

- If we serialize the sorted (sub)tree, would the result yield a grammatical sequence? Or, to ask a related question, would anything be missing if we kept only the continuous block of the head?
- If we flatten the tree by introducing a common *ordering domain* for multiple heads (which would be the result of tree flattening as proposed by Uszkoreit, 1987 or of a common argument list as advocated by Hinrichs and Nakazawa, 1989; flattening the sentence is also the solution used in the German LFG grammar of Forst, 2007), would we have gotten rid of the problem?

Making these distinctions gives us three rather large categories that we can use to classify nonprojectivity phenomena:

Extraposition[8] is phenomenon where the sorted subtree would (usually) be grammatical, and where the continuous part only would (usually) be acceptable:

[6] sentences 40698, 40788, 40836, 41003, 41174, 41218, 41356, 41399, 41544, 41665
[7] sentences 40698, 40749, 40861, 40894, 40899, 40924, 41219, 41267, 41437, 41443
[8] Sentences 40506, 40507, 40517, 40528, 40567, 40583, 40589, 40594, 40622, 40672

(2) a. Ele hat mir [ein Buch] geschenkt [über die Savanne].
Ele has me a book given about the savannah.
"*Ele gave me a book about the savannah*".
b. Ich habe [Ele] ein Buch geschenkt [und Susi].
I have Ele a book given and Susi.
"*I gave a book to Ele and Susi*".
c. Heute ist [der Staubsauger] gekommen, [den Du bestellt hast].
Today is the vacuum cleaner come, which you ordered have.
"*Today, the vacuum cleaner that you ordered came.*"

Note that extraposition can be arbitrarily deep, as NPs can embed each other recursively:

(3) a. Heute ist (die Rechnung für [den Staubsauger]) gekommen, ([den Du bestellt hast]).
Today is the invoice for the vacuum cleaner$_j$ come, which$_j$ you ordered have.
"*Today, the invoice for the vacuum cleaner you ordered came*"
b. Ich habe (die Rechnung für [den Staubsauger]) gefunden, (die Du vermißt hast).
I have the invoice$_i$ for the vacuum cleaner found, which$_i$ you missed have.
"*I found the invoice for the vacuum cleaner which you were missing*"

Scrambling[9] is the effect that occurs when two verbs that both have arguments are in the same clause, and share the ordering domain in that clause, have crossing argument dependencies:

(4) ...daß (dem Kunden) [den Kühlschrank] bisher noch niemand [zu reparieren] zu versuchen
...that the customer the fridge until now yet nobody to repair to try
(versprochen) hat.
promised has.
"*that no one has promised the customer to try repairing the fridge.*"

The example above is due to Becker et al. (1992), who claim that there is no bound on the distance over which each element can scramble, nor a bound on the number of unbounded dependencies that can occur in one sentence. Becker et al. further claim that no LCFRS can faithfully represent a sequence of m verbs which are each preceded by one argument, where the arguments can be permuted freely.[10]

Finally, **Topicalization**[11] or more generally V2-order phenomena are those where a part of the verb clause (either an argument, or an argument of a phrase within the verb clause, or part of the verb clause itself) is moved into clause-initial position.

(5) a. Ein Buch über die Savanne hat Ele mir geschenkt.
a book about the savannah has Ele me given.
"*Ele gave me a book about the savannah.*"
b. Über die Savanne hat mir Ele ein Buch geschenkt.
about the savannah has me Ele a book given.
"*Ele gave me a book about the savannah.*"
c. Ein Buch geschenkt hat Ele mir.
a book given has Ele me.
"*Give me a book, Ele did.*"

[9]Sentences 40524, 40567, 40572, 40588, 40594, 40595, 40601, 40885, 40966, 41025

[10]The practical consequence is that any LCFRS extracted from a treebank will either underspecify the dependencies in such a construction – this is the flattening solution – or yield rules with growing block-degree. van Cranenburgh (2012) shows that the sentences with up to 25 words in Negra can be parsed with an LCFRS that leads to $O(n^9)$ time complexity when a suitable binarization is used, where the original treebank grammar would mean a parsing complexity of $O(n^{19})$. Maier et al. (2012) point out that the observed time complexity of the arbitrary-block-degree parser used by Maier (2010) and Kallmeyer and Maier (2013) is due to necessary bookkeeping, and that their variant with fixed block degree yields a polynomial time complexity.

[11]Sentences 40513, 40521, 40528, 40544, 40546, 40548, 40551, 40572, 40580, 40585

5.3 Analysis of Parser behaviour

Using the movement actions, the parser is able to correctly attach topicalized nodes in simple sentences, and to sort out in most cases which nodes belong to the VP and which ones to the S node. In the presence of complex sentence structure, the very local view on the sentence that the parser has quickly becomes a hindrance. Extraposed material is attached correctly in the case of relative clauses, whereas infinitival constructions (which can plausibly attach to the verb) are often missed, and clauses that are extraposed modifiers of adverbs or adjectives are mostly missed. As with early treebank-based parsers, the presence of multiple verbs (as in coherent constructions) can mislead the parser into assuming a more complex structure than is actually present.

In general, verbless copula clauses, asyndetic coordination, and gapping/ellipsis, which are difficult for dependency parsing, are also especially prone to confuse the very local view of the easy-first parser, which is a rather anticlimactic, yet commonsensical conclusion.

In summary, simple material is often handled surprisingly well, whereas sentences with a complex topological structure – i.e., coordination, clauses embedded in a nominal phrase, or correlations, are rather challenging for easy-first parsing. Parsing algorithms with more context such as Sartorio et al. (2013) or an application of beam search might help in some of these cases.

6 Summary and Future Work

In this article, we presented a deterministic parser that uses an easy-first strategy to perform non-projective constituent parsing in expected linear time, with results that perform in a similar range as results for discontinuous treebank grammars, and provides a means to provide rather fast parsing in cases where discontinuous structure is required. We introduced the *barrier* formulation as an alternative to the lazy reordering of Nivre et al. (2009), which shows similar performance but which may reveal a closer connection to formalisms with restricted discontinuities.

While all experiments and the phenomen-oriented analysis have been performed on German data, the reordering oracle approach does not make any language-specific assumptions and constitutes a general technique for deterministic parsing of discontinuous constituent trees.

Acknowledgements The author would like to thank the three anonymous reviewers for their valuable comments, and Thomas Müller for providing the Marmot-tagged version of the SPMRL dataset.

References

Angelov, Krasimir and Peter Ljunglöf. 2014. Fast statistical parsing with multiple context-free grammars. In *Proceedings of EACL 2014*.

Ballesteros, Miguel and Joakim Nivre. 2012. MaltOptimizer: A system for MaltParser optimization. In *Proceedings of the Eigth International Conference on Language Resources and Evaluation (LREC 2012)*.

Becker, Tilman, Owen Rambow, and Michael Niv. 1992. The derivational generative power, or, scrambling is beyond LCFRS. Technical report, University of Pennsylvania. A version of this paper was presented at MOL3, Austin, Texas, November 1992.

Björkelund, Anders, Özlem Çetinoglu, Richard Farkas, Thomas Müller, and Wolfgang Seeker. 2013. (re)ranking meets morphosyntax: State-of-the-art results from the SPMRL 2013 shared task. In *Proc. SPMRL 2013*.

Bodenstab, Nathan, Aaron Dunlop, Keith Hall, and Brian Roark. 2011. Adaptive beam-width prediction for efficient CYK parsing. In *Proceedings of ACL/HLT 2011*.

Böhmova, A., Jan Hajič, Eva Hajičová, and B. Hladká. 2001. The Prague dependency treebank: Three-level annotaion scenario. In *Treebanks: Building and using syntactically annotated corpora*, Kluwer Academic Publishers, pages 103–127.

Bosco, Cristina and Vincenzo Lombardo. 2006. Comparing linguistic information in treebank annotations. In *LREC 2006*.

Brants, Sabine, Stefanie Dipper, Silvia Hansen, Wolfgang Lezius, and George Smith. 2002. The TIGER treebank. In *Proc. TLT 2002.*

Cai, Shu, David Chiang, and Yoav Goldberg. 2011. Language-independent parsing with empty elements. In *Proceedings of ACL 2011.*

Carreras, Xavier, Michael Collins, and Terry Koo. 2008. TAG, dynamic programming, and the perceptron for efficient, feature-rich parsing. In *Proceedings of CoNLL.*

Collins, Michael. 2003. Head-Driven statistical models for Natural Language parsing. *Computational Linguistics* 29(4):589–637.

Collins, Michael and Brian Roark. 2004. Incremental parsing with the perceptron algorithm. In *ACL-04.*

Dipper, Stefanie, Anke Lüdeling, and Marc Resnicek. 2013. NoSta-D: A corpus of german non-standard varieties. In Marcos Zampieri and Sascha Diwersy, editors, *Non-standard DataSources in Corpus-based Research*, Shaker Verlag.

Dubey, Amit and Frank Keller. 2003. Probabilistic parsing for German using sister-head dependencies. In *ACL'2003.*

Duchi, John, Elad Hazan, and Yoram Singer. 2011. Adaptive subgradient methods for online learning and stochastic optimization. *Journal of Machine Learning Research* 12:2121–2159.

Forst, Martin. 2007. Filling statistics with linguistics - property design for the disambiguation of German LFG parses. In *ACL 2007 workshop on deep linguistic processing.*

Foth, Kilian. 2006. Eine umfassende Dependenzgrammatik des Deutschen. Technical report, Fachbereich Informatik, Universität Hamburg.

Foth, Kilian, Arne Köhn, Niels Beuck, and Wolfgang Menzel. 2014. Because size does matter: The Hamburg dependency treebank. In *Proceedings of the Language Resources and Evaluation Conference (LREC 2014).*

Goldberg, Yoav and Michael Elhalad. 2010. An efficient algorithm for easy-first non-directional dependency parsing. In *Proceedings of NAACL-2010.*

Hall, Johann and Joakim Nivre. 2008. Parsing discontinuous phrase structure with grammatical functions. In *Proceedings of the 6th International Conference on Natural Language Processing (GoTAL 2008).*

Hinrichs, Erhard and Tsuneko Nakazawa. 1989. Flipped out: AUX in German. In *Papers from the 25th Annual Regional Meeting of the Chicago Linguistic Society.*

Hockenmaier, Julia. 2007. CCG grammar extraction from treebanks: translation algorithms and applications. Presentation from the Treebank Workshop, 2007, Rochester NY.

Huang, Liang and David Chiang. 2007. Forest rescoring: Faster decoding with integrated language models. In *Proceedings of ACL 2007.*

Huang, Liang and Kenji Sagae. 2010. Dynamic programming for linear-time incremental parsing. In *Proceedings of ACL 2010.*

Kallmeyer, Laura and Wolfgang Maier. 2013. Data-driven parsing using probabilistic linear context-free rewriting systems. *Computational Linguistics* 39:87–119.

Kapanadze, Oleg. 2012. Building parallel treebanks for the lesser-resourced languages. Technical report, Tbilisi State University.

Koo, Terry, Alexander M. Rush, Michael Collins, Tommi Jaakkola, and David Sontag. 2010. Dual decomposition for parsing with non-projective head automata. In *Proceedings of EMNLP 2010.*

Kornai, Andras and Geoff Pullum. 1990. The X-bar theory of phrase structure. *Language* 66:24–50.

Magerman, David M. 1995. Statistical decision-tree models for parsing. In *ACL'1995.*

Maier, Wolfgang. 2010. Direct parsing of discontinuous constituents in German. In *Proceedings of the NAACL-HLT First Workshop on Statistical Parsing of Morphologically Rich Languages.*

Maier, Wolfgang, Miriam Kaeshammer, Peter Baumann, and Sandra Kübler. 2014. Discosuite – a parser test suite for German discontinuous structures. In *Proceedings of LREC 2014*.

Maier, Wolfgang, Miriam Kaeshammer, and Laura Kallmeyer. 2012. PLCFRS parsing revisited: Restricting the fan-out to two. In *Proceedings of the 11th International Workshop on Tree Adjoining Grammar and Related Formalisms (TAG+11)*.

Miyao, Yusuke, Rune Sætre, Kenji Sagae, Takuya Matsuzaki, and Jun'ichi Tsujii. 2008. Task-oriented evaluation of syntactic parsers and their representations. In *ACL 2008*.

Müller, Thomas, Helmut Schmid, and Hinrich Schütze. 2013. Efficient higher-order CRFs for morphological tagging. In *Proceedings fo EMNLP 2013*.

Nivre, Joakim. 2003. An efficient algorithm for projective dependency parsing. In *8th International Workshop on Parsing Technologies*.

Nivre, Joakim. 2009. Non-projective dependency parsing in expected linear time. In *Proc. Joint ACL-AFNLP 2009*.

Nivre, Joakim. 2011. Bare-bones dependency parsing - a case for occam's razor? In *Nodalida 2011*.

Nivre, Joakim, Marco Kuhlmann, and Johan Hall. 2009. An improved oracle for dependency parsing with online reordering. In *Proceedings of the 11th International Conference on Parsing Technologies (IWPT)*.

Nivre, Joakim and Jens Nilsson. 2005. Pseudo-projective dependency parsing. In *Proceedings of ACL 2005*.

Pauly, Dennis, Ulyana Senyuk, and Ulrike Demske. 2012. Strukturelle Mehrdeutigkeit in frühneuhochdeutschen Texten. *Journal for Language Technology and Computational Linguistics* 27(2):65–82.

Plaehn, Oliver. 2000. Computing the most probable parse for a discontinuous phrase structure grammar. In *Proceedings of the 6th International Workshop on Parsing Technologies*.

Sagae, Kenji and Alon Lavie. 2006. A best-first probabilistic shift-reduce parser. In *Proceedings of the Human Language Technology Conference of the NAACL (NAACL/HLT 2006)*.

Sartorio, Francesco, Giorgio Satta, and Joakim Nivre. 2013. A transition-based dependency parser using a dynamic parsing strategy. In *Proceedings of ACL 2013*.

Schmid, Helmut. 2006. Trace prediction and recovery with unlexicalized PCFGs and slash features. In *Proceedings of COLING-ACL 2006*.

Seddah, Djamé. 2010. Exploring the spinal-tig model for parsing French. In *Proceedings of LREC 2010*.

Seddah, Djamé, Reut Tsarfaty, Sandra Kübler, Marie Candito, Jinho D. Choi, Richárd Farkas, Jennifer Foster, Iakes Goenaga, Koldo Gojenola Galletebeitia, Yoav Goldberg, Spence Green, Nizar Habash, Marco Kuhlmann, Wolfgang Maier, Joakim Nivre, Adam Przepiórkowski, Ryan Roth, Wolfgang Seeker, Yannick Versley, Veronika Vincze, Marcin Woliński, Alina Wróblewska, and Eric Villemonte de la Clergerie. 2013. Overview of the SPMRL 2013 Shared Task: A Cross-Framework Evaluation of Parsing Morphologically Rich Languages. In *Proceedings of the Fourth Workshop on Statistical Parsing of Morphologically-Rich Languages*. Seattle, WA, pages 146–182.

Seeker, Wolfgang, Richárd Farkas, Bernd Bohnet, Helmut Schmid, and Jonas Kuhn. 2012. Data-driven dependency parsing with empty heads. In *Proceedings of Coling 2012*.

Seeker, Wolfgang and Jonas Kuhn. 2012. Making ellipses explicit in dependency conversion for a german treebank. In *Proceedings of the Eight International Conference on Language Resources and Evaluation (LREC'12)*.

Stolcke, Andreas. 1995. An efficient probabilistic context-free parsing algorithm that computes prefix probabilities. *Computational Linguistics* 21(2):165–201.

Telljohann, Heike, Erhard W. Hinrichs, Sandra Kübler, Heike Zinsmeister, and Kathrin Beck. 2009. Stylebook for the Tübingen Treebank of Written German (TüBa-D/Z). Technical report, Seminar für Sprachwissenschaft, Universität Tübingen.

Tratz, Stephen and Eduard Hovy. 2011. A fast, accurate, non-projective, semantically-enriched parser. In *Proceedings of the 2011 Conference on Empirical Methods in Natural Language Processing (EMNLP 2011)*.

Uszkoreit, Hans. 1987. *Word order and constituent structure in German*. Number 8 in CSLI Lecture Notes. Center for the Study of Language and Information.

van Cranenburgh, Andreas. 2012. Efficient parsing with linear context-free rewriting systems. In *EACL 2012*.

van Cranenburgh, Andreas and Rens Bod. 2013. Discontinuous parsing with an efficient and accurate DOP model. In *Proceedings of the International Conference on Parsing Technologies (IWPT 2013)*.

van Noord, Geertjan. 1991. Head corner parsing for discontinuous constituency. In *Proceedings of ACL 1991*.

Versley, Yannick and Heike Zinsmeister. 2006. From dependency parsing to deep(er) semantics. In *Proceedings of the Fifth International Workshop on Treebanks and Linguistic Theories (TLT 2006)*.

Vincze, Veronika, Dóra Szauter, Attila Almási adn György Móra, Zoltán Alexin, and János Csirik. 2010. Hungarian dependency treebank. In *Proceedings of the Seventh Conference on International Language Resources and Evaluation (LREC 2010)*.

Volk, Martin and Yvonne Samuelsson. 2004. Bootstrapping parallel treebanks. In *Proceedings of the 5th International Workshop on Linguistically Interpreted Corpora (LINC) at Coling 2004*.

Exploring Options for Fast Domain Adaptation of Dependency Parsers

Viktor Pekar, Juntao Yu, Mohab El-karef, Bernd Bohnet
School of Computer Science
University of Birmingham
Birmingham, UK
{v.pekar,jxy362,mxe346,b.bohnet}@cs.bham.ac.uk

Abstract

The paper explores different domain-independent techniques to adapt a dependency parser trained on a general-language corpus to parse web texts (online reviews, newsgroup posts, weblogs): co-training, word clusters, and a crowd-sourced dictionary. We examine the relative utility of these techniques as well as different ways to put them together to achieve maximum parsing accuracy. While we find that co-training and word clusters produce the most promising results, there is little additive improvement when combining the two techniques, which suggests that in the absence of large grammatical discrepancies between the training and test domains, they address largely the same problem, that of unknown vocabulary, with word clusters being a somewhat more effective solution for it. Our highest results were achieved by a combination of word clusters and co-training, significantly improving on the baseline, by up to 1.67%. Evaluation of the best configurations on the SANCL-2012 test data (Petrov and McDonald, 2012) showed that they outperform all the shared task submissions that used a single parser to parse test data, averaging the results across all the test sets.

1 Introduction

Domain adaptation of a statistical dependency parser is a problem that is of much importance for many practical NLP applications. Previous research has shown that the accuracy of parsing significantly drops when a general-language model is applied to narrow domains like financial news (Gildea, 2001), biomedical texts (Lease and Charniak, 2005), web data (Petrov and McDonald, 2012), or patents (Burga et al., 2013). In a preliminary experiment, we looked at the effect of cross-domain parsing on three state-of-the-art parsers – Malt (Nivre, 2009), MST (McDonald and Pereira, 2006), and Mate parser (Bohnet et al., 2013) – trained on the CoNLL09 dataset and tested on texts from different domains in the OntoNotes v5.0 corpus as well as the in-domain CoNLL09 test set. The results (see Table 1) indicate that depending on the application domain, the parsing accuracy can suffer an absolute drop of as much as 16%.

Domain	**MST**	**MALT**	**Mate**
Newswire	84.8	81.7	87.1
Pivot Texts	84.9	83.0	86.6
Broadcast News	79.4	78.1	81.2
Magazines	77.1	74.7	79.3
Broadcast Conversation	73.4	70.5	74.4
CoNLL09 test	86.9	84.7	90.1

Table 1: Labelled accuracy scores achieved by the MST, Malt, and Mate parsers trained on CoNLL09 data and tested on different specialist domains.

In a typical domain adaptation scenario, there are **in-domain texts** that are manually annotated and that are used to train a general-language parser, and **out-of-domain** or **target domain texts** that are

First Joint Workshop on Statistical Parsing of Morphologically Rich Languages and Syntactic Analysis of Non-Canonical Languages, pages 54–65 Dublin, Ireland, August 23-29 2014.

parsed during parser testing. In addition, a certain amount of unlabelled target domain texts may be available that can be leveraged in this or that way to facilitate domain adaptation. To address the problem of domain adaption, previous work focused on weakly supervised methods to re-train parsers on automatically parsed out-of-domain texts, through techniques such as co-training (Sarkar, 2001; Steedman et al., 2003), self-training (McClosky and Charniak, 2008; Rehbein, 2011), and uptraining (Petrov et al., 2010); selecting or weighting sentences from annotated in-domain data that fit best with the target domain (Plank and Van Noord, 2011; Søgaard and Plank, 2012; Khan et al., 2013b). Another line of research aims specifically to overcome the lexical gap between the training data and the target domain texts. These approaches include techniques such as text pre-processing and normalization (Foster, 2010), the use of external lexica and morphological clues to predict PoS tags of unknown target domain words (Szolovits, 2003; Pyysalo et al., 2006), discrete or continuous word clusters computed from unlabelled target domain texts (Candito et al., 2011; Bansal et al., 2014), selectional preferences modelled from word co-occurrences obtained from unannotated texts (Zhou et al., 2011).

The goal of this paper is to investigate a combination of such techniques to adapt a general-language parser to parse web data (weblogs, online reviews, newsgroups, and answers) without resorting to manual annotation. In our study we include several techniques that have been shown to be reasonably effective for domain adaptation: text normalization, the use of word clusters, an external crowd-sourced lexicon, as well as automatically annotated texts produced with the help of co-training. All these techniques are domain-independent and can be applied to new target domains given unlabelled texts form these domains. We explore the relative utility of these methods and ways to combine them for maximum parser accuracy.

2 Related work

2.1 Text normalization

User-generated content on the web is notoriously low-quality, containing slang, abbreviations, inconsistent grammar and spelling. Foster (2010) investigated lexical phenomena that appear on online discussion forums that present common problems for parsing and compiled a list of such phenomena along with their transformations. Applying the transformations to test sentences helped to bring the F-score up by 2.7%. A similar approach was taken by Khan *et al.* (2013a) who found that it performed better than spelling correction based on the Levenshtein distance. Gadde *et al.* (2011) use a word clustering method and language modelling in order to align misspelled words with their regular spelling. Their method of cleaning noisy text helped to increase the accuracy of PoS tagging of SMS data by 3.5%.

2.2 External lexica

To adapt the Link parser to the medical domain, Szolovitz (2003) extended its lexicon with terms from the UMLS Specialist Lexicon. Pyysalo *et al.* (2006) take the same approach and together with predicting the PoS tags for out-of-vocabulary words based on their morphology this allowed them to achieve a 10% reduction in the error rate of parsing. External lexica have also been used to improve out-of-domain PoS tagging (Li et al., 2012).

2.3 Word clusters

In order to reduce the amount of annotated data to train a dependency parser, Koo *et al.* (2008) used word clusters computed from unlabelled data as features for training a parser. The same approach has proved to be effective for out-of-domain parsing, where there are many words in the test data unseen during training, and word clusters computed from in-domain data similarly help to deal with the vocabulary discrepancies between the training and test datasets. Discrete word clusters produced by Brown *et al.* (1992) method have been shown to be beneficial for adapting dependency parsers to biomedical texts (Candito et al., 2011) and web texts (Øvrelid and Skjærholt, 2012). Word clusters created with Brown clustering method have also been used to adapt a PoS tagger to Twitter posts (Owoputi et al., 2013). Bansal *et al.* (2014) introduced continuous word representations and showed them to increase parsing accuracy both on the Penn Treebank and on web data.

2.4 Co-training

Co-training (Blum and Mitchell, 1998) is a paradigm for weakly supervised learning of a classification problem from a limited amount of labelled data and a large amount of unlabelled data, whereby two or more views on the data, i.e. feature subsets, or two or more different learning algorithms are employed that complement each other to bootstrap additional training data from the unlabelled dataset. Co-training algorithms have been successfully used in NLP tasks, and specifically for parsing. Sarkar (2001) showed the both precision and recall of a phrase structure parser can be increased using a co-training procedure that iteratively adds the most confidently parsed sentences from two different views to the training set. Steedman *et al.*(2003) used two different parsers that supplied training data to each other in a bootstrapping manner.

A number of studies specifically aimed to use co-training for domain adaptation of a dependency parser. Sagae (2007) used two different learning algorithms of their graph-based parser to complete a one iteration of co-training, getting an improvement of 2-3%, which was the best result on the out-of-domain track of the CoNLL07 shared task (Nilsson et al., 2007). An interesting finding of their work was that the agreement between the two classifiers during testing was a very good predictor of accuracy. More recently, Zhang *et al.* (2012) used a tri-training algorithm for parser domain adaptation. The algorithm uses three learners and each learner was designed to learn from those automatically classified unlabelled data where the other two learners agreed on the classification label.

3 Experimental set-up

3.1 Parsers

In the experiments we included the Malt parser (Nivre, 2009), the MST parser (McDonald and Pereira, 2006), the transition-based Mate parser (Bohnet et al., 2013), and the graph-based Turbo parser (Martins et al., 2010). All the parsers were used with their default settings, and PoS tags used in the input of all the parsers were the same and came from the Mate parser.

3.2 Baseline

As the baseline we used the Mate parser, as it showed the highest accuracy when no domain adaptation techniques were used, i.e. trained on an in-domain training dataset and applied directly to out-of-domain test data.

3.3 Data

The experiments were conducted on annotated data on web-related domains available in the Ontonotes v.5 and SANCL datasets, since a large amount of unlabelled data required for most domain adaptation techniques is widely available.

OntoNotes. In experiments with weblog texts, we used the CoNLL09 training dataset (Hajič et al., 2009) as the general-language training data. The CoNLL09 test dataset was used to evaluate in-domain parsing. To create an out-of-domain test set, we selected the last 10% of the weblogs section of the OntoNotes v5.0 corpus[1], in order to make the size of the out-of-domain test data comparable to that of the in-domain test data, i.e. of CoNLL09 test. The OntoNotes corpus was converted to the CoNLL09 format using the LTH constituent-to-dependency conversion tool (Johansson and Nugues, 2007).

SANCL. In order to compare our results with the results achieved by participants in the SANCL-2012 shared task, we also ran experiments on the Stanford dependences of three SANCL test sets (`answers`, `newsgroups` and `reviews`). In these experiments we used the training set, test sets, unlabelled data, as well as the evaluation script provided by SANCL-2012 organizers (Petrov and McDonald, 2012).

Tables 2 and 3 show the sizes of the OntoNotes and SANCL datasets as well as several measures of lexical and grammatical characteristics of the data. The average sentence length (in tokens) and the average number of subjects, roughly corresponding to the number of clauses in the sentence, aim to characterize the syntactic complexity of the sentences: the higher these values, the more complex the

[1]https://catalog.ldc.upenn.edu/LDC2013T19

structure of the sentences is likely to be. The ratio of word forms absent from training data describes how different the train and test data are in terms of vocabulary.

We see that in the OntoNotes test set the average sentence length and the number of subjects per sentence is very similar to those in the train data. In SANCL test sets, these measures are more different, but the values indicate a smaller syntactic complexity than in the train data. The amount of unknown vocabulary in all the four test sets is between 5% and 8%.

	CoNLL09 train	**CoNLL09 test**	**OntoNotes test**
Sentences	39,279	2,399	2,150
Tokens	958,167	57,676	42,144
Sentence length	24.61	24.59	23.4
Subjects	1.8	1.83	1.89
Unk. wordforms ratio	0.0	0.011	0.05

Table 2: The size of OntoNotes train and test datasets.

	SANCL train	**Answers test**	**Newsgroups test**	**Reviews test**
Sentences	30,060	1,744	1,195	1,906
Tokens	731,678	28,823	20,651	28,086
Sentence length	24.56	18.44	22.79	16.35
Subjects	1.69	1.78	1.62	1.5
Unk. wordforms ratio	0.0	0.064	0.084	0.051

Table 3: The size of SANCL train and test datasets.

Unlabelled Data. As unlabelled target domain data we used the unlabelled dataset from the SANCL-2012 shared task. In experiments with word clusters, the entire dataset was used without any pre-processing. In the co-training experiments, we pre-processed the data by removing sentences that are longer than 500 tokens, or contained non-English words (this reduced the test set by 2%). Table 4 describes the size of the subsets of the unlabelled data.

	Emails	**Weblogs**	**Answers**	**Newsgroups**	**Reviews**
Sentences	1,194,173	524,834	27,274	1,000,000	1,965,350
Tokens	17,047,731	10,356,284	424,299	18,424,657	29,289,169

Table 4: The size of unlabelled datasets.

3.4 Evaluation method

As a measure of parser accuracy, we report labeled attachment scores (LAS), the percentage of dependencies which are attached and labeled correctly. Significance testing was performed using paired t-test.

4 Results and Discussion

4.1 Text normalization

We used a manually compiled lexicon containing Internet-specific spellings of certain words aligned with their traditional spellings, e.g. *u* ⇒ *you*, *gr8* ⇒ *great*, *don,t* ⇒ *don't*, as well as a number of regular expressions to deal with extra symbols usually added for emphasis (*This is sooooo good.*, *This *is* great.*). After the original word forms were read by the parser, the lexicon and the regular expressions were applied to normalize the spelling of the words. This produced only a very insignificant gain on the baseline. A manual examination of the test data in both OntoNotes and SANCL has shown that in fact although it comes from the web it contains very few examples of "Internet speak".

4.2 Word clusters

We used Liang's (2005) implementation of the Brown clustering algorithm to create clusters of words found in unlabelled domain texts. The output of the algorithm are word types assigned to discrete hierarchical clusters, with clusters assigned ids in the form of bit strings of varying length corresponding to clusters of different granularity. We experimentally set the maximum length of the bit string to 6, collapsing more fine-grained clusters. Instead of replacing the original word forms and/or PoS tags with cluster ids as was done in some previous studies (Koo et al., 2008; Candito et al., 2011; Täckström et al., 2013), the ids of clusters were used to generate additional features in the representations of the word forms, as this also produced better results in the preliminary runs. Below we describe experiments with several other parameters of the clustering algorithm.

Number of clusters. As an input parameter, the Brown clustering algorithm requires a desired number of clusters. Initially discarding all word types with a count of less than 3, we experimented with different numbers of clusters and found that an optimal settings lies around 600 and 800 clusters, which gives an improvement on the baseline of 0.9% for out-of-domain texts; but there does not seem to be noticeable differences between specific numbers of clusters (see Table 5, statistically significant differences to the baseline are indicated by stars[2]).

Number of clusters	CoNLL09	OntoNotes
50	90.46**	78.10*
100	90.28*	78.40**
200	90.27	78.39**
400	90.37**	78.20**
600	90.40**	78.43**
800	90.30*	78.14**
Baseline	90.07	77.54

Table 5: The effect of the number of word clusters on in- and out-of-domain parsing, using the reviews and weblogs subsets of the SANCL-2012 unlabelled data.

Filtering rare words. Due to the inevitable data sparseness, the algorithm is likely to mis-cluster infrequent words. At the same time, it is rare words that are not seen during parser training and are potentially of greatest value if included into word clusters. We examined several thresholds on word frequency and their impact on parsing accuracy (see Table 6; statistically significant differences to the baseline are indicated by stars). We found very slight differences between these three thresholds, although the cut-off point of 3 showed the best results. Hence in further experiments with word clusters we used this cut-off point.

Min. freq.	CoNLL09	OntoNotes
1	90.36**	78.12*
3	**90.40****	**78.43****
5	90.22	78.24**

Table 6: The effect of filtering out rare words on word clusters, using the reviews and weblogs subsets of the SANCL-2012 unlabelled data.

Amount of unlabelled data. To examine the effect that the size of unlabelled data from which word clusters are computed, has on parser accuracy, we compared parser accuracy achieved when using only the reviews and weblogs subsets of the SANCL corpus (39.6 mln word tokens), and when using the entire SANCL dataset (75.2 mln tokens). These results are shown in Table 7, significant improvements on the smaller set are indicated by stars. As expected, a larger amount of data does improve the parsing accuracy, and the improvement is greater for out-of-domain parsing (+0.55% vs. +0.32%).

[2]In this and the following tables, one star indicates significance at the $p < 0.05$ level, two stars at the $p < 0.01$ level.

	CoNLL09	OntoNotes
Reviews and Weblogs	90.30	78.14
Entire SANCL dataset	**90.62***	**78.69***

Table 7: The effect of the size of unlabelled data on word clusters, discarding word types with count less than 3.

Relevant domain data. Furthermore, we were interested if simply adding more unlabelled data, not necessarily from the relevant domain, produced the same increase in accuracy. We obtained the plain-text claims and description parts of 13,600 patents freely available in the Global IP Database which is based on the Espacenet[3], creating a corpus with 42.5 mln tokens, i.e. which was similar in size to the reviews and weblogs sections of the SANCL unlabelled dataset. Table 8 compares results achieved when building clusters from the patents corpus and when using the reviews and weblogs texts from the SANCL unlabelled dataset. Despite the fact that the size of the two datasets is comparable, we find that while creating clusters from an irrelevant domain does gain on the baseline (+0.25%), the improvement for clusters built from the relevant domain texts is noticeably higher (+0.6%). The difference between the accuracy on the legal texts and the accuracy on the reviews and weblogs texts is significant at the $p < 0.05$ level.

	CoNLL09	OntoNotes
Legal texts	90.19	77.77
Reviews and Weblogs	**90.30**	**78.14***

Table 8: The effect of the domain of unlabelled data on word clusters, discarding word types with count less than 3.

4.3 External lexicon

It is possible to supply to the dependency parser an external lexicon, where word forms are provided with PoS tags. Wiktionary, a companion project for Wikipedia that aims to produce a free, large-scale multilingual dictionary, is a large and constantly growing crowd-sourced resource that appears attractive for NLP research. Wiktionary encodes word definitions, pronunciation, translations, etymology, word forms and part-of-speech information. PoS tag dictionaries derived from Wiktionary have been previously used for out-of-domain PoS tagging (Li et al., 2012) and for PoS tagging of resource-poor languages (Täckström et al., 2013).

To create a lexicon for the parser, we extracted 753,970 English word forms and their PoS tags from a dump of Wiktionary[4]. Wiktionary uses a rather informal set of PoS labels; to convert them to the CoNLL09 tag set, we manually aligned all unique PoS tags found in Wiktionary with those of the CoNLL09 tag set. We compared the accuracy achieved by the parser when the lexicon was supplied, as well as when the lexicon was supplied together with the best configuration word clusters (800 clusters built from the entire SANCL dataset after filtering words with the count less than 3). Table 9 shows results achieved with these settings in comparison to the baseline (improvements on the baseline are indicated with stars). When the lexicon is used on its own, we observe only slight gains on the baseline, on both in-domain and out-domain data, and neither are statistically significant. When combining the lexicon and word clusters, the accuracy actually decreases compared to using word clusters on their own.

Thus the best combination of domain adaptation techniques so far included the use of 800 word clusters built from the entire SANCL unlabelled dataset, after filtering out word forms with the count less than 3, with text normalization, but without the Wiktionary lexicon (+1.15% on the baseline).

[3]http://www.epo.org/searching/free/espacenet.html
[4]http://wiki.dbpedia.org/Wiktionary

	CoNLL09	OntoNotes
Wiktionary	90.22	77.73
Clusters	**90.62****	**78.69****
Wiktionary+Clusters	90.44	78.49**
Baseline	90.07	77.54

Table 9: The effect of the Wiktionary lexicon on parsing accuracy.

4.4 Co-Training

Following Sagae (2007), the overall approach to parser co-training we adopted was as follows. First, several parsers were combined to generate additional training data from unlabelled data, i.e. were used as **source learners** for co-training. Then, the Mate parser was re-trained on the augmented training set and tested on a test set, i.e. used as the **evaluation learner**. The reason Mate was selected the evaluation learner was that it achieved the best results on the test data in its default settings (see Table 10).

	CoNLL09	OntoNotes
Mate	90.07	77.54
MST	86.9	75.35
Turbo	85.94	74.85
Malt	84.72	72.63

Table 10: The baselines of parsers used in co-training experiments.

Agreement-based co-training. We first experimented with three pairwise parser combinations: using Mate as one source learner and each of the other three parsers as the other source learner in order to obtain additional training data. If two learners agreed on the parse of an unlabelled sentence, i.e. assigned each word form the same dependency label and attached it to the same head, this was taken as an indication of a correct parse, and the sentence was added to the training set. We experimented with different amounts of the additional training sentences added to the main training set in such a manner: 10k, 20k, and 30k sentences. The results of these experiments are shown in Table 11 (significant differences to the baseline results are indicated by stars). The best result is obtained by Mate Malt pair, which outperforms the baseline by just above 1%.

	+10k	+20k	+30k
Mate+Malt	**78.22****	**78.61****	**78.61****
Mate+MST	78.10**	78.23**	78.31**
Mate+Turbo	77.94**	77.84*	77.99**
Baseline		77.54	

Table 11: Agreement-based co-training using two parsers.

Removing short sentences from unlabelled data. We noticed that among those sentences where two parsers agreed, many tended to be very short: the average number of tokens in generated additional training data was 8 per sentence, while both the training and test set contain much longer sentences on average: the OntoNotes test set had 19.6 tokens/sentence and the CoNLL09 training set had 24.4 tokens/sentence. Such short sentences in the additional training data may be less useful or even harmful for learning an accurate model of the target domain, than those that approximate both training and test data. We experimented with several thresholds (4, 5, and 6 tokens) on the sentence length below which sentences were removed from the additional training data. Table 12 shows that discarding short sentences did improve accuracy by up to 0.25%, though none of the improvements were significant.

Three learners co-training. In the previous experiments, the Mate parser was used both as a **source learner** and as the **evaluation learner**. Therefore it was likely that the additional training data did not

	Mate+Malt, +30k	Avg. Length
>6 tokens	**78.88**	13.1
>5 tokens	78.61	12.67
>4 tokens	78.67	11.94
All sentences	78.61	8.35

Table 12: The effect of removing short sentences from generated training data.

contain sufficiently novel examples based on which the evaluation parser could adapt better to the new domain. Thus we next tried the tri-training algorithm (Zhou and Li, 2005), where two parsers are used as source learners and a third as the evalaution learner. We used Malt and MST as source learners, identifying sentences which they parsed in the same manner, and using these sentences to retrain the Mate parser. We find that the tri-training algorithm performs better than the set-up with two parsers: on 10k and 20k additional sentences, it achieves an accuracy increase on Mate+Malt, significant at the $p < 0.05$ level (see Table 13).

	+10k	+20k	+30k
Mate+Malt+MST	78.70*	**79.12***	78.95
Mate+Malt	78.43	78.70	78.88

Table 13: Accuracy scores for tri-training (Mate+Malt+MST) and the best two-parser co-training algorithm (Mate+Malt).

5 Combining co-training with clusters and an external lexicon

5.1 OntoNotes test set

We explored several possibilities to combine co-training with word clusters and an external lexicon, each time supplying word clusters and/or the lexicon to the Mate parser when it is being retrained on additional training data and applied to the test data. The following configurations of each of the techniques were used:

- Word clusters: 800 clusters generated from the entire SANCL unlabelled dataset, after discarding word types with the count less than 3.
- Lexicon: Wiktionary
- Co-training: Retraining the Mate parser on the combination of initial training set and 20k automatically parsed sentences (agreed by Malt and MST) which contained more than 6 tokens.

The results showed that all three combinations failed to obtain significant improvements over co-training alone. The best result is achieved by combining co-training and clusters, which obtains an increase of only 0.09% on co-training; this is however, the greatest overall improvement on the baseline (+1.67%). The combination of co-training and a Wiktionary lexicon in fact harms accuracy (see Table 14).

5.2 SANCL test set

In order to compare different technique combinations with the results achieved by participants of the SANCL-2012 shared task, we evaluated them on the SANCL test set[5].

As the results in Table 15 indicate, similarly to the results on OntoNotes, word clusters usually fare much better than the Wiktionary-based lexicon, while the latter fails to produce statistically significant

[5]Note that the data was annotated in the Stanford format.

	OntoNotes
Co-training	79.12**
Clusters	78.69**
Wiktionary	77.73
Co-training+Clusters	**79.21****
Co-training+Wiktionary	78.89*
Co-training+Clusters+Wiktionary	79.19**
Baseline	77.54

Table 14: Combination of co-training with word clusters and an external lexicon, OntoNotes test set.

improvements on the baseline. The best accuracy overall was achieved by combinations of techniques, in all the three subdomains, improving on the baseline by up to 1.3%.

Comparing the results achieved by our best configurations with the results of the shared task, we see that our labelled accuracy averaged across the subdomains was just above the Stanford-2 system (80.31 vs. 80.25), which ranked 5th of all the twelve submissions (Petrov and McDonald, 2012). Although our results are still 3.15% lower than DCU-Paris13, the best system at SANCL-2012, the top four results were all generated by combination systems (Le Roux et al., 2012; Zhang et al., 2012; McClosky et al., 2012); our highest results only produced by the Mate parser, hence our best configuration achieved the best performance of a single parser.

	Answers	**Newsgroups**	**Reviews**	**Average**
Co-training	77.18	82.72**	78.21	79.37
Clusters	78.04**	83.06*	79.03**	80.04
Wiktionary	77.61	82.8	78.32	79.57
Clusters+Wiktionary	78.19**	**83.38***	**79.36****	**80.31**
Co-training+Clusters	78.05*	83.29**	78.8**	80.04
Co-training+Clusters+Wiktionary	**78.33****	83.35**	78.84*	80.17
Baseline	77.03	82.4	78.12	79.18
SANCL Stanford-2	77.5	83.56	79.7	80.25
SANCL Best (DCU-Paris13)	81.15	85.38	83.86	83.46

Table 15: Combination of co-training with word clusters and an external lexicon, SANCL test set.

The results on both the OntoNotes and SANCL datasets show that on their own, word clusters and co-training often improve significantly on the baseline, but their combination results only in minor further improvements (only up to 0.32%). Word clusters aim specifically to deal with the unknown vocabulary problem, and, since there seem to be no major grammatical differences between the train and test domains (see Section 3.3), it is likely that the main benefit derived from co-training is the compensation for unknown domain vocabulary. Word clusters also seem a better way to approach this problem: they perform better than co-training on three out of four subdomains. The explanation that unknown vocabulary is the main issue for domain adaptation in this domain pair is further supported by the fact that combinations of word clusters with a Wiktionary lexicon sometimes performed better than combinations involving co-training (on `newsgroups` and `reviews`).

6 Conclusion

In this paper we described experiments with several domain adaptation techniques, in order to quickly adapt a general-language parser to parse web data. We find that the best combination of the techniques improves significantly on the baseline (up to 1.67%), and achieves very promising results on the SANCL-2012 shared task data, outperforming all submissions that used a single parser, in terms of labelled accuracy score averaged across three test sets.

Our experiments with word clusters showed that word clusters derived from unlabelled domain texts consistently contribute to a greater parsing accuracy, and that both the domain relevance of the unlabelled data and its quantity are major factors for successful exploitation of word clusters. Experiments with a crowd-sourced PoS lexicon however were not as conclusive: whereas supplying the lexicon to the parser often resulted in certain accuracy gains, they were not as large as those for word clusters. This suggests word clusters created automatically from relevant domain texts are a better tool to deal with unknown vocabulary than a generic hand-crafted and wide-coverage lexicon. Another interesting finding was that co-training was most effective when the evaluation parser was not used for creating extra training data (the so-called tri-training technique), and when removing very short sentences from automatically labelled data before re-training the evaluation parser.

With respect to combining co-training with word clusters, we could not find clear evidence for additive improvement. This suggests that co-training solves largely the same problem as word clusters, i.e., unknown target domain vocabulary, and that for the web texts under study unknown vocabulary is a much more significant impediment for domain adaptation than grammatical differences between domains.

Acknowledgements

The research was supported by FP7 ICT project "Workbench for Interactive Contrastive Analysis of Patent Documentation" under grant no. FP7-SME-606163.

References

Mohit Bansal, Kevin Gimpel, and Karen Livescu. 2014. Tailoring continuous word representations for dependency parsing. In *Proceedings of the 52nd annual meeting of the Association for Computational Linguistics*.

Avrim Blum and Tom Mitchell. 1998. Combining labeled and unlabeled data with co-training. In *Proceedings of the Eleventh Annual Conference on Computational Learning Theory*, COLT' 98, pages 92–100, New York, NY, USA. ACM.

Bernd Bohnet, Joakim Nivre, Igor Boguslavsky, Richárd Farkas Filip Ginter, and Jan Hajic. 2013. Joint morphological and syntactic analysis for richly inflected languages. *Transactions of the Associtation for Computational Linguistics*, 1.

Peter F. Brown, Peter V. deSouza, Robert L. Mercer, Vincent J. Della Pietra, and Jenifer C. Lai. 1992. Class-based n-gram models of natural language. *Computational Linguistics*, 18:467–479.

Alicia Burga, Joan Codina, Gabriella Ferraro, Horacio Saggion, and Leo Wanner. 2013. The challenge of syntactic dependency parsing adaptation for the patent domain. In *ESSLLI-13 Workshop on Extrinsic Parse Improvement*.

Marie Candito, Enrique Henestroza Anguiano, and Djam Seddah. 2011. A word clustering approach to domain adaptation: Effective parsing of biomedical texts. In *IWPT*, pages 37–42. The Association for Computational Linguistics.

Jennifer Foster. 2010. "cba to check the spelling": Investigating parser performance on discussion forum posts. In *HLT-NAACL*, pages 381–384. The Association for Computational Linguistics.

Phani Gadde, L. V. Subramaniam, and Tanveer A. Faruquie. 2011. Adapting a WSJ trained part-of-speech tagger to noisy text: Preliminary results. In *Proceedings of the 2011 Joint Workshop on Multilingual OCR and Analytics for Noisy Unstructured Text Data*, MOCRAND11, pages 51–58, New York, NY, USA. ACM.

Daniel Gildea. 2001. Corpus variation and parser performance. In Lillian Lee and Donna Harman, editors, *Proceedings of the 2001 Conference on Empirical Methods in Natural Language Processing*, EMNLP '01, pages 167–202, Stroudsburg. Association for Computational Linguistics.

Jan Hajič, Massimiliano Ciaramita, Richard Johansson, Daisuke Kawahara, Maria Antònia Martí, Lluís Màrquez, Adam Meyers, Joakim Nivre, Sebastian Padó, Jan Štěpánek, Pavel Straňák, Mihai Surdeanu, Nianwen Xue, and Yi Zhang. 2009. The CoNLL-2009 shared task: Syntactic and semantic dependencies in multiple languages. In *Proceedings of the 13th Conference on Computational Natural Language Learning (CoNLL-2009), June 4-5*, Boulder, Colorado, USA.

Richard Johansson and Pierre Nugues. 2007. Extended constituent-to-dependency conversion for english. In *16th Nordic Conference of Computational Linguistics*, pages 105–112. University of Tartu.

Mohammad Khan, Markus Dickinson, and Sandra Kübler. 2013a. Does size matter? text and grammar revision for parsing social media data. In *Proceedings of the Workshop on Language Analysis in Social Media*, pages 1–10, Atlanta, Georgia, June. Association for Computational Linguistics.

Mohammad Khan, Markus Dickinson, and Sandra Kübler. 2013b. Towards domain adaptation for parsing web data. In Galia Angelova, Kalina Bontcheva, and Ruslan Mitkov, editors, *RANLP*, pages 357–364. RANLP 2011 Organising Committee / ACL.

Terry Koo, Xavier Carreras, and Michael Collins. 2008. Simple semi-supervised dependency parsing. In *In Proc. ACL/HLT*.

Joseph Le Roux, Jennifer Foster, Joachim Wagner, Rasul Samad Zadeh Kaljahi, and Anton Bryl. 2012. Dcu-paris13 systems for the sancl 2012 shared task.

Matthew Lease and Eugene Charniak. 2005. Parsing biomedical literature. In Robert Dale, Kam-Fai Wong, Jian Su, and Oi Yee Kwong, editors, *IJCNLP*, volume 3651 of *Lecture Notes in Computer Science*, pages 58–69. Springer.

Shen Li, Joo Graa, and Ben Taskar. 2012. Wiki-ly supervised part-of-speech tagging. In *EMNLP-CoNLL*, pages 1389–1398. ACL.

Percy Liang. 2005. Semi-supervised learning for natural language. In *MASTERS THESIS, MIT*.

André FT Martins, Noah A Smith, Eric P Xing, Pedro MQ Aguiar, and Mário AT Figueiredo. 2010. Turbo parsers: Dependency parsing by approximate variational inference. In *Proceedings of the 2010 Conference on Empirical Methods in Natural Language Processing*, pages 34–44. Association for Computational Linguistics.

David McClosky and Eugene Charniak. 2008. Self-training for biomedical parsing. In *ACL (Short Papers)*, pages 101–104. The Association for Computer Linguistics.

David McClosky, Wanxiang Che, Marta Recasens, Mengqiu Wang, Richard Socher, and Christopher Manning. 2012. Stanfords system for parsing the english web. In *Workshop on the Syntactic Analysis of Non-Canonical Language (SANCL 2012). Montreal, Canada.*

Ryan T McDonald and Fernando CN Pereira. 2006. Online learning of approximate dependency parsing algorithms. In *EACL*.

Jens Nilsson, Sebastian Riedel, and Deniz Yuret. 2007. The conll 2007 shared task on dependency parsing. In *Proceedings of the CoNLL Shared Task Session of EMNLP-CoNLL*, pages 915–932. sn.

Joakim Nivre. 2009. Non-projective dependency parsing in expected linear time. In *Proceedings of the Joint Conference of the 47th Annual Meeting of the ACL and the 4th International Joint Conference on Natural Language Processing of the AFNLP: Volume 1-Volume 1*, pages 351–359. Association for Computational Linguistics.

Lilja Øvrelid and Arne Skjærholt. 2012. Lexical categories for improved parsing of web data. In *Proceedings of COLING 2012: Posters*, pages 903–912, Mumbai, India, December. The COLING 2012 Organizing Committee.

Olutobi Owoputi, Brendan O'Connor, Chris Dyer, Kevin Gimpel, Nathan Schneider, and Noah A. Smith. 2013. Improved part-of-speech tagging for online conversational text with word clusters. In *HLT-NAACL*, pages 380–390. The Association for Computational Linguistics.

Slav Petrov and Ryan McDonald. 2012. Overview of the 2012 shared task on parsing the web. In *Notes of the First Workshop on Syntactic Analysis of Non-Canonical Language (SANCL)*, volume 59.

Slav Petrov, Pi-Chuan Chang, Michael Ringgaard, and Hiyan Alshawi. 2010. Uptraining for accurate deterministic question parsing. In *Proceedings of the 2010 Conference on Empirical Methods in Natural Language Processing*, EMNLP '10, pages 705–713, Stroudsburg, PA, USA. Association for Computational Linguistics.

Barbara Plank and Gertjan Van Noord. 2011. Effective measures of domain similarity for parsing. In *Proceedings of the 49th Annual Meeting of the Association for Computational Linguistics: Human Language Technologies-Volume 1*, pages 1566–1576. Association for Computational Linguistics.

Sampo Pyysalo, Tapio Salakoski, Sophie Aubin, and Adeline Nazarenko. 2006. Lexical adaptation of link grammar to the biomedical sublanguage: a comparative evaluation of three approaches. *BMC Bioinformatics*, 7(Suppl 3).

Ines Rehbein. 2011. Data point selection for self-training. In *Proceedings of the Second Workshop on Statistical Parsing of Morphologically Rich Languages*, SPMRL '11, pages 62–67, Stroudsburg, PA, USA. Association for Computational Linguistics.

Kenji Sagae. 2007. Dependency parsing and domain adaptation with lr models and parser ensembles. In *In Proceedings of the Eleventh Conference on Computational Natural Language Learning*.

Anoop Sarkar. 2001. Applying co-training methods to statistical parsing. In *Proceedings of the Second Meeting of the North American Chapter of the Association for Computational Linguistics on Language Technologies*, NAACL '01, pages 1–8, Stroudsburg, PA, USA. Association for Computational Linguistics.

Anders Søgaard and Barbara Plank. 2012. Parsing the web as covariate shift. In *Workshop on the Syntactic Analysis of Non-Canonical Language (SANCL2012)*, Montreal, Canada.

Mark Steedman, Anoop Sarkar, Miles Osborne, Rebecca Hwa, Stephen Clark, Julia Hockenmaier, Paul Ruhlen, Steven Baker, and Jeremiah Crim. 2003. Bootstrapping statistical parsers from small datasets. In *EACL*, pages 331–338. The Association for Computer Linguistics.

Peter Szolovits. 2003. Adding a medical lexicon to an English parser. In *AMIA Annual Symposium Proceedings*, volume 2003, page 639. American Medical Informatics Association.

Oscar Täckström, Dipanjan Das, Slav Petrov, Ryan T. McDonald, and Joakim Nivre. 2013. Token and type constraints for cross-lingual part-of-speech tagging. *TACL*, 1:1–12.

Meishan Zhang, Wanxiang Che, Yijia Liu, Zhenghua Li, and Ting Liu. 2012. Hit dependency parsing: Bootstrap aggregating heterogeneous parsers. In *Notes of the First Workshop on Syntactic Analysis of Non-Canonical Language (SANCL)*.

Zhi-Hua Zhou and Ming Li. 2005. Tri-training: Exploiting unlabeled data using three classifiers. *Knowledge and Data Engineering, IEEE Transactions on*, 17(11):1529–1541.

Guangyou Zhou, Jun Zhao, Kang Liu, and Li Cai. 2011. Exploiting web-derived selectional preference to improve statistical dependency parsing. In *Proceedings of the 49th Annual Meeting of the Association for Computational Linguistics: Human Language Technologies - Volume 1*, HLT '11, pages 1556–1565, Stroudsburg, PA, USA. Association for Computational Linguistics.

Self-Training for Parsing Learner Text

Aoife Cahill, Binod Gyawali and James V. Bruno
Educational Testing Service,
660 Rosedale Road,
Princeton, NJ 08541,
USA
{acahill, bgyawali, jbruno}@ets.org

Abstract

We apply the well-known parsing technique of self-training to a new type of text: language-learner text. This type of text often contains grammatical and other errors which can cause problems for traditional treebank-based parsers. Evaluation on a small test set of student data shows improvement over the baseline, both by training on native or non-native text. The main contribution of this paper adds additional support for the claim that the new self-trained parser has improved over the baseline by carrying out a qualitative linguistic analysis of the kinds of differences between two parsers on non-native text. We show that for a number of linguistically interesting cases, the self-trained parser is able to provide better analyses, despite the sometimes ungrammatical nature of the text.

1 Introduction

The vast majority of treebank-based parsing research assumes that the text to be parsed is well-formed. In this paper, we are concerned with parsing text written by non-native speakers of English into phrase structure trees, as a precursor for applications in automated scoring and error detection. Non-native text often contains grammatical errors ranging in severity from minor collocational differences to extremely garbled strings that are difficult to interpret. These kinds of errors are known to cause difficulty for automated analyses (De Felice and Pulman, 2007; Lee and Knutsson, 2008).

We explore a previously documented technique for adapting a state-of-the-art parser to be able to better parse learner text: domain adaptation using self-training. Self-training is a semi-supervised learning technique that relies on some labeled data to train an initial model, and then uses large amounts of unlabeled data to iteratively improve that model. Self-training was first successfully applied in the newspaper parsing domain by McClosky et al. (2006) who used the Penn Treebank WSJ as their labeled data and unlabeled data from the North American News Text corpus. Previous attempts (Charniak, 1997; Steedman et al., 2003) had not shown encouraging results, and McClosky et al. (2006) hypothesize that the gain they saw was due to the two-phase nature of the BLLIP parser used in their experiments. In a follow-up study (McClosky et al., 2008) they find that one major factor leading to successful self-training is when the process sees known words in new combinations.

2 Related Work

Foster et al. (2011) compare edited newspaper text and unedited forum posts in a self-training parsing experiment, evaluating on a treebank of informal discussion forum entries about football. They find that both data sources perform about equally well on their small test set overall, but that the underlying grammars learned from the two sources were different. Ott and Ziai (2010) apply an out-of-the-box German dependency parser to learner text and analyze the impact on down-stream semantic interpretation. They find that core functions such as subject and object can generally be reliably detected, but that when there are key elements (e.g. main verbs) missing from the sentence that the parses are less reliable. They

First Joint Workshop on Statistical Parsing of Morphologically Rich Languages and Syntactic Analysis of Non-Canonical Languages, pages 66–73 Dublin, Ireland, August 23-29 2014.

also found that less-severe grammatical errors such as agreement did not tend to cause problems for the parser.

An alternative approach to parsing learner text is to modify the underlying dependency scheme used in parsing to account for any grammatical errors. This can be useful because it is not always clear what the syntactic analysis of ungrammatical text should be, given some scheme designed for native text. Dickinson and Ragheb (2009) present such a modified scheme for English, designed for annotating syntactic dependencies over a modified POS tagset. Dickinson and Lee (2009) retrain a Korean dependency parser, but rather than adding additional unlabeled data as we do, they modify the original annotated training data. The modifications are specifically targeted to be able to detect errors relating to Korean postpositional particles. They show that the modified parser can be useful in detecting those kinds of particle errors and in their conclusion suggest self-training as an alternative approach to parsing of learner text. A similar alternative approach is to directly integrate error detection into the parsing process (Menzel and Schröder, 1999; Vandeventer Faltin, 2003).

3 Self-training a new parser

We first describe the data that we use for both training and evaluating our parsers, and then we describe our experiments and results.

We take the standard portion of the Penn Treebank (sections 02–21) as our seed labeled data. We then compare two different unlabeled training data sets. The first data set consists of 480,000 sentences of newspaper text extracted from the LA Times portion of the North American News Corpus (NANC). The second is a corpus of non-native written English text randomly sampled from a large dataset of student essays. It consists of 480,900 sentences from 33,637 essays written as part of a test of English proficiency, usually administered to non-native college-level students. The essays have been written to 422 different prompts (topics) and so cover a wide range of vocabulary and usage. Each essay has been assigned a proficiency level (high, medium, low) by a trained human grader. 17.5% of the sentences were from low proficiency essays, 42% from medium proficiency and 40.5% from high proficiency essays.

In order to determine the optimal number of self-training iterations and carry out our final evaluations we use a small corpus of manually treebanked sentences. The corpus consists of 1,731 sentences written by secondary level students which we randomly split into a development set (865 sentences) and a test set (866 sentences). The native language of the students is unknown, but it is likely that many spoke English as their first language. In addition, this corpus had originally been developed for another purpose and therefore contains modifications that are not ideal for our experiments. The main changes are that spelling and punctuation errors were corrected before the trees were annotated (and we do not have access to the original text). Although the treebanked corpus does not align perfectly with our requirements, we believe that it is a more useful evaluation data set than any other existing treebanked corpus.

We used the Charniak and Johnson (2005) (BLLIP) parser[1] to perform the self training experiments. Our experiment is setup as follows: first we train a baseline model on the Penn Treebank WSJ data (sections 02-21). Then, iteratively, sentences are selected from the unlabeled data sets, parsed by the parser, and combined with the previously annotated data to retrain the parser. The parser also requires development data, for which we use section 22 of the WSJ data. After each iteration we evaluate the parser using our 865-sentence development set. Parser evaluation was done using the EVALB[2] tool and we report the performance in terms of F1 score.

There are two main parameters in our self-training setup: the size of the unlabeled data set added at each iteration and the weight given to the original labeled data.[3] In preliminary experiments, we found that a block size of 40,000 sentences per each iteration and a weight of 5 on the original labeled data performed best. Given our training data, and a block size of 40K, this results in 12 iterations. In each iteration, the training data consists of the PTB data repeated 5 times, plus the parsed output of previous blocks of unlabeled data.

[1]https://github.com/BLLIP/bllip-parser

[2]http://nlp.cs.nyu.edu/evalb/

[3]Note that this approach differs to that outlined in McClosky et al. (2006) who only perform one self-training iteration. It is more similar to the approach described in Reichart and Rappoport (2007).

The results of our experiments are as shown in Figure 1. Iteration 0 corresponds to the baseline parser while iterations 1–12 are the self trained parsers. We see that the F1 score of the baseline parser is 80.9%.[4] The self trained parsers have higher accuracies compared to the baseline parser starting at the first iteration. The highest score training on non-native text (82.3%) was achieved on the 11th iteration, and the highest score training on newspaper text (81.8%) was achieved on the 8th iteration. Both of these results are statistically significantly better than the baseline parser only trained on WSJ text.[5] The graph also shows that the non-native training results in slightly higher overall f-scores than the parser trained on the native data after iteration 5, however these differences are not statistically significant.

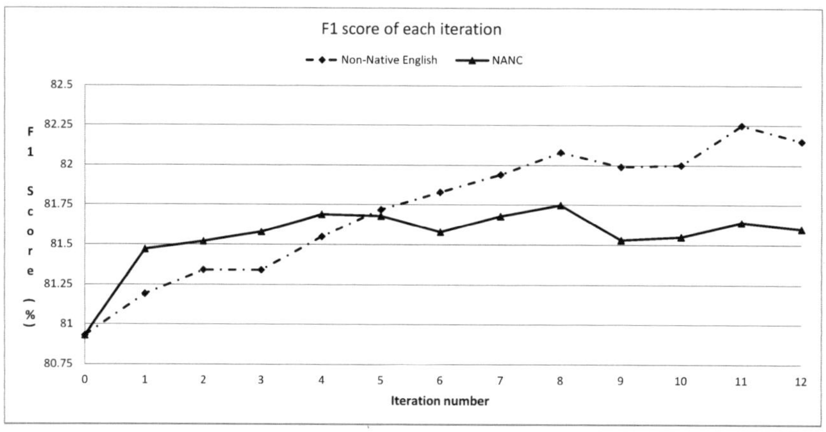

Figure 1: Performance of parsers after each iteration. Parsers used WSJ Section 22 as development data and were evaluated on the student response development data.

The final evaluation was carried out by evaluating on the student test corpus of 866 sentences, using the parsing model that performed best on the student dev corpus. The parser trained on native text achieved an f-score of 82.4% and the parser trained on the non-native text achieved an f-score of 82.6%. This difference is not statistically significant and is a similar finding to Foster et al. (2011). In another experiment, we found that if the development data used during self-training is similar to the test data, we see even smaller differences between the two different kinds of training data.[6]

4 Analysis

We carry out a qualitative analysis of the differences in parses between the original parser and one of the best-performing self-trained ones, trained on non-native text. We randomly sample 5 essays written by non-native speakers (but not overlapping with the data used to self-train the parser). Table 1 shows the number of sentences and the number of parse trees that differ, according to each proficiency level.

Proficiency	# Essays	# Sentences	# Words	# Differing Parses	% Differing Parses
High	2	30	694	12	40
Mid	1	22	389	12	54
Low	2	17	374	8	47
Totals	**5**	**69**	**1457**	**32**	**46**

Table 1: Descriptive Statistics for Essays in the Qualitative Sample

[4] Note that these overall f-scores are considerably lower than current state-of-the-art for newspaper text, indicating that this set of student texts are considerably different.

[5] Significance testing was carried out using Dan Bikel's Randomized Parsing Evaluation Comparator script for comparing `evalb` output files. We performed 1000 random shuffles and tested for p-values < 0.01.

[6] These data sets were all quite small, however, so further investigation is required to fully assess this finding.

Figure 2 reports the number of differences by proficiency level. It is important to note that these differences only included ones that were considered to be independent (e.g. a change in POS tag that necessitated a change in constituent label was only counted once). We note a trend in which the self-trained parser produces better parses than the baseline more often; however, at the highest proficiency level the baseline parser produces better parses more often. In some applications it might be possible to take the proficiency level into account before running the parser. However for many applications this will present a challenge since the parser output plays a role in predicting the proficiency level. A possible alternative would be to approximate proficiency using frequencies of spelling and other grammatical errors that can be automatically detected without relying on parser output and use this information to decide which version of the parser to use.

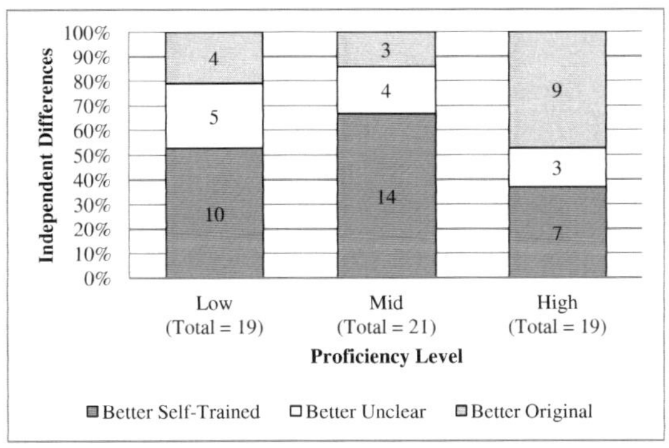

Figure 2: Unrelated Differences by Proficiency Level.

We systematically examine each of the 32 pairs of differing parse trees in the sample and manually categorize the differences. Figure 3 shows the 5 most frequent types of differences, their breakdown by proficiency level, as well as the results of a subjective evaluation on which parse was better. These judgements were made by one of the authors of this paper who is a trained linguist.

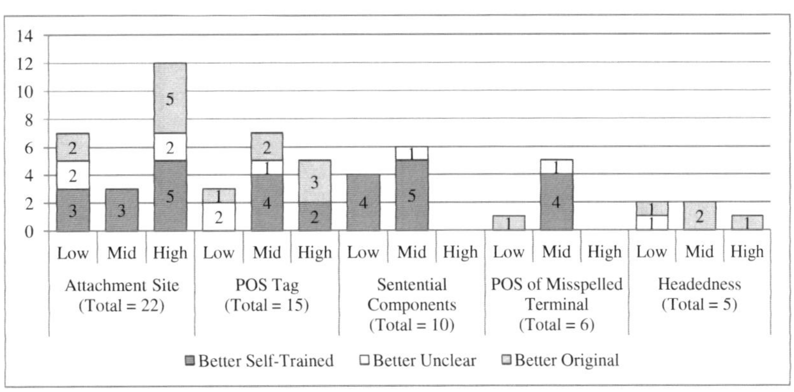

Figure 3: Parse Tree Differences by Proficiency Level.

The differences in Figure 3 are defined as follows. *Attachment Site*: the same constituent is attached to different nodes in each parse; *POS Tag*: the same terminal bears a different POS tag in each parse, where the terminal exists in our dictionary of known English[7] words; *Sentential Components*: One parse groups a set of constituents exhaustively into an S-node, while the other does not; *POS of misspelled terminal*: the same terminal bears a different POS tag in each parse, where the terminal has been flagged as a misspelling; *Headedness*: a terminal heads a maximal projection of a different syntactic category in one parse but not the other, (e.g. a VP headed by a nominal).

[7]We use the python package `enchant` with US spelling dictionaries to carry out spelling error detection.

We characterized the differences according to whether the better output was produced by the original parser, the self trained parser, or if it was not clear that either parse was better than the other. *Attachment Site* differences were evaluated according to whether or not they were attached to the constituent they modified; *POS Tag* differences were evaluated according to the Penn Treebank Guidelines (Santorini, 1995); *Sentential Components* differences were evaluated according to whether or not the terminals should indeed form a clausal constituent, infinitive, or gerund; *POS of Misspelled Terminal* differences were evaluated according to the evaluator's perception of the writer's intended target. We note that the most abundant differences are in *Attachment Site*, that the biggest improvements resulting from self-training are in the recognition of *Sentential Components* and in the identification of the *POS of Misspelled Terminals*, and that the biggest degradation is in *Headedness*.

4.1 General Difference Patterns

Using the categories defined during the manual analysis of the 5 essays, we develop rules to automatically detect these kinds of differences in a large dataset. We expect that the automatic rules will identify more differences than the linguist, however we hope to see the same general patterns. We apply our rules to an additional set of data consisting of roughly 10,000 sentences written by non-native speakers of English. Table 2 shows the number of sentences for which the parsers found different parses at each proficiency level, and Table 3 gives the totals for each of the five difference categories described above.

Proficiency	# Essays	# Sentences	# Words	# Differing Parses	% Differing Parses
High	256	4178	266543	2214	53
Mid	285	4168	263685	2364	57
Low	149	1657	93466	971	59
Totals	**690**	**10003**	**623694**	**5549**	**55**

Table 2: Descriptive Statistics for Essays in the Larger Sample

Difference	Total	Low	Medium	High
Attachment Site	7805	1331	3474	3000
POS Tag	6827	1205	3238	2384
Sentential Components	4103	778	1786	1539
POS of Misspelled Terminal	2040	346	894	800
Headedness	1357	353	568	436

Table 3: Total number of differences detected automatically by proficiency level

We see that the proportion of sentences with different parses is similar to the 5-essay sample and also that the relative ordering of the five difference categories is identical. This at least indicates that the 5-essay sample does not differ largely in its general properties from a larger set.

4.2 Illustrative Observations

We highlight some of the most interesting differences between the baseline parser and the self-trained parser, using examples from our 5-essay sample described above.

Ambiguity of subordinating conjunctions: Figure 4 shows an example from a lower proficiency essay that contains multiple interacting differences, primarily stemming from the fact that the POS tag for a subordinating conjunction is the same as the POS tag for a regular preposition according to the Penn Treebank guidelines (Santorini, 1995). The original parser (4a) treats it as a preposition: it is dominated by PP and takes NP as a complement. The self-trained parser (4b) correctly treats *because* as a subordinating conjunction: it is dominated by SBAR and takes S as a complement. In addition, the original parser identified *suffer* as the main verb in the sentence. The self-trained parser correctly analyzes this as part of the dependent clause, however this results in no main verb being identified and an overall FRAGMENT analysis. Since it is unclear what the original intention of the writer was, this fragment analysis could be more useful for identifying grammatical errors and giving feedback.

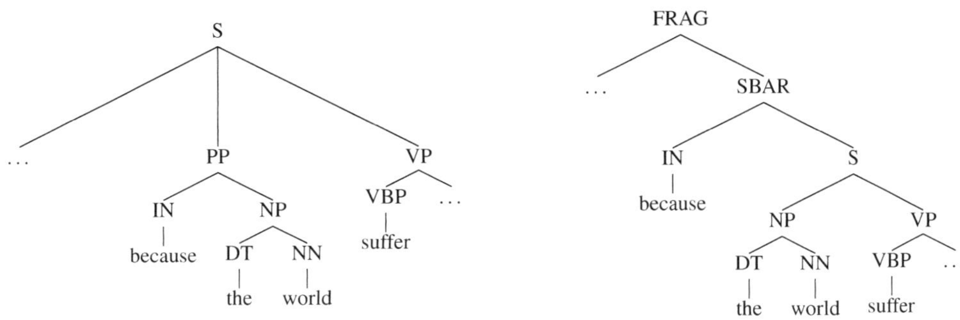

(a) Original Parser

(b) Self-Trained Parser

Figure 4: Parses for *Especaily, in this time, because the world suffer, the economy empress.*

Ambiguity of *to*: Figure 5 exemplifies a difference related to the analysis of infinitives. Here we can see that the original parser analyzed the *to* phrase as a PP (c.f. *afraid of*) whereas the self-trained parser analyzes it as an infinitival. We believe that the infinitival interpretation is slightly more likely (with a missing verb *do*), though of course it is difficult to say for sure what the intended meaning is. Here there are two interacting difference types: *Sentential Components* and *Headedness*. In the self-trained parse, *anything* is an NN that heads a VP, whereas it is an NN that appropriately heads an NP in the original parse. However, it is important to note that the self-trained parse treats *to anything* as an infinitive: a TO dominated by a VP, which is dominated by a unary-branching S. The original parse treats *to anything* as a regular PP. The fact that the self-trained parse contains a set of terminals exhaustively dominated by an S-node that does not exist in the original parse constitutes a *Sentential Components* difference. We believe that it is more useful to correctly identify infinitives and gerunds as sentential constituents, even at the cost of an XP that is apparently headed by an inappropriate terminal (VP headed by NN).

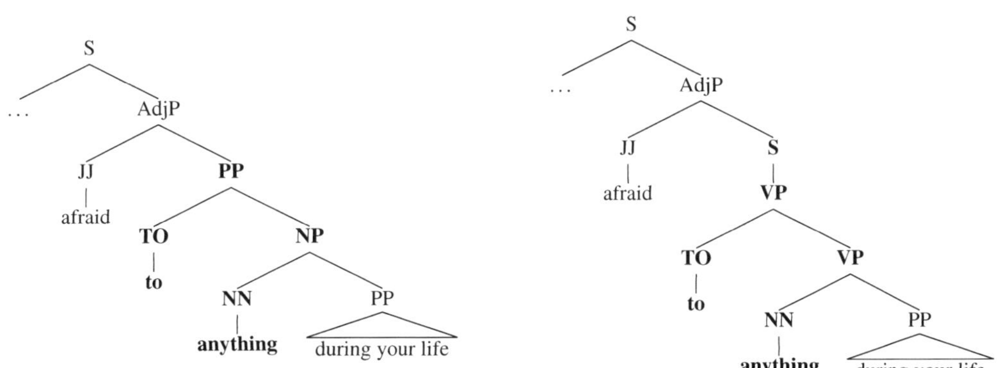

(a) Original Parser

(b) Self-Trained Parser

Figure 5: Parses for *If you have this experience, you will do not afraid to anything during your life.*

Attachment ambiguity: We turn now to Figure 6. The main difference has to do with the attachment of the phrase *that you think it worth*: the SBAR is attached to the VP in the original parse (as a clausal complement) and to the NP in the self-trained parse (as a relative clause). This example also shows that a change in POS-tag can have a significant impact on the final parse tree.

5 Future Work and Conclusions

We have shown that it is possible to apply self-training techniques in order to adapt a state-of-the-art parser to be able to better parse English language learner text. We experimented with training the parser on native text as well as non-native text. In an evaluation on student data (not necessarily language-

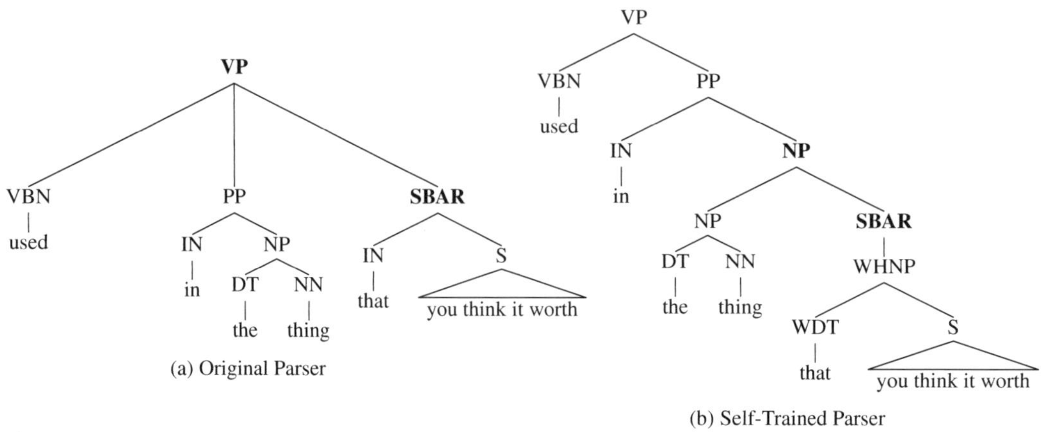

Figure 6: Parses for *So I support that the money should be* *used in the thing that you think it worth.*

learner data) we found that both training sets performed at about the same level, but that both significantly out-performed the baseline parser trained only on WSJ text.

We carry out an in-depth study on a small data set of 5 learner essays and define a set of difference categories in order to describe the parse-tree differences from a linguistic perspective. We implement rules to automatically detect these parse-tree differences and show that the general proportions of errors found in the small data set are similar to that of a larger data set. We highlight some of the most interesting improvements of the parser, and we show that despite various grammatical errors present in sentences, the self-trained parser is, in general, able to assign better analyses than the baseline parser.

Of course, the self-trained parser does sometimes choose a parse that is less appropriate than the baseline one. In particular, we noticed that this happened most frequently for the highest proficiency essays. Further investigation is required to be able to better understand the reasons for this. In future work, the most informative evaluation of the self-trained parser would be in a task-based setting. We plan to investigate whether the self-trained parser improves the overall performance of tasks such as automated essay scoring or automated error detection, which internally rely on parser output.

References

Eugene Charniak and Mark Johnson. 2005. Coarse-to-Fine n-Best Parsing and MaxEnt Discriminative Reranking. In *Proceedings of the 43rd Annual Meeting of the Association for Computational Linguistics (ACL'05)*, pages 173–180, Ann Arbor, Michigan, June. Association for Computational Linguistics.

Eugene Charniak. 1997. Statistical parsing with a context-free grammar and word statistics. In *Proceedings of the Fourteenth National Conference on Artificial Intelligence*, pages 598–603, Menlo Park, CA. AAAI Press/MIT Press.

Rachele De Felice and Stephen Pulman. 2007. Automatically Acquiring Models of Preposition Use. In *Proceedings of the Fourth ACL-SIGSEM Workshop on Prepositions*, pages 45–50, Prague, Czech Republic, June. Association for Computational Linguistics.

Markus Dickinson and Chong Min Lee. 2009. Modifying corpus annotation to support the analysis of learner language. *CALICO Journal*, 26(3):545–561.

Markus Dickinson and Marwa Ragheb. 2009. Dependency Annotation for Learner Corpora. In *Proceedings of the Eighth Workshop on Treebanks and Linguistic Theories (TLT-8)*, pages 59–70, Milan, Italy.

Jennifer Foster, Özlem Çetinoğlu, Joachim Wagner, and Josef van Genabith. 2011. Comparing the Use of Edited and Unedited Text in Parser Self-Training. In *Proceedings of the 12th International Conference on Parsing Technologies*, pages 215–219, Dublin, Ireland. Association for Computational Linguistics.

John Lee and Ola Knutsson. 2008. The Role of PP Attachment in Preposition Generation. In *Proceedings of CICLing 2008, 9th International Conference on Intelligent Text Processing and Computational Linguistics*, pages 643–654, Haifa, Israel.

David McClosky, Eugene Charniak, and Mark Johnson. 2006. Effective Self-Training for Parsing. In *Proceedings of the Human Language Technology Conference of the NAACL, Main Conference*, pages 152–159, New York City, USA, June. Association for Computational Linguistics.

David McClosky, Eugene Charniak, and Mark Johnson. 2008. When is Self-Training Effective for Parsing? In *Proceedings of the 22nd International Conference on Computational Linguistics (Coling 2008)*, pages 561–568, Manchester, UK, August. Coling 2008 Organizing Committee.

Wolfgang Menzel and Ingo Schröder. 1999. Error diagnosis for language learning systems. *ReCALL*, 11:20–30.

Niels Ott and Ramon Ziai. 2010. Evaluating dependency parsing performance on German learner language. In *Proceedings of the Ninth Workshop on Treebanks and Linguistic Theories (TLT-9)*, pages 175–186.

Roi Reichart and Ari Rappoport. 2007. Self-Training for Enhancement and Domain Adaptation of Statistical Parsers Trained on Small Datasets. In *Proceedings of the 45th Annual Meeting of the Association of Computational Linguistics*, pages 616–623, Prague, Czech Republic, June. Association for Computational Linguistics.

Beatrice Santorini. 1995. Part-of-speech tagging guidelines for the Penn Treebank Project (3rd revision). Technical Report, Department of Computer and Information Science, University of Pennsylvania.

Mark Steedman, Miles Osborne, Anoop Sarkar, Stephen Clark, Rebecca Hwa, Julia Hockenmaier, Paul Ruhlen, Steven Baker, and Jeremiah Crim. 2003. Bootstrapping statistical parsers from small datasets. In *Proceedings of EACL 03*, pages 331–228.

Anne Vandeventer Faltin. 2003. *Syntactic Error Diagnosis in the context of Computer Assisted Language Learning*. Ph.D. thesis, Université de Genève.

The effect of disfluencies and learner errors on the parsing of spoken learner language

Andrew Caines **Paula Buttery**
Institute for Automated Language Teaching and Assessment
Department of Theoretical and Applied Linguistics
University of Cambridge, Cambridge, U.K.
(apc38|pjb48)@cam.ac.uk

Abstract

NLP tools are typically trained on *written* data from *native speakers*. However, research into language acquisition and tools for language teaching & proficiency assessment would benefit from accurate processing of *spoken* data from *second language learners*. In this paper we discuss manual annotation schemes for various features of spoken language; we also evaluate the automatic tagging of one particular feature (filled pauses) – finding a success rate of 81%; and we evaluate the effect of using our manual annotations to 'clean up' the transcriptions for sentence parsing, resulting in a 25% improvement in parse success rate by completely cleaning the texts of disfluencies and errors. We discuss the need to adapt existing NLP technology to non-canonical domains such as spoken learner language, while emphasising the worth of continued integration of manual and automatic annotation.

1 Introduction

Natural language processing (NLP) tools are typically trained on *written* data from *native speakers*. However, research into language acquisition and tools for language proficiency assessment & language teaching – such as learner dialogue and feedback systems – would benefit from accurate processing of *spoken* data from *second language learners*. Being able to convert the text from unparseable to parseable form will enable us to (a) posit a target hypothesis that the learner intended to produce, and (b) provide feedback on this target based on the information removed or repaired in achieving that parseable form.

To proceed towards this goal, we need to adapt current NLP tools to the non-canonical domain of spoken learner language in a persistent fashion rather than use ad hoc post-processing steps to 'correct' the non-canonical data. Outcomes of this approach have been reported in the literature (*e.g.* Rimell & Clark (2009) in the biomedical domain; Caines & Buttery (2010) for spoken language). These fully adaptive approaches require large amounts of annotated data to be successful and, as we intend to work along these lines in future, the discussion in this paper is pointed in that direction.

The work presented here will act as a foundation for more permanent adaptations to existing tools. We annotate transcriptions of speech for linguistic features that are known to interfere with standard NLP to assess whether large-scale annotation of these features will be useful for training purposes. Obvious instances of this include disfluencies (*e.g.* filled pauses, false starts, repetition), formal errors of morphology and syntax, as well as 'errors' of word and phrase selection[1].

Since manual annotation is costly in terms of time and often money, one might question whether so many feature types are strictly necessary or even helpful for the task in hand. Indeed, filled pauses such as 'oh' and 'um' are already accounted for in the part-of-speech (POS) tagset we use (CLAWS2 (Garside, 1987)); and one might also argue that lexico-semantic errors might be dismissed *a priori* on the assumption that both the original and proposed forms are of the same POS (and thus won't affect a parser that performs tagging before the parse). We investigate the contribution of these features to

[1]The word 'error' appears here in quotes as it might be argued that questionable lexical selections are more a matter of infelicity and improbability than any strict dichotomy; we put this concern aside for now as a matter for future research.

First Joint Workshop on Statistical Parsing of Morphologically Rich Languages and Syntactic Analysis of Non-Canonical Languages, pages 74–81 Dublin, Ireland, August 23-29 2014.

parsing success. From a theoretical perspective we are interested in these features with regard to second language acquisition and therefore need to analyse them closely.

In this paper we describe our initial efforts to address the challenge of parsing learner speech with tools trained on native speaker writing. We also present empirical results that demonstrate the utility of annotated spoken transcription with respect to both tagging and parsing. We investigate: [i] the frequency of disfluencies, formal errors of morpho-syntax, and idiomatic errors of lexico-semantics in a corpus of spoken learner language; [ii] the accuracy of part-of-speech labels produced by the tagger associated with the Robust Accurate Statistical Parsing System (RASP (Briscoe et al., 2006)) for a particular type of disfluency (the filled pause)[2]; [iii] parse success rates and parse likelihoods using the RASP System with the texts in various 'modes' ranging from unaltered transcription to fully edited and corrected[3].

We find that in our spoken learner corpus of 2262 words, (i) around a quarter of words are annotated as disfluencies or errors; (ii) 81% of filled pauses were correctly tagged, meaning 1 in 5 are incorrectly tagged; (iii) mean parse likelihood for the text 'as is', unaltered, is –2.599 with a parse success rate of 47%, whereas completely 'cleaned up' text improves those scores to –1.995 and 72%[4]. We discuss the implications of these results below, along with the background context for our study and a more detailed description of our investigations.

2 Background

Previous analyses of the NLP of learner language include various experiments on the tagging and parsing of errorful text. Geertzen et al. (2013) employed the Stanford parser on written English learner data and achieved labelled and unlabelled attachment scores (LAS, UAS)[5] of 89.6% and 92.1%. They found that errors at the morphological level lead to incorrect POS-tagging, which in turn can result in an erroneous parse. Others have focused only on the POS-tagging of written learner corpora – for example with English (van Rooy and Schäfer, 2003) and French learner data (Thouësny, 2011) – demonstrating that post-hoc corrections for the most frequent tagging errors results in significant parse error reduction.

In other investigations of standard NLP tools on learner corpora, Ott & Ziai (2010) report general robustness using MaltParser on written German learner language; however, they found that by manually correcting POS tags, LAS improved from 79.15% to 85.71% and UAS from 84.81% to 90.22%. Wagner & Foster (2009) ran a series of parsing experiments using parallel errorful/corrected corpora, including a spoken learner corpus in which the likelihood of the highest ranked tree for corrected sentences was higher than that of uncorrected sentences in 69.6% of 500 instances. Taken together, these studies suggest that existing NLP tools remain robust to learner data, even more so if the original texts can be corrected and if the tagging stage is in some way verified, or adapted (*e.g.* Zinsmeister et al. (2014)).

On the other hand, Díaz-Negrillo et al. (2010) argue that treating learner data as a 'noisy variant' of native language glosses over systematic differences between the two, and instead call for a dedicated tagging format for 'interlanguage', one that encodes distributional, morphological and lexical information. For instance, 'walks' in 'John has walks' would morphologically be tagged as a present tense 3rd-person verb, but distributionally tagged as a past participle[6]. This is the kind of adaptation of existing tools that we advocate, though we would add that this system should be available for not just interlanguage but all data, allowing for non-canonical language use by native speakers as much as learners.

As for spoken language, Caines & Buttery (2010) among others suggest that adaptation can also be made to the parser, such that it enters a 'speech-aware mode' in which the parser refers to additional and/or replacement rules adapted to the particular features of spoken language. They demonstrated this with the omission of auxiliary verbs in progressive aspect sentences ('you talking to me?', 'how you

[2]The RASP POS-tagger was evaluated on the 560 randomly selected sentences from *The Wall Street Journal* that constitute the PARC dependency bank (DepBank; (King et al., 2003)) and achieved 97% accuracy (Briscoe et al., 2006).

[3]The RASP parser achieves a 79.7% microaveraged F_1 score on grammatical relations in DepBank (Briscoe and Carroll, 2006).

[4]*N.B.* the closer the parse likelihood to zero, the more probable the parse in the English language.

[5]LAS indicates the proportion of tokens that are assigned both the correct head and the correct dependency label; UAS indicates the proportion of tokens assigned the correct head, irrespective of dependency label.

[6]We thank reviewer #1 for this example.

doing?') and achieved a 30% improvement in parsing success rate for this construction type.

3 The corpus

Our speech data consist of recordings from Business Language Testing Service (BULATS) speaking tests[7]. In the test, learners are required to undertake five tasks; we exclude the tasks involving brief question-answering ('can you tell me your full name?', 'where are you from?', etc) and elicited imitation, leaving us with three free-form speech tasks. For this particular test the tasks were: [a] talk about some advice from a colleague (monologue), [b] talk about a series of charts from *Business Today* magazine (monologue), [c] give advice on starting a new retail business (dialogue with examiner).

In our full dataset the candidates come from India, Pakistan and Brazil, with various first languages (L1) including Hindi, Gujarati, Malayalam, Urdu, Pashto and Portuguese, and an age range of 16 to 47 at the time of taking the test. However, in this analysis we have only sampled recordings from candidates deemed to be at 'B2' upper intermediate level on the CEFR scale[8], so that the proficiency level of language used (and how that relates to NLP) is controlled for. In addition the L1s in our sample are Gujarati, Punjabi and Urdu only. This gives us a sample corpus of 2262 tokens in 'as-is' format (*i.e.* the true transcriptions before any corrections are made).

4 Manual annotation

The recordings were manually transcribed and annotated for various features falling into three categories described and exemplified in the following non-exhaustive list.

- *disfluencies* – interruptions to the flow of otherwise fluent speech;
  - <fp> filled pauses (tokens such as *uh, er, um* that serve to fill time and hold the turn) and <rep n="n"> repetition (the speaker repeats a word or phrase one or several times): "or the other way is to <fp>um</fp> <rep n="1">is to</rep> raise finance"
  - <false> false starts – the speaker begins to express a word or phrase which he then corrects: "in two thousand eight it was <false>thirty five p</false> thirty percent"
- *formal errors* of morpho-syntax, such as number agreement, verb inflection and word order errors;
  - noun form: "for becoming a chartered <NS type="FN"><i>accountants</i><c>accountant </c></NS>"
  - missing verb: "as the charts <NS type="MV"><c>show</c></NS> its sales increased"
  - word order: "<NS type="W"><i>how it would be help for you mention</i><c>mention how it helped you</c></NS>"
- *idiomatic 'errors'* – infelicities in lexical selection, failure to express intended meaning, or less-than-natural phrasing;
  - idiomatic: "all my class <NS type="ID"><i>fellows</i><c>mates</c></NS>"
  - idiomatic: "to <NS type="ID"><i>get in</i><c>make a</c></NS> profit"
  - replace quantifier: "for a bank to grant us <NS type="RQ"><i>some</i><c>a</c></NS> loan"

The annotation scheme for formal and idiomatic errors comes from the project to annotate the Cambridge Learner Corpus (Briscoe et al., 2010). The 'error zone' is denoted by <NS> tags, with any original token(s) enclosed by <i> and any proposed correction enclosed by <c>. The various error types are defined in Nicholls (2003) and the categories are similar to the ones given: either self-defining ('ID' for idiom error, 'W' for word order, *etc*) or a combination of operation plus part-of-speech ('FN' form of noun, 'MV' missing verb, 'RQ' replace quantifier, *etc*).

In Table 1 we report the number of errors and disfluencies found in our corpus along with a relative frequency per 100 words. Just under a quarter of the thousand tokens in our corpus are affected by disfluencies and errors, with the former being far more prevalent.

[7]We thank Cambridge English Language Assessment for releasing these recordings for this pilot study; for further information on BULATS go to `http://www.bulats.org/`

[8]The 'Common European Framework of Reference for Languages': a schema for grading an individual learner's language level. For further information go to `http://www.coe.int/lang-CEFR`

All transcription and annotation has been carried out by a single annotator (the first author). It would be interesting to obtain measures of inter-annotator agreement to assess the extent to which the nature of error judgement (particularly in judgements as to idiomaticity) is subjective.

type	**instances in corpus**	**relative frequency (per 100 words)**
disfluency	316	14
formal error	143	6
idiomatic error	70	3
total	529	23

Table 1: Error counts in our corpus

5 Automated annotation: part-of-speech tagging

Since filled pauses such as 'er' and 'um' are included in the CLAWS2 tagset used by the RASP System as UH, 'interjection', one might question the worth of manually annotating filled pauses (FPs). Of the disfluency set, it might be one small time-saving to leave these to the tagger. However, 'interjection' is not a homogeneous set, as UH also covers exclamations of surprise ('oh') and assent ('yes'). Moreover, we find that the POS-tagging of tokens annotated as FPs is not entirely appropriate in this non-canonical domain. Table 2 shows that the majority of FPs are correctly tagged UH, though others are tagged as nouns (NN), verbs (VV), adjectives (JJ), adverbs (RR) and foreign words (&FW)[9].

Token	UH	&FW	JJ	NN	RR	VV	*total*
er	104	0	0	0	0	0	104
mm	0	0	0	8	0	0	8
uh	0	0	0	1	2	4	7
um	2	5	0	0	0	0	7
nuh	0	0	0	0	2	1	3
buh	0	0	0	1	0	1	2
other	2	0	1	0	0	0	3
total	108	5	1	10	6	9	134

Table 2: POS tagging of filled pauses

One possible solution is to append a dictionary of known FP tokens to the tagger, and specify that they should be tagged UH, or even better, a new tag such as FP. But as the Table demonstrates, there are standard, highly frequent FPs such as 'er', 'uh' and 'um', and then there are novel forms such as 'nuh', 'buh' and 'nna' which we found to be rather idiosyncratic – *i.e.* there might be novel FPs for every individual. Moreover, the introduction of a closed class depends on consistent transcription practice, not necessarily a given with even a lone annotator, let alone more than one.

Automatic identification and repair of disfluencies is a well-developed research topic, with continuing refinements to joint parsing and disfluency detection models (*e.g.* Qian & Liu (2013), Rasooli & Tetreault (2014), Honnibal & Johnson (2014)), plus applied work in the domains of automatic speech recognition (Fitzgerald et al., 2009) and machine translation (Cho et al., 2014). We note the linguistic rules included in the Lease, Johnson & Charniak (2006) tree adjoining grammar (TAG) noisy-channel model – lexical, POS and syntactic rules that reduce errors in the TAG model. This is another case of improvements to NLP tools thanks to data-driven linguistic insight, and a design that we could incorporate into our work on automated assessment and feedback.

[9] The 'other' filled pauses are singleton forms: *eh, nna, ah*.

6 Automated annotation: sentence parsing

In this section we report the results of our parsing experiment in which transcribed learner utterances were processed by the RASP system in four different forms:

(A) as-is: without alteration;

(B) less-disfluency: with disfluencies removed;

(C) less-form-error: with morpho-syntactic errors corrected;

(D) less-lex-error: with semantic/idiomatic improvements.

We investigated the effect on the parsing output of each transcription format compared to the (A) format as a baseline. We processed each format in turn singularly, as well as cumulative combinations of (B), (C) and (D) in every possible order. The results are set out in Table 3, with mean likelihoods of the highest ranked parse for each sentence (μ)[10], differences between this mean and the baseline where applicable (Δ_{base}), and success rates in terms of non-fragmentary tree outputs (*i.e.* parses labelled other than 'T/frag' in the RASP System).

mode	μ	Δ_{base}	$\neg$T/frag	**mode**	μ	Δ_{base}	$\neg$T/frag	**mode**	μ	Δ_{base}	$\neg$T/frag
(A)	−2.599	0	.471	(A)	−2.599	0	.471	(A)	−2.599	0	.471
(B)	−2.094	+.505	.623	(BC)	−2.032	+.567	.689	(BCD)	−1.995	+.604	.715
(C)	−2.574	+.025	.484	(BD)	−2.049	+.550	.649		-	-	-
(D)	−2.563	+.036	.503	(CD)	−2.545	+.054	.523		-	-	-

Table 3: Mean parse likelihoods, deltas to baseline and parse success rates in all transcription modes

As can be seen in Table 3, the removal of disfluencies (B) is the single move of greatest benefit to parse likelihood scores and parse tree success rates compared to the 'as-is' baseline (A). The correction of morpho-syntactic (C) and idiomatic errors (D) have a lesser effect. All pairings have a positive effect on parse likelihoods, especially those featuring disfluency removal (B); and the three 'corrective' steps combined (BCD) have the greatest effect of all.

However, we show by analysis of two candidates in our corpus that these effects can differ on an individual basis. In Figure 1, the candidate on the left has a less pronounced effect of disfluency removal (B) compared to the baseline (A) than the candidate on the right. The effect of both formal (C) and idiomatic (D) error correction are also seen to make improvements over (A), which is not the case for the second candidate. Such observations serve as a reminder that when generalising about overall corpus patterns we collapse over so many individual language models. It may well turn out that disfluencies are an especially idiosyncratic type of language use, an avenue we will explore in future work.

7 Discussion

In this paper we have investigated NLP of transcribed learner speech, questioning how tools trained on native speaker written data would handle such data. We found that the majority (81%) of filled pauses were correctly tagged 'UH', though this only covers three of eleven FP forms (*er, um, eh*). We propose a dictionary of FPs and a specific FP POS-tag, while suggesting that the dictionary will not catch all novel FPs (since they seem to be idiosyncratic) and that we can turn to state-of-the-art research on automated disfluency detection to help us.

We also showed that sentence parsing could be improved from a 47% 'success' rate (*i.e.* non-fragmentary (T/frag in RASP parlance) parse trees) in the 'as-is' transcriptions, to 72% in transcriptions with disfluencies removed and errors corrected (see Table 3). We found that disfluency removal is the main contributor to this improvement, though this was found to be somewhat idiosyncratic (as in Figure 1).

[10]Note that parse likelihoods have been normalised for word length, as they increase in a near-linear manner according to the number of terminal nodes in a tree.

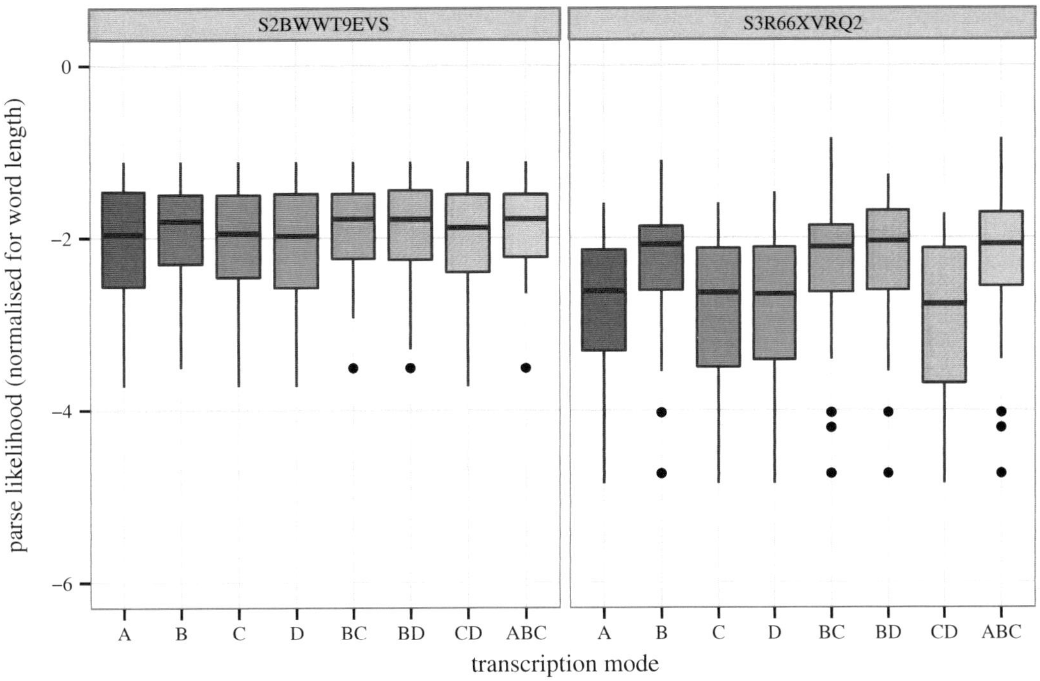

Figure 1: Parse likelihoods for each transcription mode, for two individuals in our corpus; the whiskers indicate the largest and smallest observation within $1.5 * IQR$ (inter-quartile range; the distance between first and third quartiles), while the upper hinge indicates the third quartile (75th percentile), the middle is the median, the lower hinge is the first quartile (25th percentile), and the points are outliers.

The motivation for this work is to investigate what is required to convert texts from unparseable to parseable form. The steps taken to achieve this can be used to inform automated learner dialogue or feedback systems. We note that automated assessment may be improved by parse trees but may well be performed without them: it can proceed on the basis of superficial detection of features known to correlate with high grades (possibly including certain disfluency types, for instance). But to be able to diagnose *how the learner can improve*, we need a deeper structural analysis of the text – *i.e.* requiring that the text is in parseable form. Our manual annotations are one step towards this goal.

Our annotations also indicate that spoken learner data features many disfluencies and errors, with over a quarter of the 2262-word testset affected in some way. Automatic error detection (and correction) is a burgeoning field (see for example the work on learner data by Briscoe et al. (2010), Andersen (2011) and Kochmar & Briscoe (2014), as well as the most recent shared task on grammatical error correction at CoNLL-2014 (Ng et al., 2014)). Such studies are based on written language. We envisage adding speech-specific information and adaptations to such systems on the basis of our fuller annotation project.

Indeed, it so happens that the problem of NLP in the spoken domain is one we address here with learner data. However, we do not assume that the problem of adapting or building NLP tools for spoken data is substantially different for native speaker data. We intend to collect recordings of native speakers undertaking the same tasks as the BULATS candidates, allowing for comparative studies of errors and disfluencies in native and learner data, with the task and topic variables held constant as far as possible.

Finally, we emphasise that we intend to add to the corpus with more annotated data from a wider range of L1s and a wider range of proficiency levels. We can then investigate the possible effects of more varied syntactic complexity, lexical diversity and error types.

Acknowledgments

We thank Cambridge English Language Assessment for funding this work and providing the data. We also thank Ted Briscoe, Mike McCarthy and Øistein Andersen for their support and advice, and we are grateful to the three anonymous reviewers for their helpful comments and suggestions.

References

Øistein E. Andersen. 2011. Semi-automatic ESOL error annotation. *English Profile Journal*, 2:e1.

Ted Briscoe and John Carroll. 2006. Evaluating the accuracy of an unlexicalized statistical parser on the PARC DepBank. In *Proceedings of the COLING/ACL 2006 Main Conference Poster Sessions*. Association for Computational Linguistics.

Ted Briscoe, John Carroll, and Rebecca Watson. 2006. The second release of the RASP System. In *Proceedings of the COLING/ACL 2006 Interactive Presentations Session*. Association for Computational Linguistics.

Ted Briscoe, Ben Medlock, and Øistein E. Andersen. 2010. Automated assessment of ESOL free text examinations. *University of Cambridge Computer Laboratory Technical Reports*, 790.

Andrew Caines and Paula J. Buttery. 2010. 'You talking to me?' A predictive model for zero auxiliary constructions. In *Proceedings of the Workshop on Natural Language Processing and Linguistics, Finding the Common Ground, Annual Meeting of the Association for Computational Linguistics (ACL) 2010*. Association for Computational Linguistics.

Eunah Cho, Jan Niehues, and Alex Waibel. 2014. Tight integration of speech disfluency removal into SMT. In *Proceedings of the 14th Conference of the European Chapter of the Association for Computational Linguistics (EACL 2014)*. Association for Computational Linguistics.

Ana Díaz-Negrillo, Detmar Meurers, Salvador Valera, and Holger Wunsch. 2010. Towards interlanguage POS annotation for effective learner corpora in SLA and FLT. *Language Forum*, 36:139–154.

Alison Edwards. 2014. The progressive aspect in the Netherlands and the ESL/EFL continuum. *World Englishes*, 33:173–194.

Erin Fitzgerald, Keith Hall, and Frederick Jelinek. 2009. Reconstructing false start errors in spontaneous speech text. In *Proceedings of the 12th Conference of the European Chapter of the Association for Computational Linguistics (EACL 2009)*. Association for Computational Linguistics.

Roger Garside. 1987. The CLAWS word-tagging system. In Roger Garside, Geoffrey Leech, and Geoffrey Sampson, editors, *The Computational Analysis of English: A Corpus-based Approach*. London: Longman.

Jeroen Geertzen, Theodora Alexopoulou, and Anna Korhonen. 2013. Automatic linguistic annotation of large scale L2 databases: the EF-Cambridge Open Language Database (EFCAMDAT). In *Proceedings of the 31st Second Language Research Forum*. Somerville, MA: Cascadilla Proceedings Project.

Matthew Honnibal and Mark Johnson. 2014. Joint incremental disfluency detection and dependency parsing. *Transactions of the Association for Computational Linguistics*, 2:131–142.

Tracy H. King, Richard Crouch, Stefan Riezler, Mary Dalrymple, and Ronald M. Kaplan. 2003. The PARC700 Dependency Bank. In *Proceedings of the 4th International Workshop on Linguistically Interpreted Corpora (LINC 2003)*.

Ekaterina Kochmar and Ted Briscoe. 2014. Detecting learner errors in the choice of content words using compositional distributional semantics. In *Proceedings of the 25th International Conference on Computational Linguistics (COLING 2014)*. Association for Computational Linguistics.

Matthew Lease, Mark Johnson, and Eugene Charniak. 2006. Recognizing disfluencies in conversational speech. *IEEE Transactions on Audio, Speech, and Language Processing*, 14:1566–1573.

Hwee Tou Ng, Siew Mei Wu, Ted Briscoe, Christian Hadiwinoto, Raymond Hendy Susanto, and Christopher Bryant. 2014. The CoNLL-2014 Shared Task on Grammatical Error Correction. In *Eighteenth Conference on Computational Natural Language Learning, Proceedings of the Shared Task*. Association for Computational Linguistics.

Diane Nicholls. 2003. The Cambridge Learner Corpus: error coding and analysis for lexicography and ELT. In Dawn Archer, Paul Rayson, Andrew Wilson, and Tony McEnery, editors, *Proceedings of the Corpus Linguistics 2003 conference; UCREL technical paper number 16*. Lancaster University.

Niels Ott and Ramon Ziai. 2010. Evaluating dependency parsing performance on German learner language. In *Proceedings of the Ninth International Workshop on Treebanks and Linguistic Theories (NEALT 2010)*.

Xian Qian and Yang Liu. 2013. Disfluency detection using multi-step stacked learning. In *Proceedings of the 2013 Conference of the North American Chapter of the Association for Computational Linguistics: Human Language Technologies (NAACL-HLT)*.

Mohammad Sadegh Rasooli and Joel Tetreault. 2014. Non-monotonic parsing of *Fluent umm I Mean* disfluent sentences. In *Proceedings of the 14th Conference of the European Chapter of the Association for Computational Linguistics (EACL 2014)*. Association for Computational Linguistics.

Laura Rimell and Stephen Clark. 2009. Porting a lexicalized-grammar parser to the biomedical domain. *Journal of Biomedical Informatics*, 42:852–865.

Sylvie Thouësny. 2011. Increasing the reliability of a part-of-speech tagging tool for use with learner language. In *Proceedings of the Pre-conference Workshop on Automatic Analysis of Learner Language, CALICO Conference 2009*.

Bertus van Rooy and Lande Schäfer. 2003. An evaluation of three POS taggers for the tagging of the Tswana Learner English Corpus. In *Proceedings of the Corpus Linguistics 2003 Conference*. Lancaster University.

Joachim Wagner and Jennifer Foster. 2009. The effect of correcting grammatical errors on parse probabilities. In *Proceedings of the 11th International Conference on Parsing Technologies*.

Heike Zinsmeister, Ulrich Heid, and Kathrin Beck. 2014. Adapting a part-of-speech tagset to non-standard text: the case of STTS. In *Proceedings of the Ninth International Conference on Language Resources and Evaluation (LREC 2014)*. European Language Resources Association.

Initial Explorations in Two-phase Turkish Dependency Parsing by Incorporating Constituents

İlknur Durgar El-Kahlout **Ahmet Afşın Akın** **Ertuğrul Yılmaz**

TÜBİTAK-BİLGEM
Gebze, KOCAELİ
{ilknur.durgar,akin.ahmet,yilmaz.ertugrul}@tubitak.gov.tr

Abstract

This paper describes a two-phase Turkish dependency parsing which separates dependency and labeling into two similar to (McDonald et al., 2006b). First, in order to solve the long distance dependency attachment problem, the sentences are split into constituents and the dependencies are estimated on shorter sentences. Later, for better estimation of labels, Conditional Random Fields (CRFs) are used with previously learned chunk and several dependency and morphosyntactic features. Finally, a post-processing step is applied to "correct" some of labels, if necessary.

1 Introduction

Dependency parsing, a well-studied problem in natural language processing, is the task of forming a dependency tree by attaching each word of a sentence (dependent) to another word in the same sentence (head) with a label that describes the dependency relation between these words. In the last decade, the data-driven dependency parsing approaches (Nivre et al., 2007; McDonald et al., 2006a) have received a considerable attention as it learns solely from labeled data and can be rapidly adapted to new languages and domains.

The accuracy of a dependency parser is negatively affected by two factors, among possibly others. First, a parser's accuracy is sensitive to sentence length (McDonald and Nivre, 2007). As the parsers tend to assign dependencies in relatively short distances (Nivre et al., 2006), long sentences are not easy to parse correctly. Second, wrong labels that are assigned to correct dependencies result in labeled accuracy drop.

In data-driven dependency parsing approaches (Nivre et al., 2007; McDonald et al., 2006a), the dependencies and labels are often learned at the same time. To our best knowledge, the work by McDonald et al. (2006b) is unique in that it learns the dependencies and labels in two separate stages. In this paper, we present a two-phase data-driven dependency parsing of Turkish that addresses the above-mentioned problems in consecutive steps.

In order to solve the long distance dependency attachment problem, we first split sentences into their constituents. For each constituent, we construct a sub-sentence by appending the verb group of the original sentence to the end of the constituent. We then parse all these short sentences by the MaltParser (Nivre et al., 2007) which is trained with Turkish specific parameters (Eryiğit et al., 2008). Finally, we combine the generated sentences to form the original sentence with full dependencies.

For the labeling problem, we use a CRF-based (Lafferty et al., 2001) approach with the use of chunk information and parser output for identifying dependencies. On top of our CRF-based labeling approach, we also apply a post-processing step to correct dependency labels if necessary. Our methodology improves the state-of-the-art Turkish dependency parsing (Eryiğit et al., 2008) with a 1.7% increase in the labeled attachment score (AS_L) and 0.4% increase in the unlabeled attachment score (AS_U).

There are several related research on incorporating different features during the parsing such as chunk (Attardi and Dell'Orletta, 2008) and causal (Gadde et al., 2010) and morphosyntactic features (Ambati et al., 2010). Our works differs from several aspects; first, instead of using the chunk information as a

First Joint Workshop on Statistical Parsing of Morphologically Rich Languages and Syntactic Analysis of Non-Canonical Languages, pages 82–89 Dublin, Ireland, August 23-29 2014.

	Short	**Mid**	**Long**
Gold	3188	506	815
MaltParser	3268/2881	498/298	743/537

Table 1: The Dependency Distance Statistics of the Validation Set.

feature in the parsing, we used the chunk information as a preprocessing step to split the sentences into "shorter" ones and in the second step of parsing while estimating the labels. Second, as an addition to the word's morphosyntactic features, we employed the morphosyntactic features of the head word for each token again in label estimation step.

2 Turkish Dependency Parsing

Turkish, a member of the Turkic languages, is an agglutinative language with very productive inflectional and derivational morphology. From the dependency point of view, Turkish is generally a head-final language. The dependency relation arcs are formed from left to right and do not cross each other except in some rare cases (Oflazer et al., 2003). The first investigations on a Turkish dependency parser was done by Oflazer (Oflazer, 2003). Following this grammar-based work, Turkish dependency parsing was investigated by Eryiğit et al. (Eryiğit et al., 2008) where the impact of morphological units on different types of parsers was explored. This study showed that the correct dependency representation of a Turkish sentence should use root words and inflectional groups (IGs)[1] instead of the whole words themselves. The best performing Turkish dependency parsing is obtained via the data-driven MaltParser (Nivre et al., 2007) by using Turkish-specific features.

For training the parser, we used the Turkish dependency treebank (Oflazer et al., 2003) that is also used in CoNLL-X (Buchholz and Marsi, 2006)[2]. The treebank corpus contains several features including word, lemma, POS, coarse POS[3], and IGs that reflect the morphological structure of Turkish.

Recently, Turkish dependency parsing was improved with the use of multiword expressions (Eryiğit et al., 2011) and the effects of automatic morphological analyzer and disambiguation were explored (Eryiğit, 2012).

To show that the transition-based dependency parsers are in favor of identifying dependencies in short distances, we examined the dependency attachments of the MaltParser with respect to distance on the ITU validation set (Eryiğit, 2007)[4]. We classified the dependency attachments into three categories with respect to the number of words that occur between the attached words: i) *Short*, dependency attachments at a distance of 1 or 2 words, ii) *Mid*, dependency attachments at a distance between 3 and 6 words, and iii) *Long*, dependency attachments at a distance of 6 or more words. Table 2 shows the comparison of the distances in the gold data and in the attachments identified by the dependency parser for the validation set (all/correct attachments). As can be seen from the results, the Turkish dependency parser assigns 66% of the "correct" long distance attachments and 58% of the mid distance attachments that appear in the gold data.

3 Incorporating Constituents as a Preprocessing Step

A constituent is a group of words that behave as a single unit from the structural and meaning views. Constituents can be ommitted in the sentence without influencing the sentence gramaticality. Constituents are the word groups that we can be found by asking the questions "who/what", "when", "where", etc. to the verb constituent. Most frequent Turkish constituents can be listed as Subject, Sentence (Verb), Object, and Adjunct. The main constituent of a sentence is its verb and other constituents can form a

[1] To represent the morphology, words are separated at the derivational boundaries. The inflectional morphemes with derivation (or the root word for the first IG) are called as inflectional groups.

[2] Shared Task on Multilingual Dependency Parsing

[3] The Turkish morphological analyzer gives a two-layered POS information such as *Noun+Proper* and *Num+Ordinal*. The coarse POS is the first part of this POS information. In the absence of the second layer, the POS is the coarse POS.

[4] This set was used as the test set in this work.

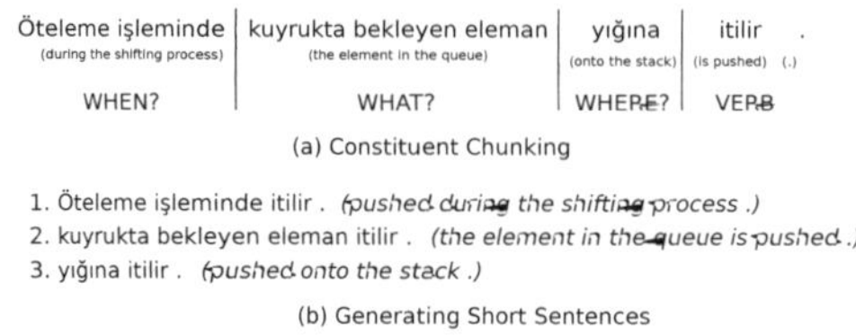

Figure 1: Constituent Chunking and Generation of Shorter Sentences.

sentence with the presence of the verb. Every word in a constituent is dependent to a word within the constituent except the head word of the constituent. Head word of the constituent is dependent to the verb. Any constituent becomes an ungrammatical and meaningless structure if its head word is removed.

Figure 1 illustrates the chunking process for the sentence *Öteleme*$_1$ *işleminde*$_2$ *kuyrukta*$_3$ *bekleyen*$_4$ *eleman*$_5$ *yığına*$_6$ *itilir*$_7$ (The element$_5$ in$_3$ the$_3$ queue$_3$ is$_7$ pushed$_7$ onto$_6$ the$_6$ stack$_6$ during$_2$ the$_1$ shifting$_1$ process$_2$). This sentence contains four constituents sequentially, Locative.Adjunct, Subject, Dative.Adjunct and finally (Sentence/Verb). One can observe by dropping the head word *işleminde* in the Locative.Adjunct constituent, contituent looses its meaning completely. Each of these constituents (except the verb) are "phrases" alone and can form a sentence only with the verb chunk. After dropping any constituent (again except the verb), for example the Subject, the sentence is still a grammatical Turkish sentence as *Öteleme işleminde yığına itilir.* (is pushed onto the stack during the shifting process.)

In our work, we used the Turkish dependency treebank and ITU validation test set which is enriched with the chunk information (Durgar El-Kahlout and Akın, 2013). The chunker is reported to work with an F-measure 91.95 for verb chunks and 87.50 for the other chunks. In that work, only verb chunks are labeled separately and the other chunks are labeled with the same type such as *[CHUNK Öteleme işleminde] [CHUNK kuyrukta bekleyen eleman] [CHUNK yığına] [VERB itilir]* .

3.1 Procedure

Before the parsing process, we split each sentence of the test set into their constituents. The idea behind splitting sentences was to create synthetically shorter sentences in order to make the dependency parsing task easier by "shortening" long distance dependencies. For each constituent, we generated a sub-sentence by appending the verb to the end of the constituent. As a result, we generated $n - 1$ new sentences from a sentence with n constituents. Part (b) of Figure 1 illustrates the generation of shorter sentences from the chunked sentence shown in part (a) of the same figure. Each of these shorter sentences are grammatical for Turkish. The shorter sentences contains only the dependencies within the constituent and the dependencies of the constituent to the verb constituent.

After splitting the original sentence into a number of shorter sentences, each of these sentences are parsed by the MaltParser in order to obtain the dependencies. Finally, these parsed sentences were combined into a whole in such a way that the original sentence was generated back with identified dependency relations.

Splitting complex sentences with more than one verb group was not trivial. We classified these sentences into two groups; complex sentences with two verb groups and complex sentences with more than two verb groups. For the first case, the last verb group was considered as the dominating one and the sentence was splitted according to this verb group. In this work, we didn't split sentences that belong to the second group and kept them as whole sentences in our experiments.

Figure 2 illustrates a sample Turkish sentence, its dependency parse generated by the MaltParser (part (a)), and the gold parse (part (b)) of the sentence. As can be seen from this example, the parser mistakenly attaches the word *"işleminde"* to the word *"bekleyen"* (shown with a dotted link in part (a)). The figure also shows the parses of the shorter sentences generated from this sentence (part (c)). The generation of the original sentence from the parses of shorter sentences (part (d)) are also given in the figure. It is noteworthy to mention that splitting the original sentence and parsing shorter sentences individually enables the parser to find the correct attachment of the word *"işleminde"* to the verb *"itilir"* (as is in the

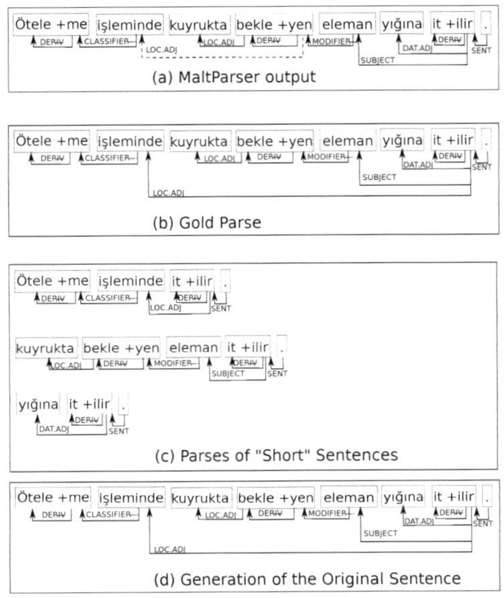

Figure 2: An Example of the Dependency Parsing by Chunks.

Distance	Original Sents.		Gold Chunks		Our Approach	
	prec.	recall	prec.	recall	prec.	recall
1	90.47	94.06	89.58	**95.45**	89.91	**95.36**
2	75.29	76.48	75.10	**79.10**	74.32	**80.08**
$3-6$	70.72	70.43	**73.61**	**73.16**	**71.75**	70.30
>6	79.48	60.86	**92.91**	**60.88**	**88.43**	58.32

Table 2: Precision and Recall Scores Relative to the Head Distance.

gold output part (b)).

3.2 Results

For our evaluations, we used the evaluation tool distributed with the MaltParser. The performance of a dependency parser is mainly evaluated with three scores; the labeled attachment score (AS_L); the unlabeled attachment score (AS_U) and the label accuracy score (LA). We conducted experiments both on the chunked sentences using Turkish constituent chunker (Durgar El-Kahlout and Akın, 2013) and gold chunks as described in Section 3.1.

Table 2 compares the precision and recall scores of the MaltParser output with original sentences and our approach relative to the dependency attachment distance. The results showed that dependency parsing with the use of constituent chunks increased the recall for all distance lengths (i.e., up to 6 points) and improved the precision approximately 3 points for dependency distances between 3 and 6 words and more than 13 points for dependency distances more than 6 words.

To see the effects of sentence lengths on parsing performance, we split sentences relative to their lengths (i.e., 1-8, 9-15, 16-30, and >30) and reported the scores with respect to different length groups. Table 3 shows the parser performance depending on sentence lengths. The results showed that AS_U was improved up to 1.5 points for all sentence lengths. For shorter sentences, the AS_L was relatively worse than the parses of original sentences but for longer sentences the performance was better with the gold chunks. For the chunker output, performance slightly better for sentences with 16 to 30 words for the chunker chunks. It is particularly noteworthy to mention that the labeling (the label accuracy result) was worse than the parses of original sentences for all sentence lengths. Our approach in a second step

# of Tokens	# of Sentences	Original Sents.			Gold Chunks			Our Approach		
		AS_L	AS_U	LA	AS_L	AS_U	LA	AS_L	AS_U	LA
$1-8$	57	79.85	88.81	83.96	79.10	**90.30**	82.46	79.48	**90.30**	82.09
$9-15$	130	76.48	83.18	86.31	75.76	**84.62**	84.62	74.96	**83.29**	84.35
$16-30$	99	67.48	76.55	80.76	**68.20**	**77.17**	80.55	**67.84**	**76.63**	**81.26**
>30	14	68.73	76.98	82.82	**69.07**	**78.69**	82.13	66.67	**76.98**	80.76
all	300	71.95	79.90	83.28	**72.05**	**81.23**	82.37	71.40	**80.23**	82.44

Table 3: Evaluation Relative to the Sentence Lengths.

improved the label accuracy as described in Section 4.

4 Relabeling the parser output

In the parses of original sentences[5], we observed that the intersection of the correct dependencies (2461) and the correct labels (2565) is only 2216 out of 3080[6] attachments. This shows us that approximately 10% of the correct dependencies are missed because of the wrong labels; this causes an accuracy drop in the AS_L score.

Assigning dependency labels can be approximated as a sequential labeling task for Turkish with the projectivity assumption, where the dependency tags are associated with every token in a sequence of tokens (Ramshaw and Marcus, 1995). Adding features of the head word's (that is learnt in the previous step) can be included to each token to create syntetically sequential data.

To assign the labels, we used CRFs (Lafferty et al., 2001) which became the state-of-the-art framework for several labeling tasks such as text segmentation, named entity recognition, part of speech tagging, and shallow parsing. They are shown to outperform the probabilistic models such as HMMs (Church, 1988; Freitag and McCallum, 2000) and MEMMs (McCallum et al., 2000) in several sequential assignment tasks.

4.1 Features

To model the label attachment problem with CRFs, we used four types of features; i) *baseline features:* the set of features that exists in the Turkish dependency treebank, ii) *morphological features:* the features that are split from the IG information, iii) *dependency features:* features that are extracted from the first phase of the dependency parsing, and iv) *chunk features:* the features from the chunk annotation. The full set of features that are used in the dependency labeling task are as follows:

- **Baseline Features:** Word, Lemma, The *main* POS of the word (CPOS), The second layer of the POS information of the word (POS), The combined inflectional morpheme information of the word's last inflectional group (IG)[7].

- **Morphological Features:** The case of the word when its POS is Noun or Pronoun (CASE). The feature can take the values *Acc, Dat, Nom, Loc, or Abl*[8].

- **Dependency Features:** The word's distance to its head (DIST); If the word is attached to a head within a distance of one or two words then the distance is **short**, otherwise it is **long**, Head word CPOS (HCPOS), lemma of the word's head (HLEM).

- **Chunk Features:** Chunk type (ChnkTYPE), Chunk type is *Verb* for the sentence/verb chunks and *Regular* for the rest of the chunks. The chunk type is *Undefined* if the token is not assigned to any chunk.

[5]The situation is more or less same in the output of our approach.

[6]This excludes the derivation and punctuation tokens.

[7]To represent the morphology, words are separated at the derivational boundaries. The inflectional morphemes with derivation (or the root word for the first IG) are called as inflectional groups.

[8]The Case information also exists in the IG feature but combined with the Person and Number information

WORD	LEM	POS	CPOS	IG	DIST	CASE	HCPOS	HLEM	ChnkTYPE
Burada	bura	Noun	Noun	A3sg|Pnon|Loc	long	Loc	Verb	var	REGULAR
çiçeklerin	çiçek	Noun	Noun	A3pl|Pnon|Gen	short	Gen	Verb	sat	REGULAR
_	sat	Verb	Verb	_	short	_	Verb	sat	REGULAR
_	_	Verb	Verb	Pass|Pos	short	_	APastPart	sat	REGULAR
satıldığı	_	Adj	APastPart	P3sg	long	_	Noun	alan	REGULAR
geniş	geniş	Adj	Adj	_	short	_	Noun	alan	REGULAR
bir	bir	Det	Det	_	short	_	Noun	alan	REGULAR
alan	alan	Noun	Noun	A3sg|Pnon|Nom	short	Nom	Verb	var	REGULAR
vardı	var	Verb	Verb	Pos|Past|A3sg	short	_	Punc	.	VERB_GROUP
.	.	Punc	Punc	_	long	_	EMPTY	EMPTY	UNDEFINED

Table 4: An Example of a Sentence with Labeling Features.

To the train the CRF relabeling, the gold labels (morphology, dependencies, etc.) are used for each type of features. Table 4 shows the complete set of features used for the Turkish sentence "*Burada çiçeklerin satıldığı geniş bir alan vardı*" (*There used to be a huge area here where the flowers were sold*).

4.2 Post-processing

To better estimate the labels, we should figure out the type of labeling errors that the dependency parser produces. In order to designate such kind of errors, we parsed 50 sentences from a Turkish corpus (different from the test set). After a manual inspection, we observed that from several others, some of the "DATIVE.ADJUNCT"s are labeled as "OBJECT". This error can be easily corrected by just controlling the *Case* feature of the token. In Turkish, specific adjuncts ends with specific case suffixes. For example, all dative adjuncts have the *Case* "Dat". Both MaltParser and our labeling procedure fails to assign the correct label for this case. So, after the relabeling procedure, we replaced every token with the label "OBJECT" and the *Case* feature "Dat" to "DATIVE.ADJUNCT". This manual post-processing corrected 41 (out of 56) of the problematic cases on the test set.

4.3 Results

We used the CRF++[9] tool, to train and test the Turkish dependency labeling. The window size of the sentence was 5 taking the preceding two words and following two words. For training, we used all Turkish dependency treebank data. As the test data, we used the output produced in the first phase of parsing. Table 5 compares the performance of the labeling according to the AS_L and LA scores for original sentences, attachments obtained by the gold chunks and chunker chunks in the previous step. As a result, we obtained same AS_L without the post-processing step score and 0.26 points in AS_L after the post-processing step with better LA scores over the MaltParser output of the original sentences with the chunker output. The performance is much better with the gold chunked assignments. Our experiments showed that using a CRF-based labeling enhanced with extra features increased the label accuracy and outperformed the Turkish dependency parser with respect to AS_L.

5 Results and Main Findings

Dependency parsers have problems in assigning long distance dependencies. They tend to assign dependencies relatively in short distances. In order to solve this problem, we offered a new chunking-based parsing methodology. Our methodology first chunks sentences into constituents. For each constituent, one grammatically correct sentence is generated with some meaning loss by attaching the verb chunk and parsed with MaltParser. First chunking a sentence and then using the dependency parser outperforms the state-of-the-art results. However, the results with respect to the AS_L is not satisfying due to wrong labeling. Thus, in a second phase, our approach treats labeling as a sequential attachment problem. CRF-based models are used with enhanced features extracted from morphological structure, chunks and dependency attachments.

In our experiments, 52 sentences out of 300 sentences were not split as either they have only one chunk or more than two verb chunks. We generated approximately 2.69 short sentences from each of

[9]CRF++: Yet Another CRF toolkit.

Method	AS_L	LA
Original Sents.	71.95	83.28
+POST	72.95	84.51
Chunks - Gold		
Shortened Sents.	72.05	82.37
+POST	73.28	83.67
CRF Feat.s	72.63	83.21
+POST	**73.86**	**84.51**
Chunks - Chunker		
Shortened Sents.	71.40	82.44
+POST	72.56	83.73
CRF Feat.s	71.95	83.51
+POST	**73.21**	**84.81**

Table 5: CRF-based Labeling and Post-processing Results.

the remaining sentence. The performance with respect to AS_L was improved from 71.95 to 73.21 (an improvement of 1.7%) and with respect to AS_U from 79.90 to 80.23 (an improvement of 0.4%) over parses of original sentences.

6 Conclusions and Future Work

In this paper, we presented a two-phase Turkish dependency parsing approach where the dependencies are identified in the first phase and the labels are identified in the second phase. We improved dependency attachments by chunking sentences into their constituents, generating shorter sentences from these constituents, finding dependencies in these shorter sentence, and finally generating the original sentence back from these dependency parses. For the labeling task, we used a CRF-based approach enriched with extra features from the morphological information, dependencies and chunking. Moreover, we performed a rule-based post-processing to correct some dependency labels, if necessary.

Future work includes splitting the dependency treebank into constituents also and train the parser with shorter sentences similar to the test data. Because the lack of different test sets for Turkish, we will also make 10-fold cross validation with the training data. Moreover, we are planning to replicate the experiments with different state-of-the-art parsers such as Bohnet parser (Bohnet and Nivre, 2012).

References

Bharat Ram Ambati, Samar Husain, Sambhav Jain, Dipti Misra Sharma, and Rajeev Sangal. 2010. Two methods to incorporate local morphosyntactic features in hindi dependency parsing. In *Proceedings of the First Workshop on Statistical Parsing of Morphologically Rich Languages in NAACL-HLT'10*, pages 22–30.

Gluseppe Attardi and Felice Dell'Orletta. 2008. Chunking and dependency parsing. In *Proceedings of LREC Workshop on Partial Parsing: Between Chunking and Deep Parsing*.

Bernd Bohnet and Joakim Nivre. 2012. A transition-based system for joint part-of-speech and labeled non-projective dependency parsing. In *Prooceedings of the EMNLP-CoNLL*, pages 1455–1465.

Sabine Buchholz and Erwin Marsi. 2006. Conll-x shared task on multilingual dependency parsing. In *Proceedings of the 10th Conference on Computational Natural Language Learning (CoNLL)*, pages 149–164, New York, NY.

Kenneth Church. 1988. A stochastic parts program and noun phrase parser for unrestricted texts. In *Proceedings of the Second Conference on Applied Natural Language Processing*, pages 136–143, Austin, Texas.

İlknur Durgar El-Kahlout and Ahmet Afşın Akın. 2013. Turkish constituent chunking with morphological and contextual features. In *Prooceedings of the Computatioanl Linguistics and Intelligent Text Processing (CICLING)*, pages 270–281.

Gülşen Eryiğit, Joakim Nivre, and Kemal Oflazer. 2008. Dependency parsing of turkish. *Computational Linguistics*, 34:357–389.

Gülşen Eryiğit, Tugay İlbay, and Ozan Arkan Can. 2011. Multiword expressions in statistical dependency parsing. In *Proceedings of the 2nd Workshop on Statistical Parsing of Morphologically-Rich Langauges (SPMRL)*, pages 45–55, Dublin, Ireland.

Gülşen Eryiğit. 2007. Itu validation set for metu-sabancı turkish treebank.

Gülşen Eryiğit. 2012. The impact of automatic morphological analysis and disambiguation on dependency parsing of turkish. In *Proceedings of the LREC*, pages 1960–1965, İstanbul, Turkey.

Dayne Freitag and Andrew McCallum. 2000. Information extraction with hmm structures learned by stochastic optimization. In *Proceedings of 17th National Conference on Artificial Intelligence (AAAI)*, pages 584–589, Austin,Texas.

Phani Gadde, Karan Jindal, Samar Husain, Sambhav Jain, Dipti Misra Sharma, and Rajeev Sangal. 2010. Improving data driven dependency parsing using clausal information. In *Proceedings of the Human Language Technology Conference of the NAACL*, pages 657–660.

John Lafferty, Andrew McCallum, and Fernando Pereira. 2001. Conditional random fields: Probabilistic models for segmenting and labeling sequence data. In *Proceedings of the 18th International Conference on Machine Learning (ICML)*, pages 282–289, Williamstown, MA.

Andrew McCallum, Dayne Freitag, and Fernanda Pereira. 2000. Maximum entropy markov models for information extraction and segmentation. In *Proceedings of International Conference on Machine Learning (ICML)*, pages 591–598, California, CA.

Ryan McDonald and Joakim Nivre. 2007. Characterizing errors of data-driven dependency parsing models. In *Proceedings of the Conference Empirical Methods in Natural Language Processing and Computational Natural Language Learning (EMNLP-CoNLL)*, pages 122–131, Prague.

Ryan McDonald, Koby Crammer, and Fernando Pereira. 2006a. Online large-margin training of dependency parsers. In *Proceedings of the 43th Annual Meeting of the Association for Computational Linguistics (ACL)*.

Ryan McDonald, Kevin Lerman, and Fernando Pereira. 2006b. Multilingual dependency analysis with a two-stage discriminative parser. In *Proceedings of the 10th Conference on Computational Natural Language Learning (CONLL)*, New York, NY.

Joakim Nivre, Johan Hall, Jens Nilsson, Gülşen Eryiğit, and Svetoslav Marinov. 2006. Labeled pseudo-projective dependency parsing with support vector machines. In *Proceedings of the 10th Conference on Computational Natural Language Learning (CoNLL)*, pages 221–225, New York, NY.

Joakim Nivre, Johan Hall, Jens Nilsson, Atanas Chanev, Gülşen Eryiğit, Sandra Kübler, Stetoslav Marinov, and Erwin Marsi. 2007. Maltparser: A language-independent system for data-driven dependency parsing. *Natural Langauge Engineering Journal*, 2:99–135.

Kemal Oflazer, Bilge Say, Deniz Z. Hakkani-Tr, and Gökhan Tür, 2003. *Building a Turkish Treebank*, pages 261–277. Kluwer.

Kemal Oflazer. 2003. Dependency parsing with an extended finite-state approach. *Computational Linguistics*, 29:515–544.

Lance A. Ramshaw and Mitchell P. Marcus. 1995. Text chunking using transformation-based learning. In *Proceedings of the Third ACL Workshop on Very Large Corpora*, pages 88–94, Cambridge, Massachusetts.

Experiments for Dependency Parsing of Greek

Prokopis Prokopidis
Institute for Language
and Speech Processing
Athena Research Center
Athens, Greece
prokopis@ilsp.gr

Haris Papageorgiou
Institute for Language
and Speech Processing
Athena Research Center
Athens, Greece
xaris@ilsp.gr

Abstract

This paper describes experiments for statistical dependency parsing using two different parsers trained on a recently extended dependency treebank for Greek, a language with a moderately rich morphology. We show how scores obtained by the two parsers are influenced by morphology and dependency types as well as sentence and arc length. The best LAS obtained in these experiments was 80.16 on a test set with manually validated POS tags and lemmas.

1 Introduction

This work describes experiments for statistical dependency parsing using a recently extended dependency treebank for Greek, a language with a moderately rich morphology. Relatively small training resources like the one we use here can set severe sparsity obstacles for languages with flexible word order and a relatively rich morphology like Greek. This work presents ongoing efforts for evaluating ways of improving this situation. The rest of this paper is structured as follows: We describe the treebank and the tools for preprocessing it in section 2. After mentioning some relevant work, we present in section 4 different settings for experiments involving manually validated and automatically pre-processed data for morphology and lemmas. In section 5 we include a comparison of the output of two well-known statistical parsers in reference to a set of criteria. Section 6 describes work on using sentences from relatively large auto-parsed resources as additional training data.

2 Treebank

We use the Greek Dependency Treebank (Prokopidis et al., 2005) for all experiments. GDT includes texts from open-content sources and from corpora collected in the framework of research projects aiming at multilingual, multimedia information extraction. A first version of the GDT (GDT-2007) contained 70223 tokens and 2902 sentences, and it was used in the CoNLL 2007 Shared Task on Dependency Parsing (Nivre et al., 2007a). A recently extended version of the resource (henceforth GDT-2014) amounts to 130753 tokens (including punctuation) and 5668 sentences. The current version of the resource contains 21827 unique types, 11005 lemmas and 10348 hapax legomena (excluding dates, digits and proper names). The average sentence length is 23.07 tokens. GDT consists of 249 whole documents and can thus be used for the annotation of other, possibly inter-sentential, relations like coreference. Each document has 22.76 sentences on average.

The dependency-based annotation scheme used for the syntactic layer of the GDT is based on an adaptation of the guidelines for the Prague Dependency Treebank (Böhmová et al., 2003), and allows for intuitive representations of long-distance dependencies and non-configurational structures common in languages with flexible word order. Most trees are headed by a word that bears the `Pred` relation to an artificial root node. Other tokens depending on this root node include sentence-final punctuation marks

First Joint Workshop on Statistical Parsing of Morphologically Rich Languages and Syntactic Analysis of Non-Canonical Languages, pages 90–96 Dublin, Ireland, August 23-29 2014.

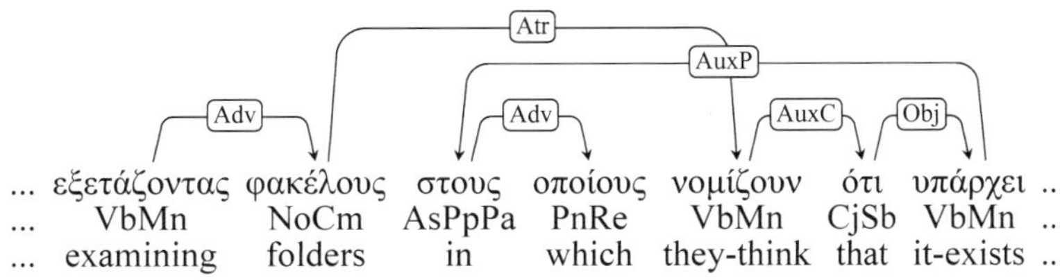

Figure 1: An analysis for a sentence fragment with a non-projective arc

and coordinating conjunctions. Coordinating conjunctions and apposition markers head participating tokens in relevant constructions. Table 1 contains some of the most common dependency relations used in the treebank, while Figure 1 presents a sentence fragment that contains a non-projective arc connecting the verb of a complement clause and its extraposed argument. In GDT-2014, 12.86% of the trees include at least one non-projective arc.

The relatively free word order of Greek can be inferred when examining typical head-dependent structures in the resource. Although nouns are almost always preceded by determiners and adjectives, the situation is different for arguments of verbs. Of the 5414 explicit subjects in GDT, 31% occur to the right of their parent. The situation is more straightforward for non-pronominal objects, of which only 4% occur to the left of their head. Of those subjects and objects appearing in "non-canonical" positions, 21% and 31%, respectively, are of neuter gender. This fact can pose problems to parsing, since the case of nominative and accusative neuter homographs is particularly difficult to disambiguate, especially due to the fact that articles and adjectives often preceding them (e.g. *το/the κόκκινο/red βιβλίο/book*) are also invariant for these two case values.

Dep. Rel	**Description**	**Dep. Rel.**	**Description**
Pred	Main sentence predicate	Adv	Adverbial dependent
Subj	Subject	Atr	Attribute
Obj	Direct object	Coord	A node governing coordination
AuxC	Subord. conjunction node	AuxP	Prepositional node

Table 1: Common dependency relations in the Greek Dependency Treebank

Apart from the addition of new material, another difference from previous versions is that GDT-2014 sentences have been manually validated for POS, morphosyntactic features and lemmas. The tagset used contains 584 combinations of basic POS tags (Table 2) and features that capture the rich morphology of the Greek language. As an example, the full tag `AjBaMaSgNm` for a word like *ταραχώδης/turbulent* denotes an adjective of basic degree, masculine gender, singular number and nominative case. The three last features are also used for nouns, articles, pronouns, and passive participles. Verb tags include features for tense and aspect, while articles are distinguished for definiteness.

Manual annotation at these levels allows to examine how the parser's accuracy is affected in realistic, automatic pre-processing scenarios. In these settings, POS tagging is conducted with a tagger (Papageorgiou et al., 2000) trained on a manually annotated corpus of Greek texts amounting to 455K tokens. During automatic processing, the tagger assigns to each token the most frequent tag in a lexicon compiled from the training corpus. A list of suffixes guides initial tagging of unknown words. When all tokens have been assigned a tag, a set of about 800 contextual rules learned during training, is applied to correct initial decisions. The tagger's accuracy reaches 97.49 when only basic POS is considered. When all features (including, for example, gender and case for nouns, and aspect and tense for verbs) are taken into account, the tagger's accuracy drops to 92.54. As an indication of the relatively rich morphology of Greek, the tags/word ratio in the tagger's lexicon is 1.82. Tags for a word typically differ in only one or two features like case and gender for adjectives. However, distinct basic parts of speech (e.g. `Vb/No`) is also a possibility.

Following POS tagging, a lemmatizer retrieves lemmas from a lexicon containing 66K lemmas, which in their expanded form extend the lexicon to approximately 2M different entries. When a token under examination is associated in the lexicon with two or more lemmas, the lemmatizer uses information from the POS tags to disambiguate. For example, the token+POS input *εξετάσεις*/VbMn guides the lemmatizer to retrieve the lemma *εξετάζω (examine)*, while the lemma *εξέταση (examination)* is returned for *εξετάσεις*/NoCm.

POS	Description	POS	Description
Ad	Adverb	AsPpPa	Prep. + Article combination
AjBa	Adjective (basic degree)	CjCo	Coordinating conjunction
AsPpSp	Preposition	CjSb	Subordinating conjunction
AtDf	Definite article	NoCm	Common noun
AtId	Indefinite article	PnPo	Possessive pronoun
VbMn	Finite verb	PnRe	Relative pronoun

Table 2: Fine grained POS tags in GDT

3 Relevant work

Nakagawa (2007) was the best system in parsing the GDT in the CoNLL 2007 shared task, showing a 76.31 Labeled Attachment Score. Nakagawa's two-stage parser first constructed unlabeled dependency structures using sentence and token features, and then labeled the arcs using SVMs. The second best score for Greek was Hall et al. (2007), who scored 74.65 LAS using an ensemble system combining the output of six different Maltparser configurations. In recent work discussing the cube-pruned dependency parsing framework, Zhang and McDonald (2014) report a 78.45 LAS on the CoNLL dataset.

4 Experiments

In this section, we report on experiments using statistical parsers trained on automatically preprocessed and manually validated versions of GDT-2014. In all experiments we report the Labeled and Unlabeled Attachment Scores (LAS and UAS) and the Label Accuracy (LACC), with punctuation tokens counting as scoring tokens. We split the data of GDT-2014 in 90% and 10% training and test sets (5,101/567 sentences; 117,581/13,172 tokens). In this partitioning scheme, unknown tokens and lemmas when parsing the test set are 27% and 16%, respectively. We performed experiments with the transition-based Maltparser (Nivre et al., 2007b) and the graph-based Mateparser (Bohnet, 2010). For Maltparser, a 5-fold cross validation on the training set using MaltOptimizer (Ballesteros and Nivre, 2012) resulted in the selection of the non-projective stacklazy parsing algorithm as the one yielding an average best 78.96 LAS. Table 3 provides an abbreviated overview of the selected feature model, which is dominated by the top and first three elements in the parser's stack and its lookahead list. For Mateparser we used default settings.

Table 4 summarizes the results of our experiments. We observe a better 79.74 LAS with Mateparser with a larger difference in UAS than in LACC (2.37 vs 1.26). This may suggest that the two parsers agree on the labels they assign but differ more in discovering node heads. Not surprisingly, testing in a more realistic scenario of using automatic PoS, features and lemmas produces more errors (Figure 2). Maltparser shows a relatively smaller decrease in accuracy (-3.05 vs -3.45) in this context. In the next two experiments with Mateparser, we see that in automatic pre-processing scenarios, the tagger clearly contributes more to error increase (-3.34) compared to the lemmatizer (-0.06).

We also trained Mateparser in the MPL setting with POS tagsets of varying granularity, by removing features that were intuitively deemed to increase sparsity without contributing to parsing accuracy. More specifically, we experimented with several combinations of removing for aspect and tense of verbs, gender of nominal elements, definiteness of articles and degree of adjectives. A best LAS of 80.16 (cf. the two final columns of Table 4) was observed after removing features for degree and definiteness. Finally, and in order to examine how the expansion of the treebank has affected performance, we also

Tokens	Form	Lem	PoS	Feats	Dep	Tokens	Form	Lem	PoS	Feats	Dep
st[0]	+	+	+	+		rd(st[0])			+		+
st[1]	+	+	+	+		rd(st[1])					+
st[2]	+		+			hd(st[0])	+				
inp[0]			+			lh[0]	+		+	+	
ld(st[0])			+		+	lh[1]	+		+	+	
ld(st[1])					+	lh[2]			+		

Table 3: Automatically selected Maltparser features. Stack/Input (st/inp) tokens refer to tokens that are/have been in the stack of partially parsed tokens. Lookahead (lh) tokens are tokens that have not been in the stack. Features ld/rd/hd refer to the leftmost/rightmost dependents and and the head. We do not show features resulting from merging two or three features (e.g. merge3(PoS(lh[0]) + PoS(lh[1]) + PoS(lh[2])))

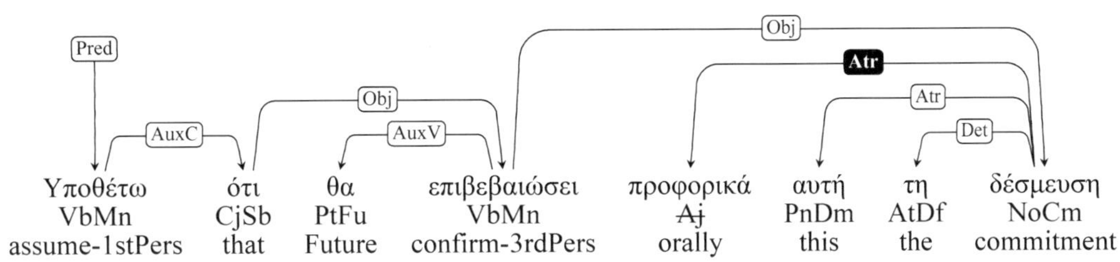

Figure 2: An example of a preprocessing error misguiding the parser: the wrong adjectival tag for the adverb *προφορικά* leads the parser in recognizing it as an attribute to a noun.

trained Mateparser in the MPL scenario using a training set equal in size to the 2.7K sentences of the CoNLL-2007 data. The results observed were 78.39 LAS and 84.77 UAS.

	MPL		APL		APML	MPAL	APL-AUTO		MFR1	MFR2
	Malt	Mate	Malt	Mate	Mate		Malt	Mate	Mate	
LAS	77.50	79.74	74.45	76.29	76.40	79.68	75.13	76.81	80.05	**80.16**
UAS	83.46	85.83	81.35	83.57	83.69	85.77	81.98	83.94	86.02	**86.29**
LACC	86.68	87.94	84.29	85.67	85.72	87.91	84.92	85.90	88.03	**88.13**

Table 4: Results from parsing GDT with Malt and Mate parsers: MPL refers to training and testing on manually validated POS, morphological features and lemmas; APL is evaluation on automatic POS, features and lemmas; APML is evaluation on automatic morphology and gold lemmas; MPAL on gold morphology and automatic lemmas. APL-AUTO is APL with training data including automatically parsed sentences. MFR1 is MPL after removing features for tense, aspect, degree and definiteness. MFR2 is MPL after removing features for degree and definiteness.

5 Error analysis

In this section we first provide a comparative analysis of errors by the two parsers on the 567 sentences test set. We use the set of length and linguistic factors proposed in the comparison between the Malt and MST parsers in McDonald and Nivre (2007). For example, in Figure 3, we plot sentence length in bins of size 10 and show, as expected, that the accuracy of both parsers decreases when analyzing longer sentences. Maltparser shows a higher accuracy for sentences of size up to 10, possibly because when parsing shorter sentences, early mistakes when making greedy decisions based on local features do not have a chance to lead to large error propagation. We omit details on UAS, where a similar pattern is observed. Figure 4 shows that Mateparser achieves better harmonic means of precision and recall, when longer dependencies are examined. This is again consistent with the fact that Maltparser favors shorter

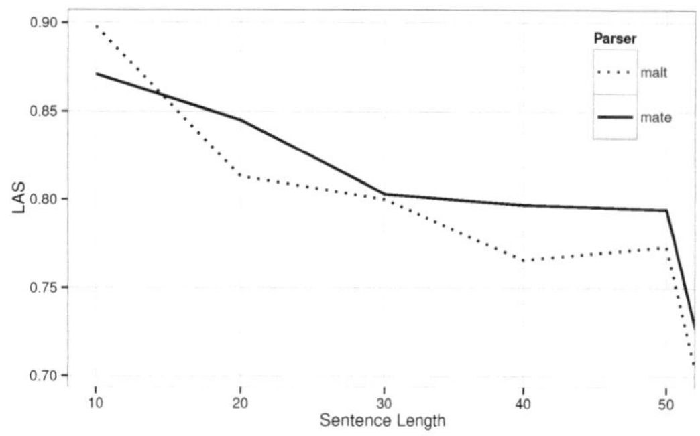

Figure 3: LAS relative to sentence length.

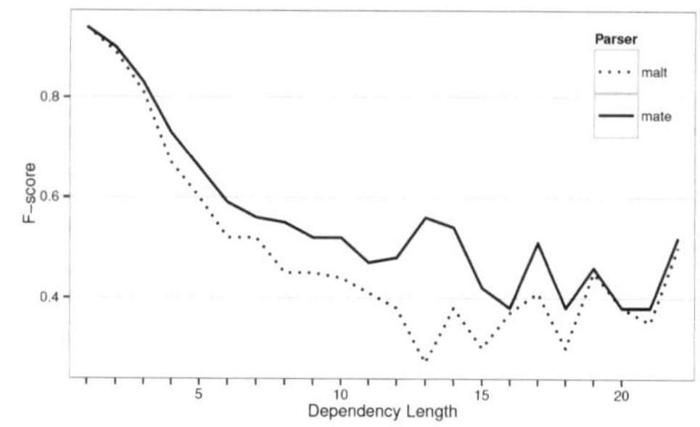

Figure 4: Dependency arc F-score relative to dependency length.

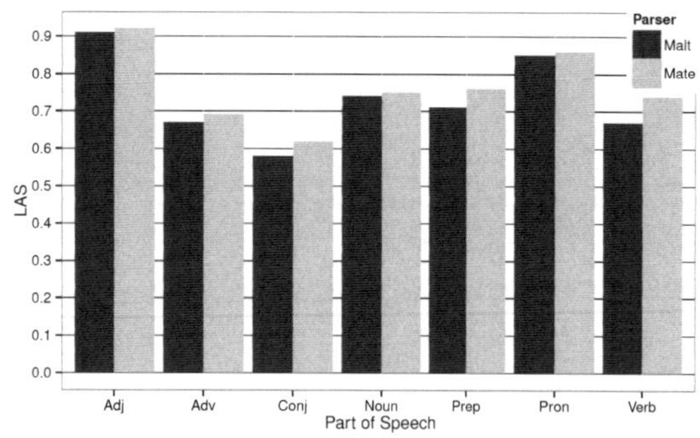

Figure 5: LAS for different POS tags.

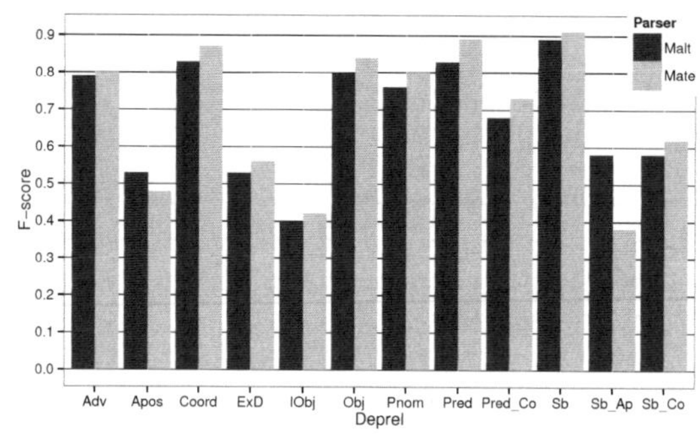

Figure 6: F-score for different relations.

arcs when making decisions based on local features only. We have seen that both parsers exhibit low F1-scores (Malt: 0.36; Mate: 0.30) in detecting non-projective heads.

In Figure 5 we see that Mate's LAS is better for all basic parts of speech. The difference is more evident for verbs, which are typically involved in longer dependencies. Finally, it is clear from Figure 6 that certain relations are particularly difficult for both parsers. For example, indirect object (`IObj`) dependents are low scoring nodes: this is because they are often attached to the correct head but are mislabeled as adverbial dependents (`Adv`) or plain objects (`Obj`). Dependents labeled as ellipsis (`ExD`) or heading appositional (`Apos`) constructions are also more error-prone. The same applies to nodes involved in coordinate structures as subjects headed by coordinative conjuctions (`Sb_Co`). The latter show an almost 0.3 drop in F1-score in comparison to simple subjects (`Sb`).

In the APL setting, errors by both parsers often involve some type of interaction between the relatively free order of Greek sentences and the case feature of nominal homographs. For example, in the case of the sentence *Διαφορετικά/different στοιχεία/figures δίνουν/provide τρεις/three επίσημες/official πηγές/sources για/on την/the ανεργία/unemployment (Three official sources provide different figures on unemployment)*, the two nominal arguments of the verb and all of their modifiers are ambiguous as far as case (Nominative/Accusative) is concerned. Both nominal arguments also agree with the verb in number. These facts, in combination with the OVS order of this and similar fragments present serious challenges to both the tagger and the parsers. In contrast, the case of the noun *ανεργία/unemployment* is easier for the tagger to disambiguate based on the preposition+article combination preceding it. However, attaching the whole subtree headed by the preposition is also problematic: it is part of a non-projective construction that would probably be disallowed in languages with a more strict order.

6 Use of autoparsed data

Following recent efforts in exploiting automatically processed data in training (Chen et al., 2012) and in accelerating treebank creation (Lynn et al., 2012), we conducted an experiment in extending the training set with similar material. We used a corpus of 66 million tokens, obtained by crawling (Papavassiliou et al., 2013) the 2009-2012 online archive of a Greek daily newspaper. We used models induced in the MPL experiment to parse all documents in the data pool with both parsers. We then appended to the original training set 30K randomly selected parsed sentences of 10 to 30 tokens length, for which identical trees were generated by both parsers. After retraining both parsers and testing on the APL test set, we observed (columns 8 and 9 of table 4) absolute LAS improvements of 0.68 and 0.52 for Maltparser and Mateparser.

7 Conclusions and future work

We described a set of experiments for dependency parsing of Greek using Maltparser and Mateparser, two well known representatives of the transition and graph-based families of parsers. Mateparser has exhibited the best accuracy on the test partition of a recently expanded version of the Greek Dependency Treebank, with Maltparser yielding higher scores on shorter sentences. After appending auto-parsed data to a training set manually validated for POS and lemmas, we observed small accuracy improvements that show room for improvement.

Scores obtained by training on datasets of different sizes in Section 4 probably indicate that apart from adding only documents or document fragments to the treebank, we should also consider selecting specific sentences for annotation, after measuring their informativeness and representativeness. In ongoing work, we are investigating ways of selecting sentences for manual annotation based on how much two or more parsers disagree, in combination with criteria like number of coordination/subordination elements and/or number of OOV words. For this purpose, we will also experiment with more members of the two parser families.

Our best LAS scores were obtained after mapping certain morphological features to default values. Since these tagset mappings may not be the most efficient ones, we plan to investigate automatic techniques for selecting optimal feature combinations.

Another line of research will be investigating semi-automatically mapping to different annotation schemes like the one proposed in McDonald et al. (2013). Finally, we plan to examine, as an additional source for resource expansion and domain adaptation, sentences from automatic dialogue transcriptions and/or product reviews.

Acknowledgments

Work by the first author was supported by the European Union Abu-MaTran project (FP7-People-IAPP, Grant 324414). Work by the second author was supported by the POLYTROPON project (KRIPIS-GSRT, MIS: 448306). We would like to thank the three anonymous reviewers and our colleague Vassilis Papavassiliou for their comments.

References

Miguel Ballesteros and Joakim Nivre. 2012. MaltOptimizer: An Optimization Tool for MaltParser. In *EACL*, pages 58–62.

Alena Böhmová, Jan Hajič, Eva Hajičová, and Barbora Hladká, 2003. *Treebanks: Building and Using Parsed Corpora*, chapter The Prague Dependency Treebank: A Three-Level Annotation Scenario. Kluwer.

Bernd Bohnet. 2010. Very High Accuracy and Fast Dependency Parsing is Not a Contradiction. In *Proceedings of the 23rd International Conference on Computational Linguistics*, COLING '10, pages 89–97. Association for Computational Linguistics.

Wenliang Chen, Jun'ichi Kazama, Kiyotaka Uchimoto, and Kentaro Torisawa. 2012. Exploiting subtrees in auto-parsed data to improve dependency parsing. *Computational Intelligence*, pages 426–451.

Johan Hall, Jens Nilsson, Joakim Nivre, Gülsen Eryigit, Beáta Megyesi, Mattias Nilsson, and Markus Saers. 2007. Single Malt or Blended? A Study in Multilingual Parser Optimization. In *Proceedings of the CoNLL Shared Task Session of EMNLP-CoNLL 2007*, pages 933–939.

Teresa Lynn, Jennifer Foster, Mark Dras, and Elaine Dhonnchadha. 2012. Active Learning and the Irish Treebank. In *Australasian Language Technology Workshop*, December.

Ryan McDonald and Joakim Nivre. 2007. Characterizing the Errors of Data-Driven Dependency Parsing Models. In *Proceedings of the 2007 Joint Conference on Empirical Methods in Natural Language Processing and Computational Natural Language Learning (EMNLP-CoNLL)*, pages 122–131.

Ryan McDonald, Joakim Nivre, Yvonne Quirmbach-Brundage, Yoav Goldberg, Dipanjan Das, Kuzman Ganchev, Keith Hall, Slav Petrov, Hao Zhang, Oscar Täckström, Claudia Bedini, Núria Bertomeu Castelló, and Jungmee Lee. 2013. Universal Dependency Annotation for Multilingual Parsing. In *Proceedings of the 51st Annual Meeting of the Association for Computational Linguistics (Volume 2: Short Papers)*, pages 92–97, Sofia, Bulgaria.

Tetsuji Nakagawa. 2007. Multilingual Dependency Parsing Using Global Features. In *Proceedings of the CoNLL Shared Task Session of EMNLP-CoNLL 2007*, pages 952–956.

Joakim Nivre, Johan Hall, Sandra Kübler, Ryan McDonald, Jens Nilsson, Sebastian Riedel, and Deniz Yuret. 2007a. The CoNLL 2007 Shared Task on Dependency Parsing. In *Proceedings of the CoNLL Shared Task Session of EMNLP-CoNLL 2007*, pages 915–932.

Joakim Nivre, Johan Hall, Jens Nilsson, Atanas Chanev, Gülsen Erygit, Sandra Kübler, Svetoslav Marinov, and Erwin Marsi. 2007b. MaltParser: A language-independent system for data-driven dependency parsing. *Natural Language Engineering*, 13:95–135, 6.

Harris Papageorgiou, Prokopis Prokopidis, Voula Giouli, and Stelios Piperidis. 2000. A Unified POS Tagging Architecture and its Application to Greek. In *Proceedings of the 2nd Language Resources and Evaluation Conference*, pages 1455–1462, Athens, June. European Language Resources Association.

Vassilis Papavassiliou, Prokopis Prokopidis, and Gregor Thurmair. 2013. A modular open-source focused crawler for mining monolingual and bilingual corpora from the web. In *Proceedings of the Sixth Workshop on Building and Using Comparable Corpora*, pages 43–51, Sofia, Bulgaria, August. Association for Computational Linguistics.

Prokopis Prokopidis, Elina Desypri, Maria Koutsombogera, Haris Papageorgiou, and Stelios Piperidis. 2005. Theoretical and practical issues in the construction of a Greek Dependency Treebank. In *Proceedings of the Fourth Workshop on Treebanks and Linguistic Theories*, Barcelona, Spain, December.

Hao Zhang and Ryan McDonald. 2014. Enforcing Structural Diversity in Cube-pruned Dependency Parsing. In *ACL*.

Introducing the IMS-Wrocław-Szeged-CIS Entry at the SPMRL 2014 Shared Task: Reranking and Morphosyntax Meet Unlabeled Data*

Anders Björkelund[§] and **Özlem Çetinoğlu**[§] and **Agnieszka Faleńska**[◇,§]

Richárd Farkas[†] and **Thomas Müller**[‡] and **Wolfgang Seeker**[§] and **Zsolt Szántó**[†]

[§]Institute for Natural Language Processing University of Stuttgart, Germany
[◇]Institute of Computer Science, University of Wrocław, Poland
[†]Department of Informatics University of Szeged, Hungary
[‡]Center for Information and Language Processing University of Munich, Germany

{anders,ozlem,muellets,seeker}@ims.uni-stuttgart.de
agnieszka.falenska@cs.uni.wroc.pl
{rfarkas,szantozs}@inf.u-szeged.hu

Abstract

We summarize our approach taken in the SPMRL 2014 Shared Task on parsing morphologically rich languages. Our approach builds upon our contribution from last year, with a number of modifications and extensions. Though this paper summarizes our contribution, a more detailed description and evaluation will be presented in the accompanying volume containing notes from the SPMRL 2014 Shared Task.

1 Introduction

This paper summarizes the approach of IMS-Wrocław-Szeged-CIS taken for the SPMRL 2014 Shared Task on parsing morphologically rich languages (Seddah et al., 2014). Since this paper is a rough summary that is written before submission of test runs we refer the reader to the full description paper which will be published after the shared task (Björkelund et al., 2014).[1]

The SPMRL 2014 Shared Task is a direct extension of the SPMRL 2013 Shared Task (Seddah et al., 2013) which targeted parsing morphologically rich languages. The task involves parsing both dependency and phrase-structure representations of 9 languages: Arabic, Basque, French, German, Hebrew, Hungarian, Korean, Polish, and Swedish. The only difference between the two tasks is that large amounts of unlabeled data are additionally available to participants for the 2014 task.

Our contribution builds upon our system from last year (Björkelund et al., 2013), with additional features and components that try to exploit the unlabeled data. Given the limited window of time to participate in this year's shared task, we only contribute to the setting with predicted preprocessing, using the largest available training data set for each language.[2] We also do not participate in the Arabic track since the shared task organizers did not provide any unlabeled data at a reasonable time.

2 Review of Last Year's System

Our current system is based on the system we participated with in the SPMRL 2013 Shared Task. We summarize the architecture of this system as three different components.

*Authors in alphabetical order

[1]Due to logistical constraints this paper had to be written before the deadlines for the actual shared task and do thus not contain a full description of the system, nor the experimental evaluation of the same.

[2]In other words, no gold preprocessing or smaller training sets.

First Joint Workshop on Statistical Parsing of Morphologically Rich Languages and Syntactic Analysis of Non-Canonical Languages, pages 97–102 Dublin, Ireland, August 23-29 2014.

2.1 Preprocessing

As the initial step of preprocessing we converted the Shared Task data from the CoNLL06 format to CoNLL09, which required a decision on using coarse or fine grained POS tags. After a set of preliminary experiments we picked fine POS tags where possible, except Basque and Korean.

We used MarMoT[3] (Müller et al., 2013) to predict POS tags and morphological features jointly. We integrated the output from external morphological analyzers as features to MarMoT. We also experimented with the integration of predicted tags provided by the organizers and observed that these *stacked* models help improve Basque, Polish, and Swedish preprocessing. The stacked models provided additional information to our tagger since the provided predictions were coming from models trained on larger training sets than the shared task training sets.

2.2 Dependency Parsing

The dependency parsing architecture of our SPMRL 2013 Shared Task contribution is summarized in Figure 1. The first step combines the n-best trees of two parsers, namely the mate parser[4] (Bohnet, 2010) and a variant of the EasyFirst parser (Goldberg and Elhadad, 2010), which we call best-first parser. We merged the 50-best analyses from these parsers into one n-best list of 50 to 100 trees. We then added parsing scores to the n-best trees from the two parsers, and additionally from the turboparser[5] (Martins et al., 2010).

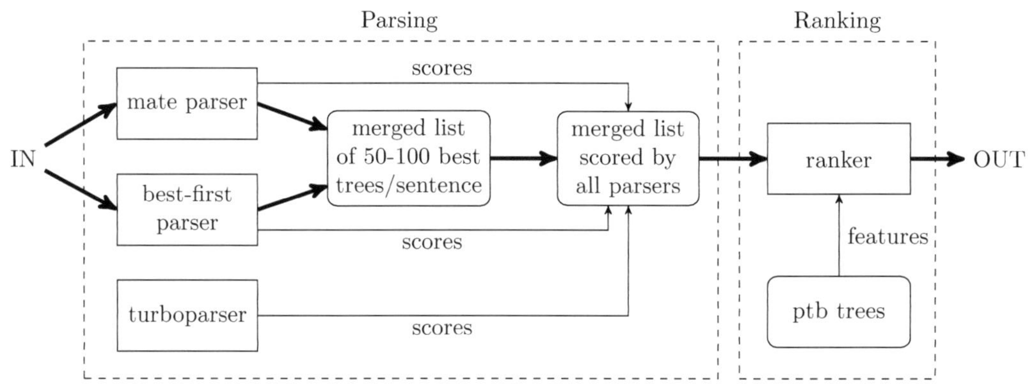

Figure 1: Architecture of the dependency ranking system from (Björkelund et al., 2013).

The scored trees are fed into the ranking system. The ranker utilizes the parsing scores and features coming from both constituency and dependency parses. We specified a default feature set and experimented with additional features for each language for optimal results. We achieved over 1% LAS improvement on all languages except a 0.3% improvement on Hungarian.

2.3 Constituency Parsing

The constituency parsing architecture advances in three steps. For all setups we removed the morphological annotation of POS tags and the function labels of non-terminals and apply the Berkeley Parser (Petrov et al., 2006) as our baseline. As the first setup, we replaced words with a frequency < 20 with their predicted part-of-speech and morphology tags and improved the PARSEVAL scores across languages. The second setup employed a product grammar (Petrov, 2010), where we combined 8 different grammars trained on the same data but with different initialization setups. As a result, the scores substantially improved on all languages.

Finally, we conducted ranking experiments on the 50-best outputs of the product grammars. We used a slightly modified version of the Mallet toolkit (McCallum, 2002), where the reranker is trained for the

[3] `https://code.google.com/p/cistern/`
[4] `https://code.google.com/p/mate-tools`
[5] `http://www.ark.cs.cmu.edu/TurboParser/`

maximum entropy objective function of Charniak and Johnson (2005) and uses the standard feature set from Charniak and Johnson (2005) and Collins (2000). Hebrew and Polish scores remained almost the same, whereas Basque, French, and Hungarian highly benefited from reranking.

3 Planned Additions to Last Year's System

This year we extend our systems for both the constituency and dependency tracks to add additional information and try to profit from unlabeled data.

3.1 Preprocessing

We use the mate-tools' lemmatizer and MarMoT to preprocess all labeled and unlabeled data. From the SPMRL 2013 Shared Task, we learned that getting as good preprocessing as possible is an important part of the overall improvements. Preprocessing consists of predicting lemmas, part-of-speech, and morphological features. Preprocessing for the training data is done via 5-fold jackknifing to produce realistic input features for the parsers. This year we do not do stacking on top of provided morphological analyses since the annotations on the labeled and unlabeled data were inconsistent for some languages.[6]

3.2 Dependency Parsing

We pursue two different ways of integrating additional information into our system from the SPMRL 2013 Shared Task (Björkelund et al., 2013): **supertags** and **co-training**.

Supertags (Bangalore and Joshi, 1999) are tags that encode more syntactic information than standard part-of-speech tags. Supertags have been used in deep grammar formalisms like CCG or HPSG to prune the search space for the parser. The idea has been applied to dependency parsing by Foth et al. (2006) and recently to statistical dependency parsing (Ouchi et al., 2014; Ambati et al., 2014), where supertags are used as features rather than to prune the search space. Since the supertag set is dynamically derived from the gold-standard syntactic structures, we can encode different kinds of information into a supertag, in particular also morphological information. Supertags are predicted before parsing using MarMoT and are then used as features in the mate parser and the turboparser.

We will use a variant of **co-training** (Blum and Mitchell, 1998) by applying two different parsers to select additional training material from unlabeled data. We use the mate parser and the turboparser to parse the unlabeled data provided by the organizers. We then select sentences where both parsers agree on the structure as additional training examples following Sagae and Tsujii (2007). We then train two more models: one on the labeled training data and the unlabeled data selected by the two parsers, and one only on the unlabeled data. These two models are then integrated into our parsing system from 2013 as additional scorers to score the n-best list. Their scores are used as features in the ranker.

Before we parse the unlabeled data to obtain the training sentences, we filter it in order to arrive at a cleaner corpus. Most importantly, we only keep sentences up to length 50, and which contain at maximum two unknown words (compared to the labeled training data).

3.3 Constituency Parsing

We experiment with two approaches for improving constituency parsing:

Preterminal labelsets play an important role in constituency parsing of morphologically rich languages (Dehdari et al., 2011). Instead of removing the morphological annotation of POS tags, we use a preterminal set which carries more linguistic information while still keeping it compact. We follow the merge procedure for morphological feature values of Szántó and Farkas (2014). This procedure outputs a clustering of full morphological descriptions and we use the cluster IDs as preterminal labels for training the Berkeley Parser.

Reranking at the constituency parsing side is enriched by novel features. We define feature templates exploiting co-occurrence statistics from the unlabeled datasets; automatic dependency parses of the sentence in question (Farkas and Bohnet, 2012); Brown clusters (Brown et al., 1992); and atomic morphological feature values (Szántó and Farkas, 2014).

[6]The organizers later resolved this issue by patching the data, although time constraints prevented us from using the patched data.

4 Conclusion

This paper describes our plans for the SPMRL 2014 Shared Task, most of which are yet to be implemented. For the actual system description and our results, we refer the interested reader to (Björkelund et al., 2014) and (Seddah et al., 2014).

Acknowledgements

Agnieszka Faleńska is funded through the Project International computer science and applied mathematics for business study programme at the University of Wrocław co-financed with European Union funds within the European Social Fund No. POKL.04.01.01-00-005/13. Richárd Farkas and Zsolt Szántó are funded by the European Union and the European Social Fund through the project FuturICT.hu (grant no.: TÁMOP-4.2.2.C-11/1/KONV-2012-0013). Thomas Müller is supported by a Google Europe Fellowship in Natural Language Processing. The remaining authors are funded by the Deutsche Forschungsgemeinschaft (DFG) via the SFB 732, projects D2 and D8 (PI: Jonas Kuhn).

We also express our gratitude to the treebank providers for each language: Arabic (Maamouri et al., 2004; Habash and Roth, 2009; Habash et al., 2009; Green and Manning, 2010), Basque (Aduriz et al., 2003), French (Abeillé et al., 2003), Hebrew (Sima'an et al., 2001; Tsarfaty, 2010; Goldberg, 2011; Tsarfaty, 2013), German (Brants et al., 2002; Seeker and Kuhn, 2012), Hungarian (Csendes et al., 2005; Vincze et al., 2010), Korean (Choi et al., 1994; Choi, 2013), Polish (Świdziński and Woliński, 2010), and Swedish (Nivre et al., 2006).

References

Anne Abeillé, Lionel Clément, and François Toussenel. 2003. Building a treebank for french. In Anne Abeillé, editor, *Treebanks*. Kluwer, Dordrecht.

I. Aduriz, M. J. Aranzabe, J. M. Arriola, A. Atutxa, A. Díaz de Ilarraza, A. Garmendia, and M. Oronoz. 2003. Construction of a Basque dependency treebank. In *TLT-03*, pages 201–204.

Bharat Ram Ambati, Tejaswini Deoskar, and Mark Steedman. 2014. Improving dependency parsers using combinatory categorial grammar. In *Proceedings of the 14th Conference of the European Chapter of the Association for Computational Linguistics, volume 2: Short Papers*, pages 159–163, Gothenburg, Sweden, April. Association for Computational Linguistics.

Srinivas Bangalore and Aravind K. Joshi. 1999. Supertagging: An approach to almost parsing. *Computational Linguistics*, 25(2):237–265.

Anders Björkelund, Özlem Çetinoğlu, Richárd Farkas, Thomas Müller, and Wolfgang Seeker. 2013. (re)ranking meets morphosyntax: State-of-the-art results from the SPMRL 2013 shared task. In *Proceedings of the Fourth Workshop on Statistical Parsing of Morphologically-Rich Languages*, pages 135–145, Seattle, Washington, USA, October. Association for Computational Linguistics.

Anders Björkelund, Özlem Çetinoğlu, Agnieszka Faleńska, Richárd Farkas, Thomas Müller, Wolfgang Seeker, and Zsolt Szántó. 2014. The IMS-Wrocław-Szeged-CIS entry at the SPMRL 2014 Shared Task: Reranking and Morphosyntax meet Unlabeled Data. In *Notes of the SPMRL 2014 Shared Task on Parsing Morphologically-Rich Languages*, Dublin, Ireland, August.

Avrim Blum and Tom Mitchell. 1998. Combining labeled and unlabeled data with co-training. In *Proceedings of the Eleventh Annual Conference on Computational Learning Theory*, COLT' 98, pages 92–100, New York, NY, USA. ACM.

Bernd Bohnet. 2010. Top Accuracy and Fast Dependency Parsing is not a Contradiction. In *Proceedings of the 23rd International Conference on Computational Linguistics (Coling 2010)*, pages 89–97, Beijing, China, August. Coling 2010 Organizing Committee.

Sabine Brants, Stefanie Dipper, Silvia Hansen, Wolfgang Lezius, and George Smith. 2002. The TIGER treebank. In Erhard Hinrichs and Kiril Simov, editors, *Proceedings of the First Workshop on Treebanks and Linguistic Theories (TLT 2002)*, pages 24–41, Sozopol, Bulgaria.

Peter F. Brown, Vincent J. Della Pietra, Peter V. deSouza, Jenifer C. Lai, and Robert L. Mercer. 1992. Class-based n-gram models of natural language. *Computational Linguistics*, 18(4):467–479.

Eugene Charniak and Mark Johnson. 2005. Coarse-to-fine n-best parsing and MaxEnt discriminative reranking. In *Proceedings of the 43rd Annual Meeting on Association for Computational Linguistics*, ACL '05, pages 173–180.

Key-Sun Choi, Young S Han, Young G Han, and Oh W Kwon. 1994. Kaist tree bank project for korean: Present and future development. In *Proceedings of the International Workshop on Sharable Natural Language Resources*, pages 7–14. Citeseer.

Jinho D. Choi. 2013. Preparing korean data for the shared task on parsing morphologically rich languages. *CoRR*, abs/1309.1649.

Michael Collins. 2000. Discriminative Reranking for Natural Language Parsing. In *Proceedings of the Seventeenth International Conference on Machine Learning*, ICML '00, pages 175–182.

Dóra Csendes, János Csirik, Tibor Gyimóthy, and András Kocsor. 2005. The Szeged treebank. In Václav Matoušek, Pavel Mautner, and Tomáš Pavelka, editors, *Text, Speech and Dialogue: Proceedings of TSD 2005*. Springer.

Jon Dehdari, Lamia Tounsi, and Josef van Genabith. 2011. Morphological features for parsing morphologically-rich languages: A case of arabic. In *Proceedings of the Second Workshop on Statistical Parsing of Morphologically Rich Languages*, pages 12–21, Dublin, Ireland, October. Association for Computational Linguistics.

Richárd Farkas and Bernd Bohnet. 2012. Stacking of dependency and phrase structure parsers. In *Proceedings of COLING 2012*, pages 849–866, Mumbai, India, December. The COLING 2012 Organizing Committee.

Kilian A. Foth, Tomas By, and Wolfgang Menzel. 2006. Guiding a constraint dependency parser with supertags. In *Proceedings of the 21st International Conference on Computational Linguistics and 44th Annual Meeting of the Association for Computational Linguistics*, pages 289–296, Sydney, Australia, July. Association for Computational Linguistics.

Yoav Goldberg and Michael Elhadad. 2010. An Efficient Algorithm for Easy-First Non-Directional Dependency Parsing. In *Human Language Technologies: The 2010 Annual Conference of the North American Chapter of the Association for Computational Linguistics*, pages 742–750, Los Angeles, California, June. Association for Computational Linguistics.

Yoav Goldberg. 2011. *Automatic syntactic processing of Modern Hebrew*. Ph.D. thesis, Ben Gurion University of the Negev.

Spence Green and Christopher D. Manning. 2010. Better arabic parsing: Baselines, evaluations, and analysis. In *Proceedings of the 23rd International Conference on Computational Linguistics (Coling 2010)*, pages 394–402, Beijing, China, August. Coling 2010 Organizing Committee.

Nizar Habash and Ryan Roth. 2009. Catib: The columbia arabic treebank. In *Proceedings of the ACL-IJCNLP 2009 Conference Short Papers*, pages 221–224, Suntec, Singapore, August. Association for Computational Linguistics.

Nizar Habash, Reem Faraj, and Ryan Roth. 2009. Syntactic Annotation in the Columbia Arabic Treebank. In *Proceedings of MEDAR International Conference on Arabic Language Resources and Tools*, Cairo, Egypt.

Mohamed Maamouri, Ann Bies, Tim Buckwalter, and Wigdan Mekki. 2004. The Penn Arabic Treebank: Building a Large-Scale Annotated Arabic Corpus. In *NEMLAR Conference on Arabic Language Resources and Tools*.

Andre Martins, Noah Smith, Eric Xing, Pedro Aguiar, and Mario Figueiredo. 2010. Turbo Parsers: Dependency Parsing by Approximate Variational Inference. In *Proceedings of the 2010 Conference on Empirical Methods in Natural Language Processing*, pages 34–44, Cambridge, MA, October. Association for Computational Linguistics.

Andrew Kachites McCallum. 2002. "mallet: A machine learning for language toolkit". http://mallet.cs.umass.edu.

Thomas Müller, Helmut Schmid, and Hinrich Schütze. 2013. Efficient Higher-Order CRFs for Morphological Tagging. In *In Proceedings of EMNLP*.

Joakim Nivre, Jens Nilsson, and Johan Hall. 2006. Talbanken05: A Swedish treebank with phrase structure and dependency annotation. In *Proceedings of LREC*, pages 1392–1395, Genoa, Italy.

Hiroki Ouchi, Kevin Duh, and Yuji Matsumoto. 2014. Improving dependency parsers with supertags. In *Proceedings of the 14th Conference of the European Chapter of the Association for Computational Linguistics, volume 2: Short Papers*, pages 154–158, Gothenburg, Sweden, April. Association for Computational Linguistics.

Slav Petrov, Leon Barrett, Romain Thibaux, and Dan Klein. 2006. Learning accurate, compact, and interpretable tree annotation. In *Proceedings of the 21st International Conference on Computational Linguistics and the 44th annual meeting of the Association for Computational Linguistics*, pages 433–440. Association for Computational Linguistics.

Slav Petrov. 2010. Products of Random Latent Variable Grammars. In *Human Language Technologies: The 2010 Annual Conference of the North American Chapter of the Association for Computational Linguistics*, pages 19–27, Los Angeles, California, June. Association for Computational Linguistics.

Kenji Sagae and Jun'ichi Tsujii. 2007. Dependency parsing and domain adaptation with LR models and parser ensembles. In *Proceedings of the CoNLL Shared Task Session of EMNLP-CoNLL 2007*, pages 1044–1050, Prague, Czech Republic, June. Association for Computational Linguistics.

Djamé Seddah, Reut Tsarfaty, Sandra Kübler, Marie Candito, Jinho D. Choi, Richárd Farkas, Jennifer Foster, Iakes Goenaga, Koldo Gojenola Galletebeitia, Yoav Goldberg, Spence Green, Nizar Habash, Marco Kuhlmann, Wolfgang Maier, Joakim Nivre, Adam Przepiórkowski, Ryan Roth, Wolfgang Seeker, Yannick Versley, Veronika Vincze, Marcin Woliński, Alina Wróblewska, and Eric Villemonte de la Clergerie. 2013. Overview of the SPMRL 2013 shared task: A cross-framework evaluation of parsing morphologically rich languages. In *Proceedings of the Fourth Workshop on Statistical Parsing of Morphologically-Rich Languages*, pages 146–182, Seattle, Washington, USA, October. Association for Computational Linguistics.

Djamé Seddah, Reut Tsarfaty, Sandra Kübler, Marie Candito, Jinho Choi, Matthieu Constant, Richárd Farkas, Iakes Goenaga, Koldo Gojenola, Yoav Goldberg, Spence Green, Nizar Habash, Marco Kuhlmann, Wolfgang Maier, Joakim Nivre, Adam Przepiorkowski, Ryan Roth, Wolfgang Seeker, Yannick Versley, Veronika Vincze, Marcin Woliński, Alina Wróblewska, and Eric Villemonte de la Clérgerie. 2014. Overview of the SPMRL 2014 shared task on parsing morphologically rich languages. In *Notes of the SPMRL 2014 Shared Task on Parsing Morphologically-Rich Languages*, Dublin, Ireland.

Wolfgang Seeker and Jonas Kuhn. 2012. Making Ellipses Explicit in Dependency Conversion for a German Treebank. In *Proceedings of the 8th International Conference on Language Resources and Evaluation*, pages 3132–3139, Istanbul, Turkey. European Language Resources Association (ELRA).

Khalil Sima'an, Alon Itai, Yoad Winter, Alon Altman, and Noa Nativ. 2001. Building a Tree-Bank for Modern Hebrew Text. In *Traitement Automatique des Langues*.

Marek Świdziński and Marcin Woliński. 2010. Towards a bank of constituent parse trees for Polish. In *Text, Speech and Dialogue: 13th International Conference (TSD)*, Lecture Notes in Artificial Intelligence, pages 197—204, Brno, Czech Republic. Springer.

Zsolt Szántó and Richárd Farkas. 2014. Special techniques for constituent parsing of morphologically rich languages. In *Proceedings of the 14th Conference of the European Chapter of the Association for Computational Linguistics*, pages 135–144, Gothenburg, Sweden, April. Association for Computational Linguistics.

Reut Tsarfaty. 2010. *Relational-Realizational Parsing*. Ph.D. thesis, University of Amsterdam.

Reut Tsarfaty. 2013. *A Unified Morpho-Syntactic Scheme of Stanford Dependencies*. Proceedings of ACL.

Veronika Vincze, Dóra Szauter, Attila Almási, György Móra, Zoltán Alexin, and János Csirik. 2010. Hungarian dependency treebank. In *LREC*.

Introducing the SPMRL 2014 Shared Task on Parsing Morphologically-Rich Languages

Djamé Seddah
INRIA & Univ. Paris Sorbonne
Paris, France
djame.seddah@paris-sorbonne.fr

Sandra Kübler
Indiana University
Bloomington, IN, USA
skuebler@indiana.edu

Reut Tsarfaty
Weizman Institute
Rehovot, Israel
reut.tsarfaty@weizmann.ac.il

1 Introduction

This first joint meeting on Statistical Parsing of Morphologically Rich Languages and Syntactic Analysis of Non-Canonical English (SPMRL-SANCL) featured a shared task on statistical parsing of morphologically rich languages (SPMRL). The goal of the shared task is to allow to train and test different participating systems on comparable data sets, thus providing an objective measure of comparison between state-of-the-art parsing systems on data data sets from a range of different languages. This 2014 SPMRL shared task is a continuation and extension of the SPMRL shared task, which was co-located with the SPMRL meeting at EMNLP 2013 (Seddah et al., 2013).

This paper provides a short overview of the 2014 SPMRL shared task goals, data sets, and evaluation setup. Since the SPMRL 2014 largely builds on the infrastructure established for the SPMRL 2013 shared task, we start by reviewing the previous shared task (§2) and then proceed to the 2014 SPMRL evaluation settings (§3), data sets (§4), and a task summary (§5). Due to organizational constraints, this overview is published prior to the submission of all system test runs, and a more detailed overview including the description of participating systems and the analysis of their results will follow as part of (Seddah et al., 2014), once the shared task is completed.

2 The SPMRL Shared Task 2013

The SPMRL Shared Task 2013 (Seddah et al., 2013) was organized with the goal of providing standard data sets, streamlined evaluation metrics, and a set of strong baselines for parsing morphologically rich languages (MRLs). The goals were both to provide a focal point for researchers interested in parsing MRLs and consequently to advance the state of the art in this area of research.

The shared task focused on parsing nine morphologically rich languages, from different typological language families, in both a constituent-based and a dependency-based format. The set of nine typologically diverse languages comprised data sets for Arabic, Basque, French, German, Hebrew, Hungarian, Korean, Polish, and Swedish. Compared to previous multilingual shared tasks (Buchholz and Marsi, 2006; Nivre et al., 2007), the SPMRL shared task targeted parsing in realistic evaluation scenarios, in which the analysis of morphologically ambiguous input tokens is not known in advance. An additional novelty of the SPMRL shared task is that it allowed for both a dependency-based and a constituent-based parse representation. This setting relied on an intricate and careful data preparation process which ensured consistency between the constituent and the dependency version by aligning the two representation types at the token level and at the level of part-of-speech tags. For all languages, we provided two versions of the data sets: an *all* data set, identical in size to the one made available by the individual treebank providers, and a *small* data set, with a training set of 5,000 sentences, and a test set of about 500 sentences. Controlling the set sizes across languages allows us to level the playing field across languages and treebanks.

First Joint Workshop on Statistical Parsing of Morphologically Rich Languages and Syntactic Analysis of Non-Canonical Languages, pages 103–109 Dublin, Ireland, August 23-29 2014.

The shared task also advanced the state of the art by introducing different levels of complexity in parsing. In general, parsing is reduced to the parsing proper step, assuming gold segmentation of the text into sentences and words as well as gold POS tags and morphological analyses. This is a serious simplification of the task since especially in Semitic languages, the segmentation into input tokens is a task that is best performed in combination with parsing because of the ambiguities involved.

The shared task deviated from this standard configuration by adding conditions in which more realistic settings were given: In the gold setting, unambiguous gold morphological segmentation, POS tags, and morphological features for each input token were given. In the predicted setting, disambiguated morphological segmentation was provided, but the POS tags and morphological features for each input segment were not. In the raw setting, there was no gold information, i.e., morphological segmentation, POS tags and morphological features for each input token had to be predicted as part of the parsing task. To lower the entry cost, participants were provided with reasonable baseline (if not state-of-the-art) morphological predictions (either disambiguated – in most cases– or ambiguous prediction in lattice forms).

As a consequence of the raw scenario, it was not possible to (only) rely on the accepted parsing metrics, labeled bracket evaluation via EVALB[1] (Black et al., 1991), Leaf-Ancestor (Sampson and Babarczy, 2003) for constituents and CoNLL X's Labeled/Unlabeled Attachment Score for dependencies (Buchholz and Marsi, 2006). When the segmentation of words into input tokens is not given, there may be discrepancies on the lexical levels, which neither EVALB and LEAF-ANCESTOR nor LAS/UAS are prepared to handle. Thus, we also used TedEval, a distance-based metric that evaluates a morphosyntactic structure as a complete whole (Tsarfaty et al., 2012b). Note that given the workload brought to the participants, we did not try to enforce function label evaluation for constituent parsing. We hope that further shared tasks will try to generalize such an evaluation. Indeed, having predicted function labels would ease labeled TEDEVAL evaluation and favor a full parsing chain evaluation. Nevertheless, the choice of TEDEVAL allowed us to go beyond the standard cross-parser evaluation within one setting and approach cross-framework (constituent vs. dependency (Tsarfaty et al., 2012a)) and cross-language evaluation, thus pushing the envelope on parsing evaluation. Additionally, we performed a specialized evaluation of multi-word expressions in the French treebank.

The SPMRL Shared Task 2013 featured seven teams who approached the dependency parsing task and one team that approached constituent parsing. The best performing system (Björkelund et al., 2013) in either framework consisted of an ensemble system, combining several dependency parsers or several instantiations of a PCFG-LA parser by a (re-)ranker, both on top of state-of-the-art morphological analyses. The results show that parser combination helps to reach a robust performance across languages. However, the integration of morphological analysis into the parsing needs to be investigated thoroughly, and new, morphologically aware approaches are needed. The cross-parser, cross-scenario, and cross-framework evaluation protocols show that performance on gold morphological input is significantly higher than that in more realistic scenarios, and more training data is beneficial. Additionally, differences between dependency and constituents are smaller than previously assumed, and languages which are typologically farthest from English, such as Semitic and Asian languages, are still amongst the hardest to parse, regardless of the parsing method used.

3 SPMRL 2014 Parsing Scenarios

As in the previous edition, this year, we consider three parsing scenarios, depending on how much of the morphological information is provided. The scenarios are listed below, in increasing order of difficulty.

- **Gold:** In this scenario, the parser is provided with unambiguous gold morphological segmentation, POS tags, and morphological features for each input token.
- **Predicted:** In this scenario, the parser is provided with disambiguated morphological segmentation. However, the POS tags and morphological features for each input segment are unknown.
- **Raw:** In this scenario, the parser is provided with morphologically ambiguous input. The morphological segmentation, POS tags, and morphological features for each input token are unknown.

[1]We extended the usualEVALB to penalize unparsed sentences.

Scenario	Segmentation	PoS+Feat.	Tree
Gold	✓	✓	–
Predicted	✓	1-best	–
Raw (1-best)	1-best	1-best	–
Raw (all)	–	–	–

Table 1: A summary of the parsing and evaluation scenarios. ✓ depicts gold information, – depicts unknown information, to be predicted by the system.

The **Predicted** and **Raw** scenarios require predicting morphological analyses. This may be done using a language-specific morphological analyzer, or it may be done jointly with parsing. We provide inputs that support these different scenarios:

- **Predicted**: Gold treebank segmentation is given to the parser. The POS tags assignment and morphological features are automatically predicted by the parser or by an external resource.
- **Raw (1-best)**: The 1-best segmentation and POS tags assignment is predicted by an external resource and given to the parser.
- **Raw (all)**: All possible segmentations and POS tags are specified by an external resource. The parser selects jointly a segmentation and a tree.

An overview of all scenarios is shown in table 1. For languages in which terminals equal tokens, only **Gold** and **Predicted** scenarios are considered. For the Semitic languages, we further provide input for both **Raw (1-best)** and **Raw (all)** scenarios.[2]

4 SPMRL 2014 Data Sets

The main innovation of the SPMRL 2014 shared task with respect to the previous edition is the availability of additional, unannotated data, for the purpose of semi-supervised training. This section provides a description of the unlabeled-data preparation that is required in the context of parsing MRLs, and the core labeled data that is used in conjunction with it.

4.1 SPMRL Unlabeled Data Set

One of the common problems when dealing with morphologically rich languages (MRLs) is lexical data sparseness due to the high level of variation in word forms (Tsarfaty et al., 2010; Tsarfaty et al., 2012c). The use of large, unlabeled corpora in a semi-supervised setting, in addition to the relatively small MRL data sets, can become a valid option to overcome such issues. For instance, using Brown clusters (Brown et al., 1992) has been shown to boost the performance of a PCFG-LA based parser for French (Candito and Crabbé, 2009; Candito and Seddah, 2010). External lexical acquisition was successfully used for Arabic (Habash, 2008) and Hebrew (Goldberg et al., 2009), self-training increased accuracy for parsing German (Rehbein, 2011), and more recently, the use of word embeddings led to some promising results for some MRLs (Cirik and Şensoy, 2013).

By releasing large, unlabeled data sets and by providing accurate pre-annotation in a format directly compatible with models trained on the SPMRL Shared Task treebanks, we hope to foster the development of interesting and feature-rich parsing models that build on larger, morphologically rich, lexicons. Table 2 presents basic facts about the data sets. Details on the unlabeled data and their pre-annotations will be provided in (Seddah et al., 2014). Note that we could not ensure the same volume of data for all languages, nor we could run the same parser, or morphology prediction, on all data. Potential future work could focus on ensuring a stricter level of comparability of these data or on investigating the feasibility of such a normalization of procedures.

[2]The raw Arabic lattices were made available later than the other data. They are now included in the shared task release.

Language	Source (main)	type	size (tree tokens)	morph	parsed
Arabic	news domain	news	120M	✓*	✓*
Basque	web	balanced	150M	✓	✓
French	news domain	newswire	120M	✓+mwe	✓*
German	Wikipedia	wiki (edited)	205M	✓	✓
Hebrew	Wikipedia	wiki (edited)	160M	✓	✓
Hungarian	news domain	newswire	100M	✓	✓
Korean	news domain	newswire	40M	✓	✓*
Polish	Wikipedia	wiki (edited)	100M	✓	✓
Swedish	PAROLE	balanced	24M	✓	✓

Table 2: Unlabeled data set properties.*: *made available mid-july*

4.2 SPMRL Core Labeled Data Set

In order to provide a faithful evaluation of the impact of these additional sets of unlabeled data, we used the exact same data sets for training and testing as in the previous edition. Specifically, we used an Arabic data set, originally provided by the LDC (Maamouri et al., 2004), in a dependency form, derived from the Columbia Catib Treebank (Habash and Roth, 2009; Habash et al., 2009) and in a constituency instance, following the Stanford pre-processing scheme (Green and Manning, 2010) and extended according to the SPMRL 2013 extension scheme (Seddah et al., 2013). For Basque, the data was provided by Aduriz et al. (2003) in both dependency and constituency, we removed sentences with non-projective trees so both instances could be aligned at the token level. Regarding French, we used a new instance of the French Treebank (Abeillé et al., 2003) that includes multi-word expression (MWE) annotations, annotated at the morpho-syntactic level in both instances. Predicted MWEs were added this year, using the same tools as Constant et al. (2013). The German data are based on the Tiger corpus (Brants et al., 2002), and converted to constituent and dependency following (Seeker and Kuhn, 2012). The Hebrew data set is based on the Modern Hebrew Treebank (Sima'an et al., 2001), with the Goldberg (2011) dependency version, in turn aligned with the phrase structure instance described in (Tsarfaty, 2010; Tsarfaty, 2013). Note that in order to match the Hebrew unlabeled data encoding, the Hebrew treebank was converted back to UTF-8. The Hungarian data are derived from the Szeged treebank (Csendes et al., 2005; Vincze et al., 2010), while the Korean data originate from the Kaist Treebank (Choi et al., 1994) which was converted to dependency for the SPMRL shared task by Choi (2013). The Polish treebank we used is described in (Woliński et al., 2011; Świdziński and Woliński, 2010; Wróblewska, 2012). Compared to the last year's edition, we added explicit feature names in the relevant data fields. The Swedish data originate from (Nivre et al., 2006), we added function labels extracted from the original Swedish XML data. Note that in addition to constituency and dependency versions, the Polish, German and Swedish data sets are also available in the Tiger XML format (Mengel and Lezius, 2000), allowing a direct representation of discontinuous structures in their phrase-based structures.

5 Conclusion

At the time of writing this short introduction, the shared task is ongoing, and neither results nor the final submitting teams are known. At this point, we can say that 15 teams registered for the 2014 shared task edition, indicating an increased awareness of and continued interest in the topic of the shared task. Results, cross-parser and cross-data analysis, and shared task description papers will be made available at `http://www.spmrl.org/spmrl2014-sharedtask.html`.

Acknowledgments

We would like to express our gratitude to the original treebank labeled and unlabeled data contributors for the considerable time they devoted to our shared task. Namely, **Arabic:** Nizar Habash, Ryan Roth (Columbia University); Spence Green (Stanford University) , Ann Bies, Seth Kulick, Mohamed Maamouri (the Linguistic Data Consortium) ; **Basque:** Koldo Gojenola, Iakes Goenaga (University of the Basque Country) ; **French:** Marie Candito (Univ. Paris 7 & Inria), Djamé Seddah (Univ. Paris Sorbonne & Inria) , Matthieu Constant (Univ. Marne la Vallée) ; **German:** Wolfgang Seeker (IMS

Stuttgart), Wolfgang Maier (Univ. of Dusseldorf), Yannick Versley (Univ. of Tuebingen) ; **Hebrew:** Yoav Goldberg (Bar Ilan Univ.), Reut Tsarfaty (Weizmann Institute of Science) ; **Hungarian:** Richàrd Farkas, Veronika Vincze (Univ. of Szeged) ; **Korean:** Jinho D. Choi (Univ. of Massachusetts Amherst), Jungyeul Park (Kaist); **Polish:** Adam Przepiórkowski, Marcin Woliński, Alina Wróblewska (Institute of Computer Science, Polish Academy of Sciences) ; **Swedish:** Joakim Nivre (Uppsala Univ.), Marco Kuhlmann (Linköping University).

We gratefully acknowledge the contribution of Språkbanken and the University of Gothenburg for providing the PAROLE corpus. We are also very grateful to the Philosophical Faculty of the Heinrich-Heine Universität Düsseldorf for hosting the shared task data via their dokuwiki.

References

Anne Abeillé, Lionel Clément, and François Toussenel. 2003. Building a treebank for French. In Anne Abeillé, editor, *Treebanks*. Kluwer, Dordrecht.

I. Aduriz, M. J. Aranzabe, J. M. Arriola, A. Atutxa, A. Díaz de Ilarraza, A. Garmendia, and M. Oronoz. 2003. Construction of a Basque dependency treebank. In *Proceedings of the Second Workshop on Treebanks and Linguistic Theories*, pages 201–204, Växjö, Sweden.

Anders Björkelund, Ozlem Cetinoglu, Richárd Farkas, Thomas Mueller, and Wolfgang Seeker. 2013. (Re)ranking meets morphosyntax: State-of-the-art results from the SPMRL 2013 shared task. In *Proceedings of the Fourth Workshop on Statistical Parsing of Morphologically-Rich Languages*, pages 134–144, Seattle, WA.

Ezra Black, Steven Abney, Dan Flickinger, Claudia Gdaniec, Ralph Grishman, Philip Harrison, Donald Hindle, Robert Ingria, Frederick Jelinek, Judith Klavans, Mark Liberman, Mitchell Marcus, Salim Roukos, Beatrice Santorini, and Tomek Strzalkowski. 1991. A procedure for quantitatively comparing the syntactic coverage of English grammars. In *Proceedings of the DARPA Speech and Natural Language Workshop 1991*, pages 306–311, Pacific Grove, CA.

Sabine Brants, Stefanie Dipper, Silvia Hansen, Wolfgang Lezius, and George Smith. 2002. The TIGER treebank. In *Proceedings of the First Workshop on Treebanks and Linguistic Theories (TLT)*, pages 24–41, Sozopol, Bulgaria.

Peter F. Brown, Vincent J. Della, Peter V. Desouza, Jennifer C. Lai, and Robert L. Mercer. 1992. Class-based n-gram models of natural language. *Computational Linguistics*, 18(4):467–479.

Sabine Buchholz and Erwin Marsi. 2006. CoNLL-X shared task on multilingual dependency parsing. In *Proceedings of CoNLL*, pages 149–164, New York, NY.

Marie Candito and Benoît Crabbé. 2009. Improving generative statistical parsing with semi-supervised word clustering. In *Proceedings of the 11th International Conference on Parsing Technologies (IWPT'09)*, pages 138–141, Paris, France.

Marie Candito and Djamé Seddah. 2010. Parsing word clusters. In *Proceedings of the NAACL/HLT Workshop on Statistical Parsing of Morphologically Rich Languages (SPMRL 2010)*, Los Angeles, CA.

Key-sun Choi, Young S. Han, Young G. Han, and Oh W. Kwon. 1994. KAIST Tree Bank Project for Korean: Present and Future Development. In *In Proceedings of the International Workshop on Sharable Natural Language Resources*, pages 7–14, Nara, Japan.

Jinho D. Choi. 2013. Preparing Korean data for the shared task on parsing morphologically rich languages. arXiv:1309.1649.

Volkan Cirik and Hüsnü Şensoy. 2013. The AI-KU system at the SPMRL 2013 shared task: Unsupervised features for dependency parsing. In *Proceedings of the Fourth Workshop on Statistical Parsing of Morphologically-Rich Languages*, pages 68–75, Seattle, WA.

Matthieu Constant, Marie Candito, and Djamé Seddah. 2013. The LIGM-Alpage architecture for the SPMRL 2013 shared task: Multiword expression analysis and dependency parsing. In *Proceedings of the Fourth Workshop on Statistical Parsing of Morphologically-Rich Languages*, pages 46–52, Seattle, WA.

Dóra Csendes, János Csirik, Tibor Gyimóthy, and András Kocsor. 2005. The Szeged treebank. In *Proceedings of the 8th International Conference on Text, Speech and Dialogue (TSD)*, Lecture Notes in Computer Science, pages 123–132, Berlin / Heidelberg. Springer.

Yoav Goldberg, Reut Tsarfaty, Meni Adler, and Michael Elhadad. 2009. Enhancing unlexicalized parsing performance using a wide coverage lexicon, fuzzy tag-set mapping, and EM-HMM-based lexical probabilities. In *Proceedings of the 12th Conference of the European Chapter of the ACL (EACL)*, pages 327–335, Athens, Greece.

Yoav Goldberg. 2011. *Automatic syntactic processing of Modern Hebrew*. Ph.D. thesis, Ben Gurion University of the Negev.

Spence Green and Christopher D. Manning. 2010. Better Arabic parsing: Baselines, evaluations, and analysis. In *Proceedings of the 23rd International Conference on Computational Linguistics (Coling 2010)*, pages 394–402, Beijing, China.

Nizar Habash and Ryan Roth. 2009. CATiB: The Columbia Arabic Treebank. In *Proceedings of ACL-IJCNLP*, pages 221–224, Suntec, Singapore.

Nizar Habash, Reem Faraj, and Ryan Roth. 2009. Syntactic Annotation in the Columbia Arabic Treebank. In *Proceedings of MEDAR International Conference on Arabic Language Resources and Tools*, Cairo, Egypt.

Nizar Habash. 2008. Four techniques for online handling of out-of-vocabulary words in Arabic-English statistical machine translation. In *Proceedings of ACL-08: HLT, Short Papers*, pages 57–60, Columbus, OH.

Mohamed Maamouri, Ann Bies, Tim Buckwalter, and Wigdan Mekki. 2004. The Penn Arabic treebank: Building a large-scale annotated Arabic corpus. In *Proceedings of NEMLAR International Conference on Arabic Language Resources and Tools*, pages 102–109, Cairo, Egypt.

Andreas Mengel and Wolfgang Lezius. 2000. An XML-based encoding format for syntactically annotated corpora. In *Proceedings of the Second International Conference on Language Resources and Engineering (LREC 2000)*, pages 121–126, Athens, Greece.

Joakim Nivre, Jens Nilsson, and Johan Hall. 2006. Talbanken05: A Swedish treebank with phrase structure and dependency annotation. In *Proceedings of LREC*, pages 1392–1395, Genoa, Italy.

Joakim Nivre, Johan Hall, Sandra Kübler, Ryan McDonald, Jens Nilsson, Sebastian Riedel, and Deniz Yuret. 2007. The CoNLL 2007 shared task on dependency parsing. In *Proceedings of the CoNLL Shared Task Session of EMNLP-CoNLL 2007*, pages 915–932, Prague, Czech Republic.

Ines Rehbein. 2011. Data point selection for self-training. In *Proceedings of the Second Workshop on Statistical Parsing of Morphologically Rich Languages*, pages 62–67, Dublin, Ireland.

Geoffrey Sampson and Anna Babarczy. 2003. A test of the leaf-ancestor metric for parse accuracy. *Natural Language Engineering*, 9(04):365–380.

Djamé Seddah, Reut Tsarfaty, Sandra Kübler, Marie Candito, Jinho D. Choi, Richárd Farkas, Jennifer Foster, Iakes Goenaga, Koldo Gojenola Galletebeitia, Yoav Goldberg, Spence Green, Nizar Habash, Marco Kuhlmann, Wolfgang Maier, Joakim Nivre, Adam Przepiórkowski, Ryan Roth, Wolfgang Seeker, Yannick Versley, Veronika Vincze, Marcin Woliński, Alina Wróblewska, and Eric Villemonte de la Clergerie. 2013. Overview of the SPMRL 2013 shared task: A cross-framework evaluation of parsing morphologically rich languages. In *Proceedings of the Fourth Workshop on Statistical Parsing of Morphologically-Rich Languages*, pages 146–182, Seattle, WA.

Djamé Seddah, Reut Tsarfaty, Sandra Kübler, Marie Candito, Jinho Choi, Matthieu Constant, Richárd Farkas, Iakes Goenaga, Koldo Gojenola, Yoav Goldberg, Spence Green, Nizar Habash, Marco Kuhlmann, Wolfgang Maier, Joakim Nivre, Adam Przepiorkowski, Ryan Roth, Wolfgang Seeker, Yannick Versley, Veronika Vincze, Marcin Woliński, Alina Wróblewska, and Eric Villemonte de la Clérgerie. 2014. Overview of the spmrl 2014 shared task on parsing morphologically rich languages. In *Notes of the SPMRL 2014 Shared Task on Parsing Morphologically-Rich Languages*, Dublin, Ireland.

Wolfgang Seeker and Jonas Kuhn. 2012. Making Ellipses Explicit in Dependency Conversion for a German Treebank. In *Proceedings of the 8th International Conference on Language Resources and Evaluation*, pages 3132–3139, Istanbul, Turkey.

Khalil Sima'an, Alon Itai, Yoad Winter, Alon Altmann, and Noa Nativ. 2001. Building a tree-bank of Modern Hebrew text. *Traitement Automatique des Langues*, 42:347–380.

Marek Świdziński and Marcin Woliński. 2010. Towards a bank of constituent parse trees for Polish. In *Proceedings of Text, Speech and Dialogue*, pages 197–204, Brno, Czech Republic.

Reut Tsarfaty, Djame Seddah, Yoav Goldberg, Sandra Kübler, Marie Candito, Jennifer Foster, Yannick Versley, Ines Rehbein, and Lamia Tounsi. 2010. Statistical parsing for morphologically rich language (SPMRL): What, how and whither. In *Proceedings of the First workshop on Statistical Parsing of Morphologically Rich Languages (SPMRL)*, Los Angeles, CA.

Reut Tsarfaty, Joakim Nivre, and Evelina Andersson. 2012a. Cross-framework evaluation for statistical parsing. In *Proceeding of EACL*, Avignon, France.

Reut Tsarfaty, Joakim Nivre, and Evelina Andersson. 2012b. Joint evaluation for segmentation and parsing. In *Proceedings of ACL*, Jeju, Korea.

Reut Tsarfaty, Djamé Seddah, Sandra Kübler, and Joakim Nivre. 2012c. Parsing morphologically rich languages: Introduction to the special issue. *Computational Linguistics*, 39(1):15–22.

Reut Tsarfaty. 2010. *Relational-Realizational Parsing*. Ph.D. thesis, University of Amsterdam.

Reut Tsarfaty. 2013. A unified morpho-syntactic scheme of Stanford dependencies. In *Proceedings of ACL*, Sofia, Bulgaria.

Veronika Vincze, Dóra Szauter, Attila Almási, György Móra, Zoltán Alexin, and János Csirik. 2010. Hungarian Dependency Treebank. In *Proceedings of LREC*, Valletta, Malta.

Marcin Woliński, Katarzyna Głowińska, and Marek Świdziński. 2011. A preliminary version of Składnica—a treebank of Polish. In *Proceedings of the 5th Language & Technology Conference*, pages 299–303, Poznań, Poland.

Alina Wróblewska. 2012. Polish Dependency Bank. *Linguistic Issues in Language Technology*, 7(1):1–15.

Author Index